The New DIY Guide to Marketing

For Charities and Voluntary Organisations

The New DIY Guide to Marketing

For Small Charities and Voluntary Organisations

Moi Ali

ICSA
PUBLISHING

Published by ICSA Publishing Ltd
16 Park Crescent
London W1B 1AH

First published 1996 by Directory of Social Change
Second edition 2001 published by ICSA Publishing Ltd
Reprinted 2007
Reprinted 2008

Designed and typeset in Swift and Bell Gothic by
Paul Barrett Book Production

Printed and bound in Great Britain by
Hobbs the Printers Ltd, Totton, Hampshire

British Library Cataloguing in Publication Data

A catalogue record for this book is available from the British Library

ISBN 978-1-86072-135-9
(ISBN 2-873860-97-8 1st edition)

Contents

Acknowledgements

Many people have helped in the writing of this book. Morag Rhodes at the Children's Hospice Association Scotland and Lorraine Gray at CHILDREN 1ST provided helpful comments on the first edition of this book, enabling me to make significant improvements to this second edition. Noelle Fletcher, Julie Beals and Jane Button at the Woodland Trust helped by allowing me to reproduce the Trust's style guidelines. Alex Kilgour at Camvista.com gave up valuable time to pass on some Internet secrets. Margaret McKay, Eileen Morrison and Lorraine Gray at CHILDREN 1ST kindly allowed me to use their website design brief and site map. Without the contributions of these people the book would not be as comprehensive as it now is. Thanks also to Clare Grist Taylor at ICSA Publishing for being so enthusiastic about publishing a second edition of *The DIY Guide to Marketing*.

About the Author

Moi Ali runs her own PR consultancy in Scotland, The Pink Anglia Public Relations Company, which specialises in public relations, communications and marketing services for the not-for-profit sector. She has more than fifteen years' experience in public relations and promotional marketing and is a member of the Institute of Public Relations.

Moi has written six books on PR and marketing, including *The DIY Guide to Public Relations for Charities* (Directory of Social Change), *Effective PR* and *Effective Marketing* (both Dorling Kindersley).

Preface

Visit any large bookshop and you will see books aplenty on marketing. A bewildering choice is available, although you may struggle to find a simple, practical, step-by-step book on voluntary sector marketing. Many marketing tomes provide serious, heavy academic reading. Their theoretical basis can make it difficult for a layperson to get to grips with them. Most are written with businesses or large organisations in mind. Few tackle the issue in a practical way, and fewer still are interested in examining marketing from a charity's unique perspective. This book is refreshing in that it does both these things.

Written especially for small organisations that are either new to marketing or very inexperienced, *The New DIY Guide to Marketing* explains how to do your own marketing on a shoestring and how to undertake cost-effective marketing with a larger budget. Discover what marketing can do for your organisation and be guided through the various aspects involved in developing an effective marketing strategy. Sit down and read it from cover to cover, or dip into this working manual whenever you need to. Keep it to hand so that you can refer to particular topics again over the coming months as your marketing activity gets underway.

This plain English, jargon-free guide is written in a clear, readable and accessible style. Although covering marketing theory, it is a very practical book, with plenty of tips and hints to make your marketing task easier. Bear in mind that this is a beginner's guide to the subject. Marketing is a huge discipline and each of the chapters could easily be a book in its own right. *The New DIY Guide to Marketing*'s aim is to introduce the subject very broadly; readers interested in undertaking a more in-depth study of marketing can follow up by reading more advanced texts.

Marketing is a must

INTRODUCTION

Marketing can be a difficult, technical and jargon-ridden subject. This book aims to demystify a complex discipline, creating a DIY manual that is light on theory, jargon and concepts, yet heavy on practice, tips and advice. Some theory is inevitable because without a basic understanding of what marketing means, no voluntary organisation can hope to get it right. That's why this introductory chapter is more theoretical than the others. It gives you the necessary information base, enabling you to get maximum benefit from the rest of the book. If this section is a bit too heavy for you, or discusses concepts that seem remote from your own experience in the voluntary sector, bear with it. The following pages provide an important foundation for the subsequent, more practical, hands-on chapters.

Defining marketing

Let's start with a definition. 'Marketing' is not just another word for selling. If it were, it would be of little relevance to the vast majority of voluntary organisations, which neither make nor sell goods. The problem is that people often use the word in everyday speech as a synonym for selling and for promotion. We talk about the marketing of a new product, when we really mean its advertising and promotion, which hopefully leads to sales. Sales and promotion are product-led: you start with a product or service, which you have to persuade customers to buy. Selling is what happens in charity shops, where there is a supply of goods and you display them in the hope that people will buy them. It is also what happens at jumble sales, bring-and-buy events, bookstalls, and so on. Marketing is an altogether more complex beast, involving both sales and promotion, but a lot more besides.

Don't Confuse Marketing and Selling

Trouble occurs when people confuse selling and marketing, setting out to attract sales before they have even thought about marketing. This was what happened with the famous – some would say infamous – Sinclair C5, the mini car-cum-trike invented by Sir Clive Sinclair and launched in 1985. He believed that his nifty little invention would revolutionise British motoring. Instead of travelling by car, we would drive the leaner, greener, cleaner and cheaper electric-powered C5 instead. The problem was that by starting with a product he was acting on his hunches rather than on objective, research-based facts. Admittedly, some have made their fortune on a hunch: take Mr Dyson and his bagless vacuum cleaner. Their 'feel' for something happened to coincide with the rest of the world's, but that's not always so. Take Sir Clive. His idea was fantastic – to him! The rest of us – his market – failed to share his enthusiasm. The C5 flopped, Sir Clive went bankrupt, and now this cute little trike is motoring history.

Establishing need

So if there's more to marketing than just selling, what is it all about? Marketing's starting point is the identification (usually using some form of research) of customers' needs and wants. Only then can a product or service be developed to satisfy those needs. Promotion comes next, to publicise the product to its target market. The final stage is sales. Find out what customers want *before* you develop a product or service and thereby avoid a potential mismatch between your service and their needs. Had Sir Clive Sinclair gone about it this way, he would probably still be a very rich man.

But what's this got to do with charities and voluntary organisations? Quite a lot. Whether you sell goods (via mail order catalogues or through a charity shop, for example) or whether you operate a service or run a pressure group, you need to understand and use marketing techniques. Why? To maximise your efficiency and minimise risk. Proper marketing will help you to develop new services to meet the real needs of the community you serve, and to attract the necessary funding to run them.

A Needs-led Organisation

Marketing is sometimes defined as 'making what you can sell, not selling what you can make'. In other words, marketing is about being needs-led, with success dependent on an organisation's ability to make what it can sell or, to use less commercial terms, to create a service to meet a need.

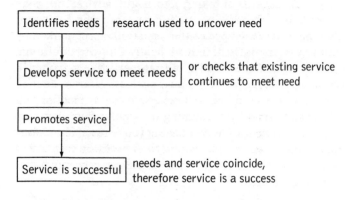

Identifies needs — research used to uncover need

Develops service to meet needs — or checks that existing service continues to meet need

Promotes service

Service is successful — needs and service coincide, therefore service is a success

A Service-led Organisation

Product-led or service-led organisations sell what they can make. Their approach is to continue doing what they have always done, without regard to the market. Such an approach is not based on meeting need, but simply on achieving sales. This is not what effective marketing is all about.

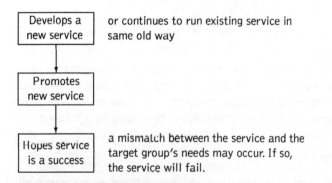

Develops a new service — or continues to run existing service in same old way

Promotes new service

Hopes service is a success — a mismatch between the service and the target group's needs may occur. If so, the service will fail.

The Exception to the Rule

Making what you can sell is a good motto, but there are charities for whom it does not so readily apply. In particular, some campaigning organisations and health promotion groups might struggle to see how it relates to them. Take the example of an anti-racism campaign. The target, surely, is racists. But give them what they will readily buy and it certainly won't be anti-racism; quite the opposite probably.

The same applies to health promotion. A campaign to get people to take more exercise, improve their diet, give up smoking and reduce their alcohol intake may aim at 'beer 'n' baccy' couch potatoes. Giving them what they want would involve developing cream cakes that make you slim, pills that replace the need for exercise and non-carcinogenic cigarettes! You know – and they know too – the benefits of taking your health advice. Your challenge is to persuade them to do something they probably don't want to do. On the surface this appears the very antithesis of marketing.

While these examples do not fit neatly into the traditional marketing model, there is still a lot that marketing can offer in such situations. Marketing techniques such as research can help uncover motivation and help shape key messages, enabling you to package and present campaigning or health promotion messages in a more persuasive way, allowing you to reach out to your intended audience and to understand their needs. So even where you may feel that marketing has no role, there may be much that the discipline can offer.

Understanding the marketing mix

To understand marketing fully you need to understand the 'marketing mix'. The marketing mix comprises 'the 4 Ps': product, price, place and promotion. Marketing planning involves:

- Developing the right product (one that meets needs).
- Charging the right price for it.
- Getting it to the right place so that it can be bought.
- Promoting it so that potential customers know about it.

'Product' is the most important element of the marketing mix; without a product you have nothing to price, place or promote. But remember that customers are the most important element in marketing. Without customers there is no need for a product.

Product

Most voluntary organisations do not sell goods, although an increasing number might sell Christmas cards, run one or more charity shops, or sell memberships. Yet even though the majority of organisations are not selling goods, they all still have products. More usually their 'product' will actually be a service, such as a helpline, drop-in centre or supported housing. Even campaigning organisations have a product: they 'sell' their campaign mission or idea. Health promotion organisations 'sell' their message – the benefits of reducing fat intake or increasing activity to combat the effects of a sedentary lifestyle. Many voluntary organisations and campaigning groups do not think of their offerings as products, yet learning to do so is vital for effective marketing. You can read more about products in Chapter 3.

Price

Regardless of whether you sell goods, run services, offer member-ship, fundraise or campaign, price is a factor for you to consider. Your 'products' may not carry a price tag, yet everything has a price, even a free service. All services cost money to establish and to run, and someone must foot the bill, even if it is not the end-user. Your funders, donors or sponsors must feel that their contribution to the service is at a price that is right. If statutory funders feel that the service is not worth the money they are paying, they will take their money elsewhere. Individual donors, too, must feel that their gift is being spent wisely. After all, there are plenty of other good causes that would be more than happy to accept their money.

Place

'Place' is the activity of bringing product and customer together. In conventional marketing 'place' refers to distribution systems – getting your goods from the factory to the shops. Organisations providing a service need to consider how to get the client to the service. Is your gay men's advice centre in a place where gay men gather? Should you consider a new venue? Is your over-fifties coffee club on a main bus route? Do you need to consider organis-ing transport? Are your collecting tins in the right places? Is there a distribution system to collect and drop off tins? How will your campaign leaflets get through the right doors?

Promotion

Often when we talk about marketing we are really just talking about promotion – advertising, websites, leaflets, posters, edito-rial, and so on. (You can read more about promotion later in this book.) Good promotional activity can help to secure the success of a service by ensuring that it is known by users and funders alike.

Why you cannot ignore marketing

Marketing may use the language of commerce and big business, but do not let that put you off using it. There are many com-pelling reasons why voluntary organisations cannot afford to ignore marketing.

Growing Competition

In an increasingly competitive environment, charities and volun-tary organisations have to compete with each other (and some-times with commercial organisations and the public sector) for their share of funding and donations, or to sell their products or services. An increasing number of charities now chase an ever-smaller pot of money. Streetwise sponsors, donors and funders demand 'value for money' and 'added value'. Only organisations able to demonstrate objectively the need for their service, and their effectiveness in delivering it, attract funding.

The Contract Culture

The statutory funding that many charities used to rely on is now subject to competition in a way that it simply wasn't in the past. Increasingly, voluntary organisations have to negotiate contracts with local authorities, health authorities/health boards and even with other voluntary organisations. Social work departments and health authorities are changing from being providers of services to purchasers of services. More and more, the voluntary sector provides mainstream services that were previously the sole responsibility of local and national government.

Consequently the operating environment for charities is more financially and 'market'-driven, and considerably more competitive, than ever before. The language some charities use reflects this. Many charity directors speak business jargon with fluency, appoint staff with business degrees or commercial experience, and produce business plans and strategies. But even for very small voluntary organisations, marketing has become a must. A good understanding of their market and well-researched products and services can make the difference between survival and extinction. That's a powerful reason for thinking marketing.

Presenting Unpopular Causes

Some voluntary organisations deal with groups, causes or issues that receive an unsympathetic and uncaring response from the public and the media: prostitution; drug misuse; ex-offenders; gay and lesbian issues, to name but a few. Such organisations can benefit from good marketing, which can help them repackage the cause and present it in a more appealing, more persuasive or more populist way. Some would call that 'selling out'; those of us who live in the real world call it survival. It is better to present your cause effectively – thereby gaining more and larger donations, attracting increased support for your campaign, or greater funding from your local authority – than to take the moral high ground and end up as a lost cause.

Meeting Need

If all this has not convinced you that you need to think marketing, this surely will. Effective marketing can help you to identify need and develop solutions to meet a need. Obviously, marketing cannot achieve miracles, creating a wonderful world at the mere swish of a magic wand. But it can take you back to basics and ensure that you develop services around the needs of your clients. Over time many organisations drift away from being needs-led and become resource-driven. They may begin to run services tailored to their budget rather than to the needs of their client group. Adopt a marketing approach and you may discover that you too are guilty of this. Marketing will help you to refocus your attention, listen to your clients and redevelop your services to meet real need.

Marketing techniques can help charities promote their work, raise money, develop services that people need and want, and run successful campaigns on important issues. Put like that, can you afford not to take marketing seriously?

Understanding 'customers'

INTRODUCTION

Successful commercial organisations recognise that customers are
vital to their well-being. Without customers there simply is no business.
Effective marketing places customers' needs and wants at the centre.
The notion of building an organisation around the needs of customers
(or clients or service-users) is one that is entirely in harmony with the
voluntary sector ethos of client-centredness.

Many of today's household name charities emerged more than a
century ago. In Victorian times charities had a very paternalistic
outlook. It never occurred to anyone to consult users for their
views on the workhouse or the almshouse. The charity knew best.
Philanthropic benefactors expected recognition from society for
their good work, gratitude from 'service-users' (a term that would
never have been used then) and their place in heaven!

We're now in the twenty-first century and paternalism is history – in most organisations at least. Today's voluntary sector
managers value the views of service-users, actively seek (and
listen to) their opinions, respond to their needs and wants, and
involve clients in the development of services and in decision-
making. However, the bigger an organisation grows, the harder it
can be to maintain a close relationship with clients. Many charities find that they have to make a special effort to ensure that
clients' involvement is secured. Marketing can help an organisation to refocus its attention on service-users, enabling it to place
clients' needs before other considerations and create a service
that is truly client-centred.

Identifying your 'customers'

Effective commercial marketing is about customers, not about products. Voluntary sector marketing is about service-users, not about services. Services exist only in order to meet clients' needs. Clients come first.

You cannot understand client need until you understand your clients. Undertake some customer analysis in order to get to know your customers. Begin by identifying your principal groups of 'customers'. Remember to distinguish between funders and service-users. We tend to think of a customer as someone who buys something – a product or a service. Yet even in commercial marketing, it is helpful to have a wider definition of customer that encompasses 'user' as well as 'payer'.

The distinction between user and payer is well illustrated with, say, children's foods: Telly Tubby custard, for example. Children eat it, but parents buy it. So who is the customer? In a sense, both are. Clever marketing targets promotional activity and packaging at children, knowing that they will use so-called 'pester power' to influence (badger?) their parents to buy it.

There are parallels in the voluntary sector. Let's take a fictitious example: BirdWatch Junior, a charity for young ornithologists. Research might reveal that adults buy membership (that is, they take the purchasing decision and pay for the product) even though BirdWatch Junior membership is aimed at children. Unlike Telly Tubby custard, which is purchased thanks to the influence of children, BirdWatch Junior is bought because adults think membership is a good idea. The product itself – the fun, comic, bird identification poster and membership pack – is produced specially for children, although promotional activity targets adults. Once you understand the purchasing process and its influencing factors, you are in a better position to know how, and to whom, you should promote your product. Two children's products – Telly Tubby custard and BirdWatch Junior – yet two very different approaches and different targets.

Another voluntary sector example. Drug-users visit needle exchanges to get clean needles, thereby protecting themselves from potentially lethal infections; the health authority or NHS Trust pays the voluntary organisation to run it. The services of the needle exchange are promoted to drug-users in the same way that Telly Tubby custard is promoted to children. The drug-user is as much a customer as the local authority, albeit in a different way.

Regard both your service-user and your service-funder as customers; without people to use your service, or without organisations to fund it, there is no service. So you instantly have two very different customers to cater for; two sets of customers to research; two lots of customers to promote to.

The notion of exchange

Marketing involves an exchange. In commercial marketing the exchange is monetary; the customer pays cash and in return receives a product or service. The concept of exchange is relevant for charities too, even though the thing received may be less tangible than a tin of baked beans: feeling worthy or contributing to society, for example. When you come to work on a marketing strategy for your organisation, you will need to be aware of the nature of the exchanges that take place. Identify your principal customers, define what exactly you receive from them, and identify what you give back in return.

Motivating factors

You probably have a range of 'customers' – donors, supporters, service-users, statutory purchasers and corporate donors. The needs, wants, motivation and influencing factors for each group will vary, as the example below shows.

'Customer' type	Gives	Example of what may be received in return
Individual donor	Money	■ A good feeling from having helped. ■ An opportunity to do some good in the world. ■ The appeasement of their guilt (at being well-off, for example, when so many people are poor). ■ Satisfaction at being able to right an injustice about which they feel strongly.
Volunteer	Time, skills, contacts and experience	■ Companionship of others. ■ Work experience for their CV. ■ A feeling of 'putting something back' into society. ■ A spiritual gain. ■ A feeling of being useful. ■ A chance to help something they care about.
Corporate donor	Staff secondment	■ Enhanced image with staff. ■ Good publicity externally. ■ An air of social responsibility.
Corporate sponsor	Money	■ Their logo on 3,000 annual reports. ■ A full page in your conference programme. ■ Positive associations from being linked with your high-profile event.
Supporters/Members	Membership fee	■ A good feeling from supporting a good cause. ■ An interesting monthly newsletter. ■ A membership/supporters' certificate or pack, or other membership benefits.

An alcohol misuse counselling service

Customer	Involvement in service	Reason for involvement
Service-user	Attends weekly counselling session.	Has a drink problem and wants help.
Health authority	Pays half the running costs.	Helps it meet one of its principal healthcare objectives.
Whisky manufacturer	Sponsors the service's promotional leaflet.	Helps it build a socially responsible image.
Local brewery	Publicises service on beer mats.	Has a policy of sponsoring locally based projects aimed at helping people overcome alcoholism.
Donor	Makes a donation every Christmas.	Donor's father was an alcoholic, so he knows the impact of this on families, especially at times when drink is freely available – such as Christmas.
Volunteer counsellor	Runs a monthly counselling session.	Used to drink too much and appreciates how close she became to becoming an alcoholic. Wants to help others in same situation.

Market segmentation

Having identified your principal customer types, you can develop individual strategies to meet their different needs and expectations: this is known as 'market segmentation'. By segmenting your market you can tailor your offerings to the specific needs of the different segments, thereby becoming more successful in meeting the individual needs of each target group.

Segmentation makes it easy for you to see what each group may need or want from you. Even within groups you may find that there are subgroups. Your 'individual donor' category, for example, might comprise quite distinct subgroups, such as:

- regular donors who give by covenant;
- high-value occasional donors;
- Christmas card customers;
- people who have promised a legacy.

Clearly, you should have a different approach to regular donors from that used with people who donate only at Christmas. Segmentation can help you to identify key groups, thereby enabling you to create a tailored approach to suit each category. You may have hundreds or even thousands of donors, but segmentation will allow you to treat each as an individual.

A children's hospice charity

Customer Segment	Needs
Donors	An individual donor might wish to know why their financial support is needed, how their money will help, and how much of their donation will go in administration.
Statutory healthcare and social work departments	Their statutory duty is to provide respite and palliative care for the public they serve. They will want to know full details of the service offered, its costs, the professional qualifications of staff providing it, care and service standards.
Volunteers	In giving their time rather than their money, volunteers' need is to help in a more practical way, perhaps in the fundraising office, by making goods to sell, or by spreading the word through speaking engagements. They will want to know that their contribution is valued by the people who run the charity. They might need training to help them perform their role.
Corporate donors	They wish to help, to have their help acknowledged in some way, and to be associated with a well-regarded and worthwhile charity. They need evidence that their charitable association will reflect well on them and create goodwill from the public.
General practitioners and other healthcare workers	GPs need information so that they know what services are available for children with life-shortening conditions and how to make referrals and thus help families.
Children with life-shortening conditions	They need a fun place for respite care, plenty of activities, good food and comfortable surroundings. They want staff they know, like and trust. Depending on their age, they might need counselling and emotional support. Medical needs will also have to be met.
Parents	They want a comfortable home from home. They may want counselling, support, a listening ear and, when the time comes, bereavement support. Parents initially want practical information – what to pack for their children, whether special diets can be catered for and whether pets are welcome. They want to know that their children are in safe hands.

Categorising Individual Customers

Marketers have developed a number of ways of categorising customers according to 'type'. Various categories have been suggested, based on social class, occupation, income and education. The categorisation that is widely accepted is that of the Institute of Practitioners in Advertising, the advertising agencies' professional body. This classification has been adopted as the standard one by advertisers, marketers, market researchers and a host of others involved in marketing:

AB Managerial and professional
C1 Supervisory and clerical
C2 Skilled manual
DE Unskilled manual and unemployed

As with any classification there are problems. When this classification was devised, most households were headed by a male 'breadwinner'. It was fairly easy to categorise a family according to his occupation. These days we have many more households comprising two males, two females, two equal breadwinners and a host of other permutations. The 'average' family no longer exists.

Sometimes classification is arrived at by asking people about their income, since there is a correlation between income and occupation. However, two families on the same income may have very different interests and lifestyles, depending on their social class and level of education. A middle-class family on £30,000 will probably live in a different area, buy a different newspaper, watch different TV programmes, eat different food and spend spare income in different ways from a working-class family on the same income. You need to be aware of any shortcomings in the classification system you opt for.

Why Classify?

It is helpful to categorise customers because it has been shown that groups of customers share characteristics. By understanding the characteristics of particular groups, you can begin to target those groups that are more likely to be disposed towards donating, joining, using your service or supporting your cause.

The discovery that 90 per cent of your donors are middle-class *Guardian* readers who give at Christmas and Easter enables you to target your fundraising appeals more effectively. By placing adverts in the *Guardian* at Christmas and Easter you can reach other people who match your existing donor profile.

In order to segment your market and build up an accurate picture of your many customer types, you will need to undertake research. This can be very basic, simply involving the analysis of information you already have (desk research) or it can be more indepth, involving the commissioning of primary research among your customers. You can read more about research in Chapter 5.

Corporate customers

When your customer is an organisation, pinpointing the decision-maker is vital. Social work departments 'buy' care in the community services from voluntary organisations. But departments are not entities in their own right; they comprise individuals, some with power and autonomy and others without any. The customer, then, is not the social work department, but certain key individuals within it. Pinpointing the real customer involves asking:

- Who decides to buy?
- Who are the key decision-makers in the buying/commissioning process?

- How do they arrive at a purchase decision? (By appraising the options in a formal way? By holding a meeting? By using personal contacts?)
- How long is the pre-purchase decision period? (Do they start considering the options six months before a final decision is reached?)
- What are the key dates in the process? (Is there a cut-off date after which they will not, for example, accept applications for funding?)
- At what stage, if any, can you influence the decision?
- Who from within influences the decision?
- Who makes the final decision?
- How often do they buy? (At the year end? Every three years?)
- What do they 'buy' (sponsor, fund or support)?

These same questions can be asked when seeking to identify key company personnel responsible for sponsorship or funding decisions. In order to answer many of these questions you need to carry out some marketing research (see Chapter 5).

Getting to Know your Corporate Customers

In-depth research may be necessary if you want to get to know your customers really well. But without spending too much time or money there are some simple ways of getting to know your organisational customers:

- List the five most important organisations (and people within them) you should interview in order to find out what they want from your service/organisation. Arrange to talk to them on the phone, or preferably face to face.
- List the principal enquiries you want to make. Ask about these when you go to see them.
- List any important magazines or journals that will tell you more about your customers and the issues that concern them. Go out and buy them or inspect them in the library.
- List any exhibitions and events that will provide a chance to get to know your customers better. Book tickets and attend them, or exhibit at them.

Understanding buying behaviour

No one buys anything for the sake of it: we buy to fulfil a need. Even the shopaholic who spends money on expensive yet unnecessary items is buying for a reason, even if the reason is merely to satisfy their addiction to shopping! Knowing your customer involves first knowing who they are (see above) and second, finding out why they buy. What motivates them? A great deal of work has been done in this area, for obvious reasons. If it were possible to unlock the reasons why people buy, it would give companies a head start in selling and it would transform charity fundraising into a job we could all do in our sleep. Sadly it is impossible to

Motivating Factor	Product Example	Comments
Need	Basic foodstuffs, loo roll, heat and light	An NHS trust might buy a service from your organisation because they have a responsibility to offer that service, and it is preferable to provide it via your organisation than to establish their own service. In other words, they need it.
Want	Perfumes, alcohol, chocolates and luxury items	Desire can be a strong motivating factor. We might not need a carved Indian casket from the Oxfam shop or a batik bedspread; we buy these things because we like and want them.
To make a statement	Save the Whale car sticker, Greenpeace T-shirt, 'Rats Have Rights' mug	Sometimes we buy an object because it is a way of making a statement about ourselves, our moral beliefs or political affiliations. Charity merchandise is frequently bought for this reason. Even practical items, such as mugs and T-shirts are bought not because we need the object, but because our possession of it says something about us.
Re-sale	Manufacturers make goods to sell to wholesalers, who buy in order to sell to retailers, who buy to sell to customers	Some charities produce guides and handbooks which others (such as bookshops) buy to re-sell. Charities may buy gifts to resell in their fundraising shops.
Entertainment	Theatre, cinema, horse races, lottery tickets	Tickets to charity balls, charity sporting events, fêtes and fairs are bought so the purchaser can both enjoy the entertainment and help the charity at the same time.
Impulse	Bargains come into this category!	Often we buy on impulse, particularly when it comes to things we don't particularly need. They catch our eye, they might come in handy later, or they are a bargain. Charity merchandise is often bought for this reason, such as a cheerful Traidcraft waistcoat or some bright Mexican earrings.
Emotional	Child sponsorship or membership of an organisation	A great deal of charity buying is done for emotional reasons. We may buy a cake from a fête stall not because we are hungry, but because we want to help raise money for the cause. That's why we might buy membership of a campaigning organisation or send donations to charity. We do it because we care about the issue or subject, whether it is a campaign to end torture in a totalitarian regime or an appeal to build a sanctuary for old donkeys.

come up with a neat set of reasons why people buy, and when it comes to supporting a charitable organisation, motivations become even more complicated. However, the table above outlines some common motivations.

Usually people buy not just for one reason, but for a complex variety of motivations. Someone might buy an enamel CND badge because they are passionately committed to nuclear disarmament, they want to support CND, they want to make a political statement by wearing the badge, they want to annoy their boss, and they think it looks stylish and attractive.

Highlighting Motivation in Publicity Materials

Find out why people buy from you. It will help you promote your product more effectively by highlighting the key motivational factor in publicity material. If most of your customers buy your silk blouses because they wish to support the work of the hostel for unmarried mothers in India that made them, your promotional material might read:

> Our Delhi Mother and Baby Centre provides a lifeline to unmarried mothers rejected by their families. It offers comfortable rooms, nutritional food for mother and child, a crèche, parenting classes, and provides employment in the community sewing room. That's where these beautiful silk blouses were made. Women from the Delhi Centre make the blouses in return for a decent wage and free lodgings. Our Centre gives them a chance to establish a relationship with their new child, to learn essential parenting skills, and to grow physically healthy. By buying one of their blouses you are helping these women to become self-sufficient and to take care of their child.

But if your research reveals that people buy the blouses primarily because they are attractive, fashionable and good value, your promotional material would take a very different slant:

> Beautiful blouses in the finest silk, the brightest jewel-like colours, the highest quality – and at a price that is much less than you might expect. These stunning silk blouses will not look out of place anywhere – teamed with a suit for the office, or dressed up with some glitzy accessories for a dinner party. Nor will they break the bank. And while wearing your blouse you can have the satisfaction of knowing that your purchase has helped single mothers in Delhi ...

If you are selling your blouses through wholesalers for re-sale, their motivation is profit. They want to buy cheap and sell dear. To them you might say:

> Quality silk blouses in a range of fashionable colours, sizes 10–14. Only £120 per dozen. Will easily retail at £20+ each.

There is no need in this case to focus on the Delhi Centre. As the motivating factor is the profit to be made from re-sale, the Delhi Centre is irrelevant unless it is likely to help boost sales to consumers.

To find out why people buy, you need to ask them. There are lots of ways of undertaking research to find out why people buy from you, and some of them are neither costly nor time-consuming. Chapter 5 on marketing research looks at how you can carry out this sort of research in-house.

Why do Organisations Buy?

While individuals buy for a whole set of different reasons, organisations generally buy in order to fulfil their organisational goals. An individual might give to a mental health charity because they care about the issues surrounding mental health, perhaps because they or a relative have experienced mental health difficulties. A social work department might support a mental health project run by a housing charity because it has a statutory responsibility for the community care of people with mental health difficulties. In funding the charity it is discharging its duty. But even here the motivation is complicated. One authority might buy services from a particular mental health charity because:

a It has to provide that service.
b It is committed to innovation in dealing with people with mental health difficulties and believes that the particular housing charity has a good track record for innovation.

Another authority might buy into the same service because:

a It also has a statutory duty to provide that service.
b It has a policy of supporting local voluntary organisations where possible.

Only by knowing your customers and their motivation can you begin to understand their purchasing decisions. To the first social work department you would need to stress the innovative nature of your work; to the second you would place more emphasis on being locally based.

Customers Have Choices

Even when the customer knows what they want to buy – let's say it's toilet tissue – they still have choices to make, such as which brand, which colour, recycled or normal, luxury or budget loo roll. Then there's where to buy it. Supermarket or corner shop? And how to pay for it. Cash or (assuming other items are being bought at the same time) cheque, debit, credit or store card.

It is the same when it comes to selecting a charity to give to. We might know that we want a children's charity, but which one? For abused children? Third World children? Disadvantaged children? Physically disabled? Mentally disabled? Sick? Holidays for children? Education? Healthcare? Local, national or international? The choice is immense. Then there's how to give. Via a collection can, a legacy, a covenant, a one-off donation, Gift Aid, payroll giving, by volunteering, by buying merchandise, by collecting door-to-door, by organising a fundraising event?

The Dilemmas of Attracting Customers

Identify what choices your customers have, try to understand why they choose what they do, and work out how you can persuade more of them to opt for you rather than the competition. There is a paradox, though. For membership organisations (such as the RSPB or National Trust, for example) and for campaigning organisations, more customers means more money. By contrast, for service charities more customers (service-users) often means less money. The more service-users a charity has, the more costly the service is to run, often without a concomitant increase in funding. So whereas a commercial body wants to get more customers, service charities need to attract more customers *and* more funding.

There is a further paradox when it comes to charities and their customers. Companies try to attract and keep their customers; their survival depends on it. For many charities, however, the philosophy is about decreasing dependence and fostering autonomy. Voluntary organisations working in the field of disability, for example, aim to create a world in which people with disabilities can be as independent as possible, by removing barriers that prevent them from getting about, working, going on holiday, studying and leading a full life. Such an approach, if successful, will put such charities out of business once their mission is achieved. No business would deliberately plan to make itself redundant.

Turning Customers Away

There are times when a voluntary organisation is asked to provide a service for which funding is available, but the organisation declines because it recognises the value of being needs-led, not resource-driven.

Let's take an example. A statutory body asks you to provide a service for older people. The funding on offer is, in your view, inadequate. You could provide a service for that amount, but it would fall far short of your own acceptable standard. You might decide to turn your customer away because doing business with them would result in:

1 Having to provide a substandard service which would, you believe, cause serious damage to your reputation for providing high quality, innovative services, thus leading to a future loss of credibility.
2 Having to compromise your principles: if you genuinely feel that older people deserve better than this, you would be a hypocrite to provide an inferior service.

Clearly, in this example you would be rejecting one customer (the statutory body) because doing business with them would result in a disservice to another group of customers: older people. By building a service around available resources, you would be failing to meet the identified needs of older people.

Customer care

It costs seven times as much to attract a new customer as to keep an existing one. It therefore makes great sense for cash-strapped charities to ensure that they have first-rate customer care, because good customer care is the best way you have of keeping your customers and, via their word of mouth, attracting new ones.

Some of our more successful companies have achieved their success by caring about their customers and having clear procedures and comprehensive training to ensure that customer care is a reality, not just rhetoric. Many charities are now wising up to customer care. The days are gone when recipients were expected to be both deserving and grateful. Today's customer culture has reached the voluntary sector, and there is a widely held view – and rightly so – that customers, whether paying or not, have rights.

Caring about customers and taking steps to provide them with a top-class service (given the limitations imposed on you due to funding restraints) are natural to charities' thinking today, although these are frequently not approached in an organised way, still less considered as part of a marketing strategy.

Meeting needs also means managing expectations. Customer care involves setting out clearly what your customers need (based on what they tell you, not on what you surmise) and explaining what you can deliver. You must provide a quality service that meets reasonable expectations and be prepared to take swift remedial action whenever you fail.

Establishing a Customer Care Culture

Everyone can tell stories of poor customer service from their own recent experience. It happens to us all every week – in restaurants, shops, railway stations and on buses, face to face, over the telephone and in writing. Poor customer service is so common that it is likely that your organisation is as guilty of it as any other.

If you visit a shop and the assistant ignores your obvious need for help because he is too busy telling his colleague about a recent football match, that gives you a bad impression not only of the shop assistant, but of the store as a whole and all the other stores in the chain. You judge it all by your one experience of one member of staff. That's how charities are judged too. If one of your staff is rude or unhelpful, that reflects on the rest of you.

Organisations do not exist as entities in their own right. They are made up of staff and viewed on the basis of the skills and attitude of those staff. For some of your staff, customer care will be second nature; others will need to learn it. Train all staff in customer care and make the training programme part of your marketing activity.

If you are an organisation with many functions, you may need to organise a range of different customer care training sessions. For example, customer care training for staff running your mail order catalogue would need to cover different issue from training for HQ fundraising staff or for volunteers who work in your charity shops.

Good customer care can be measured. You can record and evaluate it in an objective way, for example by:

- Timing how long it takes to answer the telephone.
- Timing how long it takes to reply to mail.
- Counting the number of customer complaints.
- Counting the number of complimentary letters you receive.

TRUE STORY   Getting it Wrong

I was in a charity shop when I spotted an interesting antique teapot. As a collector of teapots I was eager to inspect it with a view to buying it, despite its hefty price tag. Carefully lifting it from the shelf, I heard an angry voice from behind: 'Don't touch. It's valuable,' screeched the assistant. Shocked and surprised I put the teapot back and left the shop. Some weeks later I saw the teapot in the window. As no one had shown any interest in it, it had been reduced to half price. I would have been happy to pay the full price. Now I avoid that shop and have started giving my unwanted goods to another charity shop. How much goodwill and custom do you miss out on without ever knowing it?

TRUE STORY Getting it Right

An elderly friend of mine contacted a local charity for information on a health problem he was suffering from. The woman on the other end of the phone was very sensitive, helpful and caring. She provided lots of information, which he found extremely helpful. He is grateful for the help received and plans to leave a legacy to the charity in his will. Knowledgeable and kind individuals can enhance the image of your organisation more than any glossy publicity materials can.

THE GOOD CUSTOMER CARE CHECKLIST

☑ Set up a customer care working group to examine customer care, to come up with ideas for achieving it, and to set and monitor standards.

☑ Make sure that at least one person in your organisation (possibly a voluntary member) is charged with the task of overseeing customer care, even if you are a very small organisation. Make sure that person sees every customer complaint and is informed of the outcome.

☑ Gather information about the standard of performance within your organisation.

☑ Set demanding yet achievable standards for improving and maintaining customer care.

☑ Publicise the standards you are aiming for.

☑ Measure your performance regularly and publish this too.

☑ Explain failures to meet your standards – to other staff and to your customers.

Volunteers as Customers

Volunteers are customers too. As an extremely valuable asset you should take very special care of them. The Volunteer Centre UK conducted a survey, which revealed that Britain's 22 million volunteers contribute as much as £41 billion a year to GDP (gross domestic product) – more than that produced by the energy, construction or water supply industries! Treat them badly and charities will lose this enormous annual boost. Volunteers can generate income for you (by fundraising for example), they can help preserve your funds (by removing the need to buy in extra help) and they can make otherwise impossibly expensive services (such as a befriending or free counselling service) affordable to

tip

Draw up a customer charter which lets your clients know what they can expect. Base this on what they have told you they would like to see by way of performance.

operate. So in many ways they are one of your most important customers. Your success certainly depends on them.

Why is it, then, that so many volunteers are treated like dogsbodies or unpaid skivvies? Too few volunteers are given interesting and rewarding jobs to do. Many are taken for granted. Few are given a contract, training, a job description. It is amazing that so many put up with it! Some charities do treat their volunteers very well, appreciate and value their contribution, and ensure that their work is worthwhile and fulfilling. Are you one of those? If not, you could be losing some very valuable customers.

Building Brand Loyalty

Companies spend vast amounts of money trying to ensure that their customers remain loyal. They will continue 'buying' from you only if you treat them well (by getting your customer care right) and offer the right products (which is what marketing is all about). There are things you can do to enhance a customer's loyalty to your cause:

- Thank them for being customers and show their support is appreciated.
- Keep them up to date with news and developments.
- If feasible and appropriate, give them loyalty rewards – 10 per cent off their next membership subscription, for example.

Complaints

Customer care is not about handling complaints, it is about ensuring that you get things right in the first place, thus removing the causes of complaint. Inevitably, though, even in well-run charities things do occasionally go wrong, and you need to be ready to respond properly and to correct errors.

Complaints Fact File

- People are generally very reluctant to make formal complaints, but most will grumble to others about poor service.
- Of all dissatisfied customers, 96 per cent make no complaint!
- Most unhappy customers tell seven others how bad you are.
- Thirteen per cent of unhappy customers tell at least twenty others how bad you are.
- Commercial organisations are more likely to receive complaints because their customers have paid for something and therefore feel that they have more of a right to expect a certain standard.

- Charities are less likely to receive complaints: users of their services may be vulnerable or may regard a complaint as ingratitude.

Encourage complaints, don't regard them as threats. Complaints are a bit like free research, providing you with data on where you are failing and thus enabling you to put it right. Establish a system for copying customer complaints to relevant staff, so that there is an opportunity for a complaint to result in a policy or service delivery change or improvement. If your office is inaccessible for people with pushchairs, and no toys are available in your reception area for the many parents who need to bring their children with them, a visit to your office will be an ordeal, even if the service you offer is in other respects first-class. Perhaps you have failed to notice this shortcoming. A complaint can identify it for you and give you a chance to put it right, thus further improving your service. This will come about only if the person dealing with complaints feeds them through to someone with responsibility for taking corrective action.

Understanding your 'product'

INTRODUCTION

What is your product? Ask any manufacturer and they could answer without hesitation, but it may not always be so obvious for charities. In conventional marketing a product is the thing you produce in order to sell. Some charities sell goods proper – such as gifts and Christmas cards via mail order catalogues, aids for people with disabilities or second-hand clothes through charity shops.

What is your product?

The majority of Britain's top 200 charities trade, with more than half of them having a separate trading company. But what is their product? They probably have a range, which encompasses far more than they sell in their shops or through their catalogues. In the case of charity shops, why do charities run them? Usually, as a means of raising funds for their 'real' work, such as medical research (a cancer charity), aid (a Third World charity), campaigning (a pressure group), to fund a service (a cats' home) or whatever.

Let's look at the cancer charity. It might run shops in order to raise funds to:

- Research the causes of cancer.
- Develop cures.
- Run hospices.
- Run a service providing terminal care at home for cancer sufferers.
- Provide support and counselling to cancer sufferers.
- Provide support and bereavement care to families.

The charity could, therefore, be said to have seven products: the goods sold in the shops and the six services listed above. It needs to develop and promote each separately, and yet each needs to be linked as part of an integrated marketing strategy. There's no point appointing new medical researchers and opening new hospices if the shops are bringing in too little income to support them. The success of one product often depends on the success of another – very profitable shops might enable the charity to open another hospice or to undertake new research.

It is really important that you itemise each of your products. That way you can measure the effectiveness and performance of each, and develop separate promotional programmes. If one product is clearly in difficulty, you can take action to ensure that it does not pull down other products (or indeed the whole organisation) with it. Even charities involved in just one line of 'business' will probably have a range of different products. A charity for older people might have:

- residential homes;
- a befriending and visiting service;
- a day centre;
- a meals-on-wheels service;
- a publications division producing good practice guides for professionals who work with older people;
- an information division producing advice for old people on how to guard against crime, keep warm in winter and keep fit in old age;
- a training division running courses for professionals who work with older people;
- a campaigning wing lobbying for improved rights for older people.

All the above relate to older people, and yet clearly they are very separate and distinct products, each requiring a very different marketing approach. Some are free services; some attract a fee; some are aimed at old people, others at professionals. The example highlights why it is so important to list your products. It enables you to see how diverse your work is, even if as an organisation you have a very integrated feel. So sit down now and list all your products. Do you currently treat each separately? Is each one promoted, costed and evaluated separately? Do you run one product at a profit in order to subsidise a less profitable (or even loss-making) but nevertheless much needed service? Are you clear that this is what you are doing?

Many companies employ 'product managers' to oversee the development and promotion of individual products. For example, a bank might have a credit card product manager, one for current accounts, one for business borrowing, one for mortgages, one for e-banking and one for savings accounts. Although a bank is in the business of borrowing and lending, each of its products has an individual role to play within that.

Products within a Product

Look again at the fictitious example of the charity for older people. One of its services is an information division. This division may itself produce a range of products, such as:

- a freephone information hotline;
- a 'Keep Fit in Old Age' diet and exercise pack;
- a home security leaflet and video;
- access via its website to cut-price home insulation products.

Remember, when listing your products, to itemise the products produced by each of your services.

An Organisation as a Product

Sometimes, one of the products an organisation sells is itself or its reputation. For example, the Vegetarian Society sells its logo to food manufacturers, who use it to endorse their products and verify their non-animal composition. Companies buying this are not paying for the privilege of using someone else's logo on their products; they are paying for the beneficial associations they will get from their relationship with a respected vegetarian organisation.

The Plain English Campaign sells its 'Crystal Mark' in very much the same way. Organisations wishing to use the Crystal Mark logo must first show that the material on which they plan to use it is indeed plain English. They must also pay a fee.

Another charity, the RSPCA, markets itself as a product, as you can see from the following excerpt from one of its ads, which was placed in *Marketing*, a weekly newspaper for marketing professionals. It reads:

> HOW THE RSPCA CAN HELP YOUR COMPANY BECOME
> A TOP DOG
> We'd like to offer you another way of looking at the RSPCA.
> We may be a charity but we're also a big business
> opportunity. We have one of the highest spontaneous
> awareness measurements of any charity in the UK and
> constantly feature among the top UK organisations in the
> news. With so much public support for our work the
> RSPCA makes an ideal business partner. As over half the
> households in Britain own pets, building a relationship
> with us could help raise your company's profile, increase
> sales and present a positive image, as well as helping us in

our lifesaving work. Such a relationship certainly worked with White Horse Whisky, Superdrug, Burmah and Kellogg's.

In their ad the RSPCA names big companies it has worked with, thereby providing reassurance to readers that its product must be good – otherwise the household names quoted would not have bought it.

This technique is also used in a Red Cross promotional advert:

> ... This year, with the help of such famous names as Zeneca, Barclays Bank, British Telecom, Somerfield Stores and Selfridges, we have raised hundreds of thousands of pounds, while our corporate sponsors have enjoyed the benefits of supporting the British Red Cross ...

An Idea as a Product

For many voluntary organisations and pressure groups, their product is an idea – such as anti-racism or safe sex. Even ideas can benefit from being marketed properly. The same principles apply. You need to think about your product – the idea. You need to consider its promotion – via editorial coverage, perhaps, and campaign leaflets. You must think about place – how people will get to hear about your idea. And you need to consider price. For example, if your 'idea product' is that nobody should live in poverty in Britain, a cost will be attached to its implementation. The cost to the taxpayer would probably be enormous in terms of boosting welfare benefits. That is what is known as the 'impact cost'. If you are to stand any chance in selling any product, the price must be right. For campaigning organisations and others selling ideas, your impact cost must be considered as part of your own marketing work.

The Idea beyond the Product

A cosmetics manufacturer might make lipstick and mascara. These are its products. Yet successful cosmetics companies realise that their 'generic product' is beauty (or the hope of beauty). A washing powder manufacturer sells cleanliness, not soap powder. A deodorant-maker sells confidence, not anti-perspirant. What is the idea behind your product? If you provide supported accommodation for people leaving psychiatric hospitals, you are not just providing a community care service: you are offering hope, independence and freedom to your clients. Look behind your products and see what you are really selling. When promoting your product and seeking support for it, highlight the idea that lies behind it.

Growing through products

The aim of most companies is to grow and, through growth, to prosper. Some charities regard this as inappropriate behaviour for the voluntary sector. Growth is equated with empire-building, predatory and aggressive actions, counter to the spirit of cooperation that is believed to exist within the sector. It need not be like this. It is possible to expand and to build up a solid base without treading on others' toes or invading a fellow charity's patch. When it comes to growth, charities – like companies – have certain options. These include:

- Market penetration – this is where you take your existing products to your existing markets. Your aim is to capture a bigger share of this market, or to reach previously unreached potential customers.
- Market development – here you take your existing products, but you promote them to new target markets.
- Product development – this is where you develop brand new products, but offer them to your existing target markets.
- Diversification – this involves complete change. You must develop new products and offer them to new markets, a risky strategy for charities and businesses alike.

The low-risk option is market penetration. You do not have to develop new products or find new markets, all you need to do is ensure that you penetrate your existing market. Of course, that's easier said than done. Suppose your market is elderly wealthy women who, by and large, are the main group to leave you legacies. To penetrate the market you need to reach all the wealthy elderly women who currently have made no provision for you in their will. You can see the problem immediately. How do you know who they are? How do you reach them? There is no easy answer, though you can read more about targeting your key audiences later on in the book.

Market development involves taking your existing products to new markets. It might be that you run a confidential telephone counselling service for teenagers in Manchester. You could develop your market by offering the same service, but to teenagers in Bolton, Bury and Rochdale.

If you wanted to aim for a strategy of product development, you would need to find some new products for your existing market. Remember that marketing is not about making what you think people need, it is about finding out what people need (by asking them) and then developing the products and services that will meet that need. If you discover that the blind people for whom you run a drop-in centre have difficulties getting their weekly shopping, you might decide to develop a service to meet that need.

Diversification as a means to growth is risky. For many charities it may also be illegal, depending on what your constitution says about your aims as an organisation. Certainly for charities reading this book – those new to marketing – it is an inadvisable route.

Give an incentive

Whether you want to grow by reaching new markets or penetrating an existing one, you may want to use 'incentives' to help encourage take-up of your product. An incentive is something additional to the product that is offered as an inducement. For example, a bank might offer a free passport holder for anyone buying over £500 worth of travellers' cheques. An environmental charity might offer a free address book made from recycled, chlorine-free paper to new members.

Use incentives to:

■ Persuade people to buy from you rather than a competitor: for example, if you are selling Christmas cards (along with thousands of other charities) you might want to offer a free pack of gift tags with every box of cards. This might tip the balance in your favour, and give yours the edge over other charity cards.

■ Get people to respond: if you offer potential members a free gift, but only if they join before a certain deadline, this may prod them into action. Without an incentive to encourage a response, inertia might otherwise prevent potential supporters from signing up.

■ Get people to buy more of your product: if you offer an incentive for sales over a certain number, this can encourage people to buy more than they might otherwise do. For example, offering mail order customers free postage on orders over £30 might be enough to persuade some to increase the total of their purchases.

It is not just charities selling goods that can benefit from using incentives. Service charities can also use incentives to advantage. For example, a drop-in centre for single parents might offer free face-painting, a free crèche and free coffee and cakes, as an inducement to get parents through the door.

If you are considering offering an incentive, ask yourself:

■ What incentive would we offer?
■ What would the cost be?
■ Is the incentive appropriate?
■ Is it likely to boost sales?
■ Would it boost sales by enough to cover its costs?
■ How do we know? On what evidence are we basing our assumptions?

TRUE STORY   Getting it Wrong

A bank was promoting motor loans in July, timed to coincide with the annual spate of new car buying. It decided to offer an incentive linked with motoring and opted for snow shovels. Unfortunately, snow shovels were far from motorists' minds during one of the hottest summers in years. The incentive campaign was a flop!

Don't Bribe, Incentivise!

It can be difficult getting incentives right, especially for charities.

- ☒ Don't come across as trying to bribe customers. They will resent it.
- ☒ Don't appear lavish or wasteful.
- ☑ Do offer something appropriate, that links with your work and your members'/customers' interests.
- ☑ Do offer something that will be valued (without appearing extravagant).

Assessing an Incentive's Impact

If you plan on using incentives, work out your figures very carefully. There is no point in spending money on incentives if you do not attract enough extra 'business' as a result. But how do you know what effect an incentive will have? The only reliable way is to offer an incentive to one group but not to another similar group. Measure take-up to see if the incentivised group was significantly more responsive than the control. The easiest way to do this is to split your mailing list (see Chapter 10 on direct mail to find out more about 'test mailings'). Questionnaires too may help you find out whether an incentive is likely to affect whether someone joins you/buys from you/supports you, and can help you assess the popularity of different incentive options.

Endorsing endorsements

A certain pet food manufacturer says that it makes the dog food that top breeders recommend. This is an endorsement. The use of endorsements serves to make buyers feel reassured of the quality of the product. With an endorsement, you don't need to use a real person. For example, you could describe a resort as the place travel agents take their holidays.

What can you use to endorse your products?

The following was printed on the envelope of a direct mail appeal: 'When my mum was dying of cancer, I had to cope on my own – I support Marie Curie Cancer Care so others don't have to do the same.' Alongside the quote was a photograph of a woman; her name; and wording telling us that she has been a supporter of the charity for over ten years. This personal touch, a direct appeal from one individual to another, is far more powerful than the words of a charity officer urging people to help.

Testing testimonials

An alternative to an endorsement is the testimonial, where you quote someone's words. Some companies use famous faces to provide testimonials, but the words of ordinary people can be every bit as powerful, as this fictitious example shows:

'I was at rock bottom and could see no reason for continuing to live. I felt worthless, unloved and unwanted. Yet with the help of Listening Ear I have turned my life around and made it worthwhile. Today I have a wonderful husband and beautiful children, a job I enjoy and a fabulous home. I owe it all to Listening Ear. They gave me the will to live, helped me sort out my problems and adopt a positive approach. Without their help I dread to think where I would be now.'

tip

Handwritten testimonials add authenticity. If the author consents, use their name and a photograph too.

Understanding your market

INTRODUCTION

One of the key aspects to knowing your market is knowing your customers. But you must also know what you are up against, and in particular, who the competition is. This may sound a bit too cut and thrust, and rather unseemly, for the voluntary sector. In an ideal world charities would work together in full cooperation and harmony. Of course, in Utopia there would be no need for charities at all! But the reality is that it is a hard world out there. Other organisations are competing against you - for funding, for donations, for sales, even for staff and volunteers. Some charities will survive, they may even grow and thrive, but others will shrink or perhaps die. Those in the latter category are likely to be the ones who refused to consider marketing. Where do you want your organisation to be in five years' time? Dead, buried and long since forgotten? Or going from strength to strength, focused, successful and expanding?

The charities likely to succeed in the fierce outside world are the streetwise ones, those that understand the market and know how to sell themselves as well as their products and services. Know your market by getting to know competitors and what they are up to. Then, develop a competitive edge so that you are better, and are seen to be better, than rivals.

Who are your competitors?

Identifying your competitors is not necessarily an easy thing to do. Suppose you run a work experience scheme for people with learning disabilities. They make attractive craft products, which are sold through local shops in order to help fund the scheme.

Projects of this sort are generally not run like a mainstream business; the prices you would need to charge for your products in order to cover your overheads would price you out of the market. So such projects require external funding to act as a subsidy, unlike a commercial set-up making similar products. In a very narrow sense your competitors are those other manufacturers who make products similar to your own, and sell them through similar outlets.

But that's only part of the story. If there is a charitable project on the other side of town employing people with various disabilities, you might regard them as the competition, particularly if they are funded by the same charitable trust or local authority. They are indeed your competitor, but so too are the many other organisations funded by that trust or council, for all are seeking funding from the same finite pot of money. If you regard your competition in too narrow a way, you may lose out.

Geographic or Generic?

Competition may be geographic. A children's charity might be a competitor of a wildlife charity if both rely on the same local authority for their funding. But it can also be generic, with national children's charities up against each other, or national wildlife charities competing with local wildlife charities for the same supporters.

Competition in the voluntary sector is a funny business. Disability Charity A is not competing with Disability Charity B in the same way as Widget Factory A would be up against Widget Factory B. The chances are that the two factories would be busy chasing the same customers. In the case of the two charities, there would probably be more than enough 'user customers' for both charities. What they would be short on is someone to pay for their services, so their area of competition would not so much be to attract more users, as to attract more funding.

Some Words of Warning

Be careful not to see competition where none exists. Some charities are so preoccupied with so-called competitors that they spend too much time on warfare and not enough time on welfare. In the long run such organisations will not prosper.

Having worked out who your competitors are, monitor them. In the more aggressive world of business, monitoring the competition has been known to involve bugging the boardroom, infiltrating the organisation, even industrial theft and espionage. We're talking here about something altogether more humdrum and definitely more legal.

TRUE STORY Getting it Wrong

I write annual reports for housing associations, but lacking an in-house designer I buy in design work. Seeing an advertisement for a firm of designers specialising in housing association annual reports, I called for information with the intention of using them if I liked their work. I had recently been commissioned to produce two reports, needed a designer and was eager to try someone new. The person I spoke to was immediately suspicious of me, and let it show. He regarded me as a competitor rather than a customer: I wanted to buy his services, not steal his customers. Far from telling me about his work, he interrogated me about my intentions! Eventually I issued an ultimatum: send me some information and I will consider giving you some business, or ignore my request and lose out on some well-paid work. I never heard from the company again. They have lost out on a great deal of work, and all because they feared competition where none existed.

Six Ways to Keep your Eye on the Competition

You can monitor the competition by:

1 **Talking to them** Find out from the horse's mouth what they are up to, what the new developments are, whether any plans are afoot. Naturally you may find that in areas of real competition your rivals will not be very talkative. But by having some kind of ongoing dialogue with potential competitors, at least you are in touch, you are not isolated from what else is happening, and you have some feel for what is taking place. Remember that if you are monitoring them, they are probably monitoring you!

2 **Talking to their users and/or supporters** Sometimes you can find out quite a lot about the competition from those who use it or support it. Talking to NSPCC supporters, for example, about why they opt for that charity rather than another children's one, can be very helpful in providing you with the information you need to shape your own charity. It is, of course, not always easy, possible or, indeed, ethical to do this.

3 **Visiting exhibitions such as Charityfair** This is an excellent way of keeping in touch with developments in your field and of finding out what else is happening nationwide. It is a chance to check out the competition, but also to forge partnerships and to take forward joint initiatives (which is another important element of marketing).

4 **Monitoring local and charity/specialist press** Charities like to promote what they are doing, so building up a file of press cuttings is a good way of knowing what a particular charity, or a particular sector, has been doing over the months and years.

5 Monitoring their advertising This is particularly important with charities that attract the bulk of their donations from advertising. Your own ads may appear in the same publications, so you must know what you are up against. Look out for where else rival charities advertise. It might be in publications you would not have expected, and that in itself could be useful marketing intelligence. What imagery are your competitors using in their advertising, what messages are they promoting, what line are they taking?

6 Collecting their literature (annual reports, leaflets, brochures) Find out what they are doing that you are not. It is also useful to see what sort of image they are putting across via their publications.

Essentially, you want to know what the competition is doing. What is their 'marketing mix'? In other words, what is their product; how do they promote it; what is it sold for and to whom; how do they get customers to the product? Answer these questions and you will have a greater understanding of your competitors. Try also to discover their approach and philosophy, find out more about their staff, the conditions under which they run their service, the resources they have available and anything else that may prove useful.

Knowing the competition is just one aspect of knowing your market. It also involves developing a really good understanding of your customers, how they think, what their motivation is, what their expectations are, how they regard your organisation, and so on. Finding out about your market can be costly. Some companies spend huge sums and employ external consultancies to undertake research and monitoring. It can be done in-house, though you will need to make the time and space to do it.

UNDERSTANDING YOUR MARKET CHECKLIST

☑ Talk to your own users/clients. Conduct individual and group interviews to find out what they want from your organisation and your services.

☑ Talk to those who buy your service (such as social work departments and health authorities) to establish their reaction to your service, to find out what they think about your strengths and weaknesses.

☑ Talk to your supporters, members, volunteers and donors about why they are involved in your work and what they get out of it.

☑ Monitor competitors.

☑ Monitor trends in your market to spot changes that create opportunities or threats.

Factors affecting your market

There are always things that will affect your market and the environment in which you work. Some you can influence and others you will have no control over. Many factors will represent a threat to you, while others will offer opportunities, as long as you have an eye on the market, are flexible and ready to adapt to changing environments and changing needs. Some of the uncontrollables you may face include the following.

Science and Technology

Changes in technology have been vast and rapid. The invention and cheap mass production of the silicon chip has revolutionised our lives, bringing high-tech wizardry such as computers and Internet access into our offices and our homes. In one small object the size of a calculator we can store information that previously would have occupied a machine the size of a house. Microwave ovens have changed the way we eat (as well as providing new opportunities for 'ready meal' manufacturers). Faxes, mobile phones, WAP phones and e-mail have altered how we communicate and how our organisations are run. Today everything from meals to communication is instant.

There are new technology implications for voluntary organisations, too, and not just in terms of the impact of new products on how the office is run. There are potentially big implications for some services too. For example, the Internet shopping revolution could result in people with disabilities preferring to shop from the comfort of their armchair, making your Dial-A-Ride service redundant and causing you to rethink the needs of your customers. (Such a technological change could result in people with disabilities becoming socially isolated and confined to their homes; research would uncover this and you could develop new services to address this problem!) We already have the technology to program a computer to switch off lights, turn on the heating, close the curtains, and so on. This technology, put to use in the home of, say, someone with dementia, could alter the way you support such people in their homes. It could also have major implications for your funding, if you have to install expensive hardware in people's homes.

Scientific breakthroughs such as genetically modified foods have spawned new products containing them (as well as GM-free products), new legislation controlling them, and new campaigns opposing them.

Government Policy and Laws

The government's care in the community policy meant the closure of many NHS and voluntary sector hospitals and other long-stay institutions for people with learning disabilities and mental health difficulties. It also opened up new markets for housing providers who adapted to provide care as well as accommodation. Government policy can have the effect of putting some voluntary organisations out of business, while at the same time boosting the work of others. Keeping a close eye on policy developments, and their potential impact on your organisation, is vital if you don't want to be left behind as your competitors move swiftly to adapt to change and to grasp emerging opportunities.

Legislation, too, can create new openings for charities. For example, if drugs were legalised, there might be a need for the establishment of services to respond to this move, perhaps by explaining the pros and cons of certain substances, and by providing public health information and training. If brothels were legalised, it might be necessary to set up health promotion and safe sex initiatives for prostitutes and clients.

When legislation was introduced to enable the government to launch the National Lottery, few charities anticipated the effect a lottery and scratch cards would have on their fundraising. Charities running their own lotteries or scratch cards were particularly hard hit. A survey by NCVO at that time showed that the proportion of the population giving to charity fell by 14 per cent and the Lottery was blamed. Yet few charities had taken action to find other sources of finance in the period between lottery announcement and launch. The Lottery is no longer new yet its impact continues to be felt. Long-term drops in charities' revenue are occurring. Monitoring the market and anticipating change are important aspects of marketing. If you wait until the impact of new legislation is felt before you act, you've waited too long.

Competitors' Activities

In business the threat of new competition is always there. Many telecoms companies now supply electricity, while electricity companies supply gas! Even monopolies such as the Royal Mail are to face competition from postal operators in Europe once markets are opened up in line with EU legislation. The voluntary sector is also affected by competition. Other organisations may do similar work or specialise in your field of expertise. If one of them comes along and sets up a service in direct competition with yours, which is always a possibility, that will affect your funding and threaten your service. Increasingly, competition is coming from the private and public sectors, as competitive tendering for services grows. You might find yourself competing with brand new competition from these sectors.

Culture and Taste/Trends

A decade ago recycled toilet tissue, organic food and environmentally-friendly cleaning materials could only be found through specialist retailers. Now these things are available in every supermarket. Everyday products, such as CFC-free aerosols and mass-produced vegetarian ready-meals, were not available at all a few years ago. Commerce spotted a growing trend and created products that satisfied our need to be ethical and green. Even the financial institutions responded by creating ethical investments and other 'green' financial products. Trends can also present charities and voluntary organisations with new marketing opportunities. Campaigning organisations can tap into the public's interest in a particular issue and meet their need to take some kind of action.

Successful marketing depends on knowing your market, having a very clear picture of the competition and what they are up to, and keeping an eye out for the uncontrollables. It also relies on your ability to respond to the uncontrollables by seizing opportunities and anticipating threats. Do all this and you will be better placed to cope with any difficulties the marketplace throws at you.

Undertaking marketing research

INTRODUCTION

If the mention of 'market research' conjures up images of clipboard-clutching women on the high street, think again. Marketing research is an important tool for voluntary organisations, and some charities annually spend six figure sums on it. Research provides you with the information on which you can base your marketing decision-making, enabling you to make informed and intelligent decisions. It can even provide you with information that will help you avoid costly advertising and promotional mistakes.

Many small charities are close to their client group. The people who run it may even be part of that group. But as organisations grow, it is easy for them to lose touch with what the charity was originally set up to do. A charity providing information and support to parents of children with birth defects may have been established by those affected. Years later it might find that it has become less self-help and more professionalised, being run by paid staff with no direct experience of the issue. The more remote you are from the users (and funders) of your service, the more important it becomes to find out what those users and funders expect, want and need. That's where marketing research comes in. It enables you to keep close to your customers, whether those customers are service-users, funding bodies or individual donors, by providing you with information on them, their needs, thoughts, interests and motivations.

Marketing research can be used to help you find out:

- **About your service** What do users think about it? Can they suggest any improvements? What do funders think?

- **About your 'products'** Why do people buy/use/fund them? What do they think of them? Are there any gaps in your 'product line'?
- **About your organisation** What do people think about your name, logo and image? About your staff? About your premises?
- **About your donors** Who are they? What types of people? Where do they live? How much do they give? How can you get them to give more?
- **About your competitors** What are they up to? What are they doing that you are not?

What is marketing research?

You will be familiar with the term 'market research' which is, essentially, research into your market(s). 'Marketing research' is research that goes much wider. It involves market research, as well as other types of research designed to help you get all the information you need to make the right marketing decisions. It might, for example, cover research into your advertising and its effectiveness.

Marketing research can take many forms – questionnaires, interviews or reviewing existing material, for example – and can be carried out to uncover many different pieces of information. You might undertake research to find out why people give to your charity – or why they don't give. Perhaps you want to discover shortcomings in your service, or find out how you are regarded by your local community. Marketing research can provide you with the information you need. It can be used at the 'ideas stage' to gauge responses to your proposed new service, and it can be used

---

TRUE STORY   Getting it Right

After nearly 50 years of operation, the Scottish Council for Spastics decided to change its name. (Its sister charity in England did likewise.) The view of people with cerebral palsy, and of the charity's staff, was that the term spastic had become outdated, derogatory and offensive. Research confirmed this view and the need for a name change. Younger parents of children with cerebral palsy said that they were put off using the charity's services because its name made it sound old-fashioned and paternalistic. A marketing advisory panel comprising external experts was established to implement the name change. Now renamed Capability, it has a fresher and more positive image that is more appealing to its target audiences. Research was an essential tool in confirming gut feeling and demonstrating the need for a new name and a modern image.

again once the service is up and running to establish the level of customer satisfaction. It can be used to help you develop new services and to improve existing ones.

If you look at books on marketing research, the contents will probably be enough to make you feel that it is all too complicated to undertake. It is indeed the most technical area of marketing, requiring an understanding of statistics, or at least some mathematical bent. Added to that, there's the jargon and concepts to cope with – Z scores, finite population correction and bivariate analysis to name but three. But don't let all that put you off. You can do basic research in-house without a PhD in maths, and there are lots of friendly experts you can use if you need to commission external help.

The benefits of research

Marketing research was once the preserve of the large company. Now it is common for the public and voluntary sectors to undertake it. The benefits for not-for-profit organisations of carrying out research are clear. By finding out what people need from your services you can ensure that needs are met. Research can make you a more responsive, accountable and effective organisation. It can also be used to gather the necessary information to justify the existence of a threatened service, to prove the need for a new service, or to explain the demise of an existing one.

So, as you can see, there are many uses for marketing research in the voluntary sector. It is not just about finding out why shoppers buy Brand X soap powder rather than Brand Y. It can help you take a fundamental look at your products and services, your organisation as a whole, and the people who support it. Good research is the foundation stone of good marketing.

Using Research to Show Need

Many charities provide resource-driven services shaped by income. With available money setting the standard, this is a sure-fire way to the lowering of standards in the long run. Charities must, of course, live within their means, but by allowing resources to dictate the service, there is a risk that you will fail to meet the real needs of service-users. By contrast, a needs-led service takes need as its starting point, and then costs a service around this. If a service is to be needs-led, you must first use research to establish what the actual needs are.

Research can demonstrate need, and this in turn can be used to put pressure on statutory buyers of your service – local authorities or central funders such as government – to provide the necessary funds. It can also be used in publicity material to attract individual donors. Let's say that you want your local council to finance you to run a support service for male anorexics. First you need to prove the need for the service, both by establishing the scale of the problem and by showing the lack of alternative provision for this group. Research findings can be used to support and add weight to a funding application.

Another way of using research is to publicise it in the media, thereby educating and informing decision-makers and establishing a favourable climate of opinion for your application or fundraising appeal. You can make your approach for funding just at a time when funders are thinking about the problem. Raise the issue and then come along and offer the solution.

Gathering information

The raw material for marketing research is information. You can get information from:

- desk data (existing information within your organisation);
- secondary data (published sources of information);
- primary data (newly gathered information).

Desk Data

Start the information-gathering process by looking at what you already have. Many organisations have existing raw data, which could be extremely useful if analysed and interpreted. National charities reliant on income from individual donors might find it useful to go through their records to build up a picture of where most donors live. Donors could be classified according to town or city; county; England, Scotland, Wales and Northern Ireland; north or south, east or west. Only undertake such an exercise if you have some thoughts on how you plan to use the information. You may wish to focus your publicity drive on the parts of the country where donations are low in an attempt to boost your profile and increase donations, or to concentrate efforts on those areas where you appear to be already successful.

A simple desk analysis of donations can help you uncover all sorts of useful information, for example:

- your most profitable geographic areas;
- the preferred method of giving – credit card, cheque, standing order, etc.;
- the gender balance of donors – do you appeal to men more than women?
- the most popular time of year for giving.

A small charity held a photo-call to publicise the antics of an octogenarian grandmother who was running in the London Marathon for them. Following the media coverage, donations arrived at the charity addressed to the 'Marathon Granny', which clearly stemmed from the media coverage received. This analysis of donations has helped them with their fundraising strategy. Now they make a point of publicising fundraising events likely to capture the imagination, and monitor donations that follow. They have a very clear picture of cause and effect thanks purely to the analysis and interpretation of existing data.

Think about what information you already have which, if properly analysed, could be helpful to you in your marketing work. Why not look at your press cuttings and see whether donations received correlate with the date and place of the appearance of positive coverage of your charity in newspapers?

Secondary Data

Secondary data are often cheaper to obtain and generally more readily available than primary data. Secondary data include:

- trade journals (magazines for charities, social workers, health service professionals, housing workers, etc.);
- government publications and statistics (such as the census of population, the family expenditure survey, reports from the Registrar General, monthly digest of statistics, social trends);
- research carried out by other organisations;
- information available on the Internet;
- surveys published by market research companies.

Although secondary data can be useful, the drawback is that they are non-specific and more likely to be out of date. Use secondary data to establish the facts. For example, you can use the population census to find out what demographic age changes have or are expected to occur. This information can enable you to develop relevant services and to support applications for funding such services. Figures would reveal that we have an ageing population and you may respond by developing social projects for retired people, housing that is accessible to older people, or reminiscence projects for older people with memory impairment.

The Internet is an obvious starting point when tracking down secondary data. It contains a vast amount of information on a huge range of subjects. Search engines can help you locate the information you need. Simply type in key words and wait for a list of relevant websites to appear. Often the problem is narrowing

tip

Many professional bodies have comprehensive specialist libraries and they may allow you access if they regard your research as worthwhile. You may also be able to get access to university libraries. Ring up, explain your need and see what they say.

down the list, since searches can generate hundreds or even thousands of leads. Because anyone can publish information on the Internet, you need to be careful about accepting everything as gospel. There is a lot of valuable and reliable data in cyberspace, but you may need to make a phone call to verify it. Try to stick to the sites of organisations you know and trust.

Large reference libraries are also a good source. The twenty-first century library is much more user-friendly than in the past, and the staff will do their best to help you find the information you need. The Chartered Institute of Marketing runs a library and information service, Infomark, for general marketing information. Some of the services it offers are open to non-members for a small fee. Call Infomark on 01628-852190.

tip

MORI produce reports (based on opinion gathering) covering a wide range of issues, from social attitudes and health to government policy and the environment. It is a great deal cheaper to buy one of their reports than to commission your own survey, though obviously they will be less specific to your organisation than something you commission yourself.

Primary Data

Primary data are not ready-made. You have to gather the data yourself, or commission someone else to do it for you. As such, primary data tend to be more expensive and take longer to obtain. On the plus side it is specific to your needs. You can get primary data by:

- **consulting experts** – academics, councillors, people affected by the issue or problem;
- **observation** – watching reactions and behaviour, such as showing a group of people your proposed new adverts to see how they react;
- **survey** – postal and Internet questionnaires, telephone surveys, personal interviews and focus groups.

tip

MORI, Gallup, Harris, NOP and the other big market research companies run regular 'omnibus' surveys which track consumer attitudes. They ask a number of very wide-ranging questions and you can pay the research company to have your own question included in one of these. It will set you back around £700. This may sound a lot, but it is a cost-effective way of getting a national survey carried out by a leading market research organisation.

Getting data from observation

Here are three real-life examples of observation being used to collect important marketing information:

- **The Central Office of Information** wanted to monitor the effectiveness of its seat belt advertising campaign. Asking people if they wore a seat belt was likely to result in too many motorists lying and giving the socially acceptable (and legal!) answer. Therefore observation was used: they simply counted the number of motorists wearing and not wearing their belts.
- **Honda** watched how people load their car boots and used the information to redesign the Honda Civic hatchback.
- **Philips**, the shaver maker, watches men shaving (with their consent) through a two-way mirror. Information gained this way is used to modify and improve its products.

Try to think of examples in your own work where simple observation will provide you with valuable marketing information. For example:

- Use observation to see if clients look at your information board in reception; if they do, it could be an effective way of communicating with them.
- Use observation to see if visitors read the information (brochures, leaflets, etc.) that you leave in your waiting room.

Remember the ethical issues associated with covert observation.

Asking questions

There are numerous ways of gathering marketing information. The best way is to ask questions. You can do this in a formal way – by issuing a questionnaire, for example – or informally, perhaps by sitting down with a target group and asking them to discuss various questions and issues.

You can combine, for example, direct with closed questions to produce very structured questionnaires, which are easy to administer and analyse. On the downside, responses can be less helpful than you might wish. Take the following example:

Do you give to charity?	yes	no	
If yes, do you give at least once a	week	month	year
How much do you give in a year?	less than £5	£5–£15	more than £15

Types of question

Question Type	Example
Direct	'How much do you give to charity each year?'
Indirect	'Why do you think people are giving less money to charity now than ten years ago?'
Closed	'Yes/no' questions, or those offering multiple choice answers.
Open	'How do you think Save Seafish could improve its image?'

You may get some interesting information, but you will only get part of the picture. Closed questions will not reveal why people give, how they decide how often and how much to give, or whom they give to. Only open-ended questions will uncover this sort of information. But the trouble with open questions is that they are difficult to record. With closed questions, your interviewer or interviewee can tick boxes on the questionnaire. With anything open-ended you have to do one of the following:

- Tape record it. Respondents might object to this. Furthermore, the tapes will have to be listened to, analysed, transcribed and interpreted.
- Get the interviewee to write responses (which is time-consuming and puts people off. It also excludes people who are illiterate or whose first language is not English).
- Get the interviewer to write responses during the interview (they will need shorthand to keep up, their attention will not be as good if they are having to simultaneously write and listen, and you will be relying on their interpretation and summarising of responses, which could be unreliable).
- Get the interviewer to write it up afterwards (which means relying on their memory of events and interpretation).

In spite of all the drawbacks of open-ended questions, to which we must add time and cost, they do provide better insights. Judge which is best for you, depending on what you want to find out, how much time and money you have, whom you need to interview and where they are. In practice, many questionnaires contain a mix of open and closed questions.

Remember when designing questions that your starting point is your hypothesis. What are you trying to find out? What do you need to prove or disprove? Your questions must provide you with the answers you need to enable you to address your initial hypothesis.

Don't Lead the Way

tip

Before launching a questionnaire, first test drive it. Check for ambiguity and clarity of questions and correct any errors. Try it out on friends and colleagues, or better still on a sample of potential respondents.

Never ask leading or biased questions. Phrase all questions carefully so that you do not inadvertently suggest that certain answers are more acceptable than others. For example, if you ask: 'These days most people do not hit their children and regard it as cruel. Do you smack your children?' you will probably not find out what really happens. Certainly you must never ask: 'You don't think ... do you?' Be careful, too, of intonation when reading questions aloud to respondents. This can lead the listener to a particular answer. For example: 'Did you *agree* with the council's decision to ...?'. By stressing the word 'agree', you might influence interviewees. Always try to come across as neutral so as not to influence responses.

Use a Funnel

Many questionnaires use the 'funnel technique' to avoid bias in responses. Begin with general or unrestricted questions and gradually home in on more specific areas. In this way the respondent creates the frame of reference for his or her responses to the general questions. It should be a smooth process in going from the general to the specific and helps to warm up the respondent for more detailed questioning.

Let's suppose you want to find out how much (or how little) people give to charity, and why. Asking strangers straight out, upfront, is unlikely to provide you with the information you need. The socially acceptable answer is to cite a reasonable annual sum – even if in reality you rarely donate anything. By starting with general questions on how people divide up their weekly income, what the priorities are and what the pressures are, you are making it easier for a respondent to explain to you that as a single parent with two children and a mortgage, there is no cash left to give away. You probably would not get an answer like that without funnelling in on the issue gradually.

Opt for Filters

Filtering is a useful technique. You my ask interviewees: 'Do you use the local community centre regularly?' Respondents answering yes would then be asked a series of questions about why they use it and what they like about it. If they answer no, you move on to the next block of questions relating to why they do not use it and what might encourage them to use it.

Getting Personal

Questions about the respondent, such as age, name, income, education, marital status, and so on should be left until the end. If you start with these questions, before a rapport has been established, and you will not get far. Even at the end of the interview respondents may wonder why you need to know, so it helps to preface the questions by explaining the reason and stressing confidentiality. This applies with self-completion questionnaires as well as face-to-face and telephone interviews. The only exception to this rule is when using a 'quota sample'. This is when you decide that in order to be representative, your sample must include, for example, 20 per cent of respondents in the 18–25 age group, 25 per cent in the 26–40 age range, and so on. Here you might need to know what age respondents are at the outset, so you can meet your quota.

Sometimes you may need to ask questions that are 'difficult', threatening or on taboo subjects. For example, questions about attitudes to race, sexual orientation, religion or fears about personal health. If so, save them until the middle or near the end of the interview, so that you can build up confidence and reassurance. Unless a rapport has been established, respondents will not be willing to answer these types of question. Many may be unwilling to answer them at all. That's their right. If they terminate the interview, at least you will have gained some information from them during the first part.

What's Your Job?

Sometimes you need to find out someone's occupation as part of your survey data. This apparently straightforward enquiry may in fact be fraught with difficulty. Many people when asked their job title inflate their status and importance. One man claimed to be 'transport manager' when in reality he was in charge of trolleys at a local supermarket. You may need to probe gently to find out what people actually do. Even when people are not trying to exaggerate the importance of their role, they may give an answer that is too vague, such as 'I work in housing' or 'I'm a manager'.

Even the order in which questions are asked can have an influence on the answers received. Survey experiments have been carried out in which half the group is asked questions in one order, and half in a different order. The responses of each group to the questions were very different, where one might have expected them to be the same.

Using Questionnaires to Measure Attitudes

It is easy to measure facts using questionnaires. Questions such as 'How much do you give to charity in a year?' can be answered easily in a simple questionnaire and can be quickly collated and analysed. But what if your questions involved delving into views, such as what people think of your charity? That's where it gets harder, especially if you are using a simple, self-complete ques-

---

INTERESTING TALE

Decades ago, when the film *Gone With the Wind* was current and fashionable, a survey was carried out to investigate readership of the book. When asked: 'Have you read this book?', an overwhelming number of respondents said yes, as this was the socially acceptable answer at that time. When rephrased to: 'Do you intend to read *Gone With the Wind*?' a more accurate response to the original question was elicited. Many people who perhaps did not intend to read it said that they would, but those who really had read the book made this very clear.

tionnaire. There are two methods that are widely used in marketing research, known as the 'Likert method of rating' and the 'semantic differential technique'. Don't let the jargon put you off! They sound complicated, but they are actually very easy and you have probably seen and possibly drawn-up questionnaires using these methods.

> **tip**
>
> Avoid too many hypothetical questions; the information they reveal cannot always be relied upon. For example, a question like: 'If charity-giving were made easier by the government, would you be likely to give more to charity?' is not likely to yield information that will be useful to you in your planning. Questions relating to people's actual experience usually elicit more accurate information.

The Likert Method of Rating

Using this method, respondents are asked to state their degree of agreement or disagreement with a number of statements. For example:

Canine Carers is a warm and appealing name for a dog charity
1 *Strongly agree*
2 *Agree*
3 *Tend to agree*
4 *Tend to disagree*
5 *Disagree*
6 *Strongly disagree*

Semantic Differential Technique

Here respondents are given statements from the top and bottom of a scale and they are asked to indicate their feelings in one of seven positions offered for each set of paired statements. It sounds complicated when described like this, but the examples below show how easy it is:

7 6 5 4 3 2 1

1 *The staff at our Day Centre are:*

Friendly and   *Unfriendly and*
courteous   –   –   –   –   –   –   –   *unhelpful*

2 *The food at our Day Centre is:*

Excellent value   *Poor value*
for money   –   –   –   –   –   –   –   *for money*

Tasty and   *Unpalatable*
nutritious   –   –   –   –   –   –   –   *and unhealthy*

Surveys

When you ask people questions in order to obtain marketing information, you are conducting a survey. You can conduct your survey in a variety of ways:

- personal interviews (face-to-face questionnaires, one-to-one depth interviews and focus group interviews);
- mailed surveys;
- Internet surveys;
- telephone surveys.

Personal Interviews

These are generally regarded as the best type of surveys, for the following reasons:

- They tend to elicit the highest level of responses.
- The interviewer can prompt respondents, or help them understand questions with which they are having difficulty.
- They can be very structured (such as a questionnaire with closed questions) or only slightly structured (a focus group interview, for example – see below).
- They can take the form of a dialogue – two-way conversations allow respondents to ask questions as well as answer them.

There are three types of personal interviews:

- face-to-face questionnaires;
- one-to-one depth interviews;
- focus group interviews.

Face-to-Face Questionnaires

With face-to-face questionnaires an interviewer reads out questions from a questionnaire and records the responses. Often these take place in the street, with passers-by being stopped and invited to help (although they can be carried out elsewhere, for example at a day centre, in a library or other public building). Rapport is vital in face-to-face interviews.

THE SUCCESSFUL FACE-TO-FACE QUESTIONNAIRE CHECKLIST

- ☑ When stopping people in the street to ask them questions, you are relying on their goodwill to take part in your survey. Start with a brief introduction explaining why you are doing the survey and asking if they are willing to take part.

☑ Carry something official, such as an ID card, to reassure respondents that you are *bona fide*.

☑ Ensure your opening question is interesting and easy to answer, to give the respondent confidence. Some interviewers like to start with an open question that gets people talking.

☑ If you are doing the interviews in-house, train staff and make them aware of possible errors they could introduce.

☑ For street interviews, try to pick a sheltered spot such as a shopping centre, or a place where people have time to kill, such as a bus stop. (Remember to select a spot that will enable you to talk to a representative group.)

☑ Ensure interviewers are properly equipped for outdoor surveys, with appropriate footwear and clothing, plenty of spare pens, a clipboard and bag or briefcase.

tip

Pay attention to how interviewers dress, and what assumptions respondents might make about them on the basis of how they look. Respondents are likely to react differently to a middle-aged woman in a smart suit than they are to a man in his early twenties wearing T-shirt and jeans.

One-to-One Depth Interviews

A depth interview aims to uncover feelings, attitudes and motivations. It is structured (in so far as the interviewer has a framework and clear ideas of topics/areas to be covered) but it is far less rigid than a questionnaire-based interview. Such interviews offer opportunities to delve deeper and to get qualitative insights. They can be carried out in-house using your own staff, though training will need to be provided first, as depth interviewing is an art. Ideally interviewers should be encouraging but not leading. They should be friendly and easy to talk to.

Focus Group Interviews

This is rather like a depth interview, though it involves more people – anything up to a dozen or so. The aim is for an experienced facilitator to introduce an issue and encourage the group to discuss it and offer views, opinions and insight. The interview could, for example, focus on looking at some proposed new adverts for your charity, or it could examine one of your services by bringing together a small group of service-users.

THE SUCCESSFUL FOCUS GROUP INTERVIEW CHECKLIST

☑ Select members of the group carefully, so they are representative of your target audience.

☑ Use only a trained or experienced facilitator.

☑ Structure the session so that all the necessary issues are covered.

☑ If necessary, reassure participants about confidentiality.

☑ Ensure participants receive a copy of your findings, if appropriate, or at the very least a thank you letter and an update.

Mailed Surveys

This is where you send a questionnaire by post for completion by the recipient. There are pros and cons to mailed questionnaires. Here are some of them:

Pros

- Questions that people might not answer truthfully face-to-face – such as 'How much do you give to charity?' or 'Have you ever had a sexually transmitted infection?' – might be answered honestly in an anonymous postal questionnaire.
- Unlike personal interviews, which tend to have an urban bias – the woman in the high street with a clipboard comes to mind – postal questionnaires can be sent to more remote places. This is particularly useful for a national charity doing its research in-house. You couldn't possibly question people in Lands End from your HQ in John o' Groats, except by telephone, the Internet and by mail.
- Respondents can work through the questionnaire at their own pace.
- They can be cheaper than face-to-face interviews, though don't forget to take into account the cost of envelopes, printing and staff time to do the mailing, as well as the cost of the stamps. Questionnaire return rates are increased if a stamped addressed envelope is enclosed, though this adds considerably to the cost of the exercise. (To avoid expenditure on wasted stamps, talk to Royal Mail about a Freepost address, so that you will pay the cost of postage only on those returned.)
- You can reach many more people for the same cost as face-to-face interviews.
- If appropriate, questionnaires can be left in your reception, where you have a captive audience with nothing better to do. (Remember to have a box available in which to post the questionnaire and plenty of pens.)

Cons

- They usually generate a low response and thus may cast doubt on the validity of the sample. Professional market researchers are pleased to get a response rate of 30 per cent for postal questionnaires, though don't be surprised if you get as few as 10 per cent back. You need to be confident that the non-responders are not significantly different in their attitudes and opinions

tip

If you are conducting a postal survey and you plan to send tactful and encouraging reminders to those who have not completed their questionnaire, enclose a spare; the original may have been mislaid.

from those who have responded. This is not easy. Effectively you have a self-selecting sample.

- They have to be questionnaire-based and therefore are less flexible.
- They often comprise closed questions because respondents usually are unwilling to complete anything that will take too much time or effort.
- Attractively presented questionnaires with a layout designed to navigate the respondent are more likely to be completed and returned. This could mean the extra expense of having to pay a designer.
- You may need to go to the trouble and expense of enclosing stamped, self-addressed envelopes to encourage returns, or setting up a 'Freepost' address.
- You may also have to face the effort and cost of doing a follow-up mailing to encourage response.
- Unless you have an appropriate mailing list, you will need to construct one or hire one (see section on mailing lists in Chapter 10).
- They are not appropriate for surveying people with low literacy levels, or those whose first language is not that used in the questionnaire.
- Because these questionnaires can be read through fully before answering, it is possible for bias to creep into the answers. 'Funnelled' questions (see above) are therefore less effective.
- Sometimes the answers you get back come from more than one person. Perhaps someone in the household starts answering the questionnaire, gets bored and finds it completed by another member.
- The observations which interviewers can make when working face-to-face with respondents are impossible for a postal questionnaire.

It is usual, when sending out a questionnaire, to include a covering letter explaining who you are and what you do (if necessary), and what you hope to achieve through your research.

Research has shown that sponsored surveys can elicit a better response than identical surveys that are not sponsored. For example, a survey on nurses' views about whether personal care for

> **tip**
>
> Leave a space at the end of a questionnaire for additional comments. Sometimes this can reveal some interesting and relevant insights about issues not covered in your questions.

INTERESTING TALE

An experiment was carried out whereby identical questionnaires were issued, each with a covering letter. Half the covering letters were polite and tactful, but half were short and authoritarian. Surprisingly, the questionnaires sent with the curt covering letter elicited a slightly better response!

tip

The status of the person signing the covering letter has an effect on response rates: the higher the status, the higher the return figures.

people with dementia should be available free of charge might be more successful if backing could be obtained by one or more of the professional bodies or publications representing this sector. A covering letter accompanying such a survey would carry more weight if from the secretary of the Royal College of Nursing or the editor of *Nursing Times*, on their own headed notepaper.

Mailed Survey Fact File

- There is no significant difference in response rates between questionnaires sent in a hand-addressed envelope and those with a computer-generated label.
- Self-addressed envelopes with proper postage stamps on them, when enclosed in postal questionnaires, produce a higher response than pre-printed business reply envelopes.
- If respondents are really interested in the subject matter of your survey, they will be willing to complete even quite lengthy and detailed questionnaires.
- The more interested respondents are in the subject matter of your questionnaire, the sooner they are likely to complete and return it.
- Design of postal questionnaires is important. Research has shown that response rates can be affected by typeface and type size, type of paper used and even the choice of colours used.
- Single-sided sheets produce more responses than double-sided ones.
- Setting a deadline for returns increases the return rate.

Sample mailed questionnaire

> **Brippington Animal Welfare: Help Us to Help You to Help Us**
>
> Thank you for helping us over the past year by making a donation to BAW. We want to make it easier for you and our other donors to support our work with sick animals, and we would welcome your input into how we can achieve this. So please spare a few minutes to complete this questionnaire. We do appreciate it!
>
> Please tick any applicable responses. There is space for additional comments at the end of the questionnaire
>
> 1 Have many times have you given to BAW in the last 12 months?
>   ☐ once   ☐ twice   ☐ three times
>   ☐ more than three times (please state how many)_____
>
> 2 How have you given?
>   ☐ sent a cheque   ☐ put money in a collection can
>   ☐ held a fundraising event
>
> 3 If we made it easy for you to give us a fixed amount monthly direct from your bank account, would you use this facility?

☐ yes   ☐ no   ☐ would consider it

4   If yes, would you use it in place of the other ways of giving, or as an addition?

☐ in place of   ☐ as well as

5   Tick any of the following ways of giving to BAW that you would consider using if available.

☐ credit card   ☐ on-line donations via our website
☐ direct from your salary (for those in work)

6   Would you consider leaving money to BAW in your will?

☐ yes ☐ no ☐ have already made provision for a legacy to BAW

7   Would you consider organising fundraising events for BAW (such as jumble sales, raffles or sponsored events)?

☐ yes   ☐ no   ☐ already do so

8   Any other comments?

....

....

Thank you for completing the questionnaire. Your comments will help us to make it easier for you to support our work. You can read about the main findings of this questionnaire in the next issue of our newsletter, which will be sent to you, and there will be an update on the action we propose to take as a result of what you have said. If you have no objection to our getting back to you, please complete your name, address and telephone number. You are welcome to remain anonymous if you prefer.

OPTIONAL

Name ....

Address ....

Phone no ....

email address ....

We may wish to get in touch with you again about other issues and campaigns with which we are involved. Please tick here if you do not want us to contact you again. ☐

Please return this questionnaire by 1 July to:

Felix Thompson, Brippington Animal Welfare, Catford St, Brippington BR1 1PR

When designing your questionnaire, try to use questions and a format that will make it easier for you to collate the results in numerical or percentage terms. You want to be able to present your findings in a meaningful way – for example, 80 per cent of respondents gave to BAW just once last year, and nearly half of these people said that a direct debit facility would encourage them to donate every month.

Internet Surveys

The Internet is widely used for gathering secondary data, but it is also an invaluable tool for undertaking primary research. You can email questionnaires to people, or you can place a questionnaire on your website for completion online or for downloading and completion later. By and large the rules of postal surveys also apply to Internet surveys. However, there are a few fundamental differences. The first is cost: it is much cheaper to do an Internet survey than a postal one. The second is speed: you may begin getting responses to an Internet questionnaire the same day.

A major problem with undertaking a survey on the Internet is that your sample will be skewed. Participants of an Internet survey must be online. This rules out a large number of people, giving you a sample that is not representative of society as a whole. If you want to ensure a good response and representative findings, ensure that your target audience is online before opting for an Internet survey.

The problem with a questionnaire on your website is that it is reactive. You post the survey on your site and hope that people will complete it. The more proactive alternative, emailing it, poses problems. 'Spamming', or sending unsolicited emails, is regarded as an unacceptable practice. Therefore, an Internet survey requires an organisation to have an email list where people have opted in to receiving information from you.

Another drawback with Internet questionnaires is low response rates. Respondents are clocking up a phone bill all the time that they are online and may therefore be less inclined to swell their bill further in order to complete your questionnaire. An incentive can help boost response rates. Consider offering to email respondents a copy of the survey findings.

You can also use the Internet for online focus group surveys via a 'chat room'. A chat room is a special area on a website, which is entered using a password. Visitors 'meet' in the chat room at a specified time for discussions on a particular topic. They type their comments, thoughts and opinions into their keyboard and these are displayed on the website for view by the other chat room visitors. Rather like a face-to-face focus group, a facilitator encourages contributions and leads the discussion.

Telephone Surveys

Cold-calling by double glazing sales reps has given telephone surveys a bad name. Perhaps as a result of this, there is now a legal requirement that organisations making cold calls ensure that they do not call numbers registered with the Telephone Preference Scheme. This free service enables individuals to register their wish not to receive direct marketing calls. It is supported by, among others, the Institute of Charity Fundraising Managers and the Direct Marketing Association.

Carefully weigh up the pros and cons before opting to survey by telephone.

Pros

- You can reach out nationwide.
- You can ask open-ended questions.
- Research has shown that the quality of data obtained by telephone interviews is as good as that from personal interviews.
- It can be much faster than conducting face-to-face interviews.
- You can do away with the need for a paper record, which then needs to be keyed into a computer. Technology means that you can now use computer-assisted telephone interviewing (see below).

Cons

- You might ring at an inconvenient time and alienate the respondent.
- If you are calling someone's home, they might regard this as intrusive or wonder how you got their name and number.
- There can be difficulties in building up a list of people to ring and in ensuring representative samples, though you can buy lists.
- It can run up huge phone bills, especially if you are calling long distance or during office hours.
- People might find it difficult to answer questions honestly when speaking to a real person.
- You cannot do an anonymous survey this way.
- Depending on what time you call, you might find that you fail to get a representative sample. For example, calling a home number between 9 am and 5 pm on a weekday is not a good way of reaching working people (other than shift workers, who will not welcome being woken).
- Communication is limited to oral responses: surveyors cannot pick up on visual detail as they could if interviewing someone face-to-face. Visual cues which indicate that a respondent has perhaps not understood the question are lacking on the telephone.
- Visual aids cannot be used. For example, this technique could not be used to test the reactions of the public to three press advertisements you were considering running.
- The growth in the number of people owning answer machines and caller display devices can pose a problem.

Computer-Assisted Telephone Interviewing (CATI)

In such surveys, respondents are telephoned and questioned in the usual way, but instead of the interviewer writing their responses, they are keyed into a computer terminal. This saves the need for later having to do this with all the results collected. It is therefore faster and cheaper, although you need to develop a computer program to deal with it, the cost of which should be added to your research budget. There are a number of companies specialising in this field who will carry out a survey for you. Computers can also be used for personal interviews (CAPI), thanks to the advent of portable laptop computers. And they can be used for self-administered testing. In this case, the questionnaire is set up on a computer screen (perhaps in your waiting room or in a shopping centre) and people can complete a questionnaire directly onto the computer. This is not widely used by charities or market research companies, but it has great potential.

Methodology

This is jargon for how you intend to get the information you need. For example, you may decide to use a postal questionnaire plus depth interviews with a sample of donors.

> **tip**
>
> Sometimes survey findings can be used to attract publicity. For example, if you carry out research to discover the level of poverty in your town, because you want to use the results in support of your application to an anti-poverty trust fund, why not also compile a news release (see Chapter 9) and send it to your local media? You may be able to attract some media coverage for your work, helping you achieve one of the Ps in your marketing mix – promotion. Charities can even hit the national headlines. The Cats' Protection League did this when it carried out a survey on cat neutering, and found a newsworthy angle in the findings.

Survey Errors

When you carry out a survey, you might expect to be able to take the results at face value and act on them. It is not always that easy. Errors can creep into your survey. Here are the three main ways in which this can occur:

Errors in Interpreting

A respondent might misinterpret what is meant by the question, thus giving the wrong answer. For example:

Q: *How much do you give to charity?*
A: *(scaled response from 'a lot' to 'none')*

The first problem is that no time period is specified. Does the researcher mean over a year, a month or a week? Do they mean how much do you give in a single donation? It is not clear and respondents are left to interpret the question, inevitably leading people to different interpretations. Also, 'a lot' to one person might be 'a little' to another.

Q: How many charities do you help?

Again interpretation is required. What is meant by 'charities'? Are local community groups or church groups included in the definition? What is meant by 'help'? Money? Time? Help in kind? Again respondents are likely to interpret this question differently, leading to inconsistent answers.

It is also possible for the interviewer to misinterpret. If the respondent is ambiguous, the interviewer might misunderstand.

Errors in Reactions

Some respondents feel that in being asked to take part in a survey they have been singled out and are in some way regarded as special. They may wish to present a good impression and perhaps be tempted to give what they regard as the 'right' or socially acceptable answers. If asked whether they give to charity, or how much they give, people might be tempted to lie or exaggerate, so as not to appear mean. When asked about attitudes to controversial issues – drugs, prostitution, gay and lesbian rights, immigration, etc. – you might find yourself getting the answers people think you expect, not what they really think and believe.

Interviewer-induced Errors

A face-to-face interview is a social interaction. It has been discovered that in some survey interviews, the interviewee simply plays back to the interviewer the views and attitudes that they believe he/she will share. They pick up what they think are the interviewer's values and reflect these, not their own.

When undertaking a survey, know where errors can occur so that you can attempt to avoid them altogether or take account of them where necessary.

EFFECTIVE QUESTIONNAIRE CHECKLIST

- ☑ Put questions into a logical order.
- ☑ Avoid ambiguous wording and make your questions clear and easy to understand. One survey asked: 'How did you find your last job?' expecting the reply to be 'through the local paper' or 'at the Job Centre'. Instead many people responded 'It was really interesting' or 'I hated it'.

☑ Keep the questionnaire as short as possible: people are put off by anything too long.

☑ Make sure your address is on postal questionnaires, so respondents know where to return them.

☑ Give respondents the opportunity of returning the questionnaire anonymously if you want really truthful feedback.

☑ Ensure your questions are not biased or slanted. If respondents feel you have already made up your mind about the sort of answers you want, they may not bother to complete the questionnaire.

☑ Ensure that the layout of your questionnaire is clear and easy; if it looks a mess, it will put people off tackling it.

☑ Make it as easy as possible to complete, by giving boxes to tick or multiple choice options to circle.

☑ Limit the number of open-ended questions; they are difficult to process and off-putting to respondents.

☑ Set a deadline for the return of completed questionnaires.

Samples

With the exception of the government's ten-yearly census, no survey can cover the whole of the population. Researchers use instead a 'sample', which is a smaller group that is representative of the 'population' they wish to survey. For example, if you wished to discover how your service was viewed by minority ethnic communities, you would need to ask them. It would be impossible to ask every minority ethnic person in the country, but you could draw up a sample that included people UK-wide, with representative percentages of Bangladeshis, African Caribbeans, Chinese, Indians, and so on. By surveying a representative sample, rather than the entire relevant population, your survey is made more manageable and affordable.

INTERESTING TALE

Use plain and simple language and short, easy-to-understand questions in surveys, but always remember that what's clear to you might be gobbledegook to your respondent. Research has revealed that words in common use, such as 'incentive', 'proximity', 'discrepancy' and 'paradox' are not widely understood. In one survey, 10 per cent of respondents thought that 'devolution' was Jeramiah's brother! In another, one respondent, when asked for the definition of 'nostalgia', said it was Welsh for 'goodnight'. So remember to watch your language and keep it simple.

We'll look in a moment at how to select a sample. First you need to define your population. That can take some thought. Let's look at the example above. You would need to ask:

- Do we want to survey:
  - a sample of all ethnic minority people?
  - just a sample of those who have used the service?
  - just those who have never used the service?
- Do we want to survey only those within the catchment area of one of our services?
- What do we mean by an ethnic minority? Does it include Irish people, travellers, other groups?
- How many people will we need to interview?

Be clear on the population you wish to survey and ensure that your sample is representative of that population. Then locate your sample. If you needed to reach Irish people in Birmingham, contacting the Irish Centre in that city would be a good starting point.

There are a number of ways of selecting a sample from your population.

Random Sampling

With random sampling, every member of your survey population has an equal chance of being selected. First you start with your 'sampling frame' – this lists everyone in the population you wish to survey, which might be:

- everyone who currently uses your service;
- all adults living in Anytown;
- subscribers to your monthly campaign newsletter.

Next you need to select a random sample from the list. You can do this in one of two ways:

1 **Simple random sample** – give every name on the list a number and then get a computer to generate numbers randomly.
2 **Systematic sample** – give every name on the list a number, select your first name randomly, then select every, say, fifth or tenth name.

Judgement Samples

With such samples you use your judgement as to who to interview. This method of sampling is useful only where you are dealing, say, with an issue requiring expert judgement. You may decide that you need only speak to a handful of key people in your local social work department, and half a dozen at a nearby NHS

Trust, to get the information you need on likely developments in community care provision locally.

Quota Samples

You select people in order to be sure that you have a list that represents the population. For example, you may decide that it is necessary to interview a certain percentage of men and women, a certain number of people in particular age groups or social classes.

Undertaking a survey

So now you know the issues and you know the jargon. The next step is to undertake the research. Simply follow these five crucial steps:

1 **The research brief** – this involves developing survey objectives. What is your hypothesis? What are you trying to prove or to find out? Who are you trying to find it out from? The brief is a broad exploration of these issues. (If you are using external consultants, you will need to give them a brief and talk through it with them. If you are doing research in-house, you still need to produce a brief. This offers involved colleagues an opportunity to have an input into the research.)

2 **The research proposal** – this is where the broad discussions held previously are now firmed up. The problem is set out, the 'population' defined, a way of selecting a sample recommended, the methodology, and estimates of time and costs worked out. If you are using consultants, they will prepare a research proposal for you to approve. If the work is being done in-house, a research proposal can be used to seek approval for the project from your committee or director, if necessary. It can also be used to ensure that everyone understands what the research is about, why it is necessary and how it is being undertaken.

3 **Data collection** – this is the bit we most readily think of as marketing research. Here you put your methodology, recommended in your research proposal, into practice.

4 **Data analysis and evaluation** – having got your raw data you need to process it into a form that is meaningful. Your findings need to be analysed and related back to your original objectives.

5 **Preparing the findings report** – this is where you write up all the work you did in the preceding stage. You will also need to draw conclusions and make recommendations. Then you must ensure that your report does more than just sit on a shelf collecting dust. Action recommendations!

Using a market research company

This is a DIY book, so the focus has been on how *you* can do the work. Nowadays, though, larger charities are using marketing research companies to undertake research on their behalf. If you think that commissioning a company to undertake your research will relieve you totally of the burden, you are wrong. Undoubtedly it is easier (albeit more expensive) to get someone else to do research for you, but there are still a number of tasks that have to be undertaken by you, namely:

1 Drawing up a research brief.
2 Selecting a market research consultancy.
3 Interpreting the findings (although you can pay your research company to do this for you).
4 Deciding what action to take as a result of the research (you can ask your researchers to make recommendations as part of their brief).

Drawing up a Research Brief

You should draw up a research brief so that you are clear about why you need the research, what you wish to discover, and how you will use the findings. Also, it is important to have a brief so that your researchers understand what exactly they are doing and to what end.

Sample research brief

Williston Family Drop-in Centre

Our drop-In centre is based in the old church hall on the Williston estate, a housing estate with over 1,500 residents. It offers a range of activities free of charge for families and opens weekdays from 10 am to 4 pm. We were established five years ago and we are funded by the local authority.

Need for the research

At its peak two years ago the Centre attracted over 500 families every week. Now just 200 families are regularly using the Centre and numbers are gradually trailing off. The drop in usage may jeopardise our funding, leading to the closure of the Centre. We want to know why people are not using the centre in order that we can meet the needs and expectations of local people. We also wish to know from people using the Centre what they like most about it as well as what they dislike.

What we want to know

We would like to find out the following:

- How many people on the Williston estate and the surrounding area have heard of our drop-in centre.
- How these people came to hear about us.
- Whether they have ever used the Centre and, if so, how often.
- Whether they still use it.
- If they have stopped coming, why.
- If they have not used it, why not. What sort of activities would we need to offer to get them to consider attending.
- Do non-users know what we offer at the Centre.
- Would non-users use it if it were open in the evenings.
- Of those who use the Centre, what do they value and enjoy about it and what they would like to see changed.

What action we are considering/how we will use the research

We are considering extending our opening times and increasing the range of activities on offer. The research will provide us with the information we need to take these decisions. If activities are identified by users as being unpopular, we will consider changing, scrapping or replacing them. We intend to use some of the research findings in our funding application to the Council. For example, if evening opening would boost usage, we would need to seek additional funding in order to be able to provide extended opening hours. Our application is due in by the end of September.

Sample

We wish to seek the views of people aged ten years and over. We want equal numbers of males and females interviewed. 80 per cent of the sample should live on the estate and the rest in the surrounding area (Blimpton and Ecclesford). Of the overall sample, we would like 25–30 per cent to be regular users of the Centre (that is, visit it at least once a week). We would require our researchers to indicate how they would select the sample.

Methodology

We would like our researchers to recommend an appropriate and cost-effective methodology for this assignment.

Report

We require a detailed report setting out all the findings plus a summary report that shows the main points in an easy to digest way. We require visual presentation on the main findings (bar charts, pie charts, etc.) plus accompanying explanatory narrative. Any qualitative observations picked up during the survey may be included, in addition to the quantitative findings. We also require our researchers to make recommendations to us on future action.

Time scale

We require tenders for this assignment to be with us by midday, 30 April. We intend to have appointed a market research agency by 31

> May and to have the research underway by the end of June. The
> research report must be with us by 31 July.

Selecting a Consultancy

Always discuss your brief with more than one consultancy. Each
will have its own style and a distinctive approach to carrying out
your brief, so aim to speak initially with three or four to give you
a range of perspectives. Go by recommendation if you can.
Alternatively, talk to the market researchers' trade body, the
Association of Market Survey Organisations (AMSO). They can be
contacted on 020-7235 1277 and will provide you with information on the types of research on offer and companies with expertise in specific sectors. There is also an organisation for those who
commission marketing research, the Association of Users of
Research Agencies, who can be contacted on 020-7283 7500 ext.
28323. And if all of this sounds like a headache, why not take
ASPIRIN. This is an acronym that summarises the stages involved
in choosing a consultancy:

A Ask around.
S Source the market.
P Prepare a brief.
I   Invite market research consultancies to present to you (at your
    premises or at theirs).
R Review their approach, proposals and presentations. Decide
    who to use.
I   Invite the successful consultancy to start.
N Negotiate and agree the project plan and contract.

Interviewing Consultants

When you come to interview consultants, ask the following questions:

- Was our brief clear? Do you understand what we are looking
  for and why?
- How would you tackle the assignment? (Consider whether
  their suggestions are practical and cost-effective.)
- How many consultants would be involved? (You need to find
  out who these would be – they may not be the people presenting to you – and what their relevant experience is for the job.)
- Would you use trained interviewers? (Ask what training interviewers receive.)
- What experience do you have of working with the non-for-
  profit sector?
- What would your fee be? (Ask whether this would be inclusive,
  and if not, what the extras would be.)

- Do you anticipate any problems or difficulties, and if so, how do you propose to solve them?
- How flexible are you? Can you cope with a brief that may change, or a timescale that might differ from the original?
- How long have you been established?
- Who else have you worked for?
- If successful, what other projects or commitments would you be undertaking at the same time as this project?
- Can you provide references?

Remember that your meeting with consultants should be two-way; you need to find out what they can do, and they need to find out more about you. If you aim for a meeting format that is informal yet structured, you will make it easier to achieve this.

Making your Choice
After the selection interviews, ask yourself of each consultancy:

- Did they appear knowledgeable and professional?
- Were they able to think on their feet?
- Did they impress us with their understanding of our organisation and the need for this research?
- Were they enthusiastic and keen to do the work?
- Did they have any interesting and helpful observations to make on the brief?

> **tip**
>
> Ask consultants which other charities they have carried out research for and take up references. Ask referees what work was undertaken, whether they were any good at it, whether the work was carried out on time, whether the consultants were helpful and whether they under-performed in any of the tasks.

Once you have made a decision, call the successful company and commission them. Ask them to sign a contract with you which sets out your terms, expectations, deadlines, performance measures, payment details, and so on. Write to the unsuccessful firms to notify them of the outcome and to thank them for their time.

THE EFFECTIVE MARKETING RESEARCH CHECKLIST

- ☑ If using consultants, choose a reputable company.
- ☑ If doing it in-house, ensure your staff are properly trained and know what they are doing.
- ☑ Check that your questions are not slanted.

☑ Ensure the sample is a valid one and large enough to be both relevant and credible.

☑ Be aware of how errors can creep in.

☑ Select the right survey method.

Have a go yourself

Think about what you have read on questionnaires and then take a critical look at the questionnaire below. It has been prepared by a fictitious donkey sanctuary in order to discover how the charity can improve the service it offers to members. What mistakes does it make?

Twilight Donkeys

We value your membership and wish to further improve the service we offer to members. So that we know what you think of what you get, what else you want and what you are willing to pay for it, we have produced this questionnaire. Your assistance in filling and returning it would be appreciated.

1   Do you like the monthly newsletter?

☐ Yes   ☐ No

2   Would you mind if we scrapped the newsletter or reduced it to a quarterly publication?

3   Would you favour the introduction of an 'adopt a donkey' scheme as part of your membership? (This would give you a chance to give a donkey a name and to receive a photo and regular updates on your very own donkey.)

☐ Yes   ☐ No

4   Would you be willing to pay an extra £5 in order to adopt a donkey?

☐ Yes   ☐ No

5   Would you be more likely to renew your annual subscription if we were to give away a free poster?

☐ Yes   ☐ It would make no difference
☐ It might make a difference

6   Do you have any other comments?

....

....

....

Return this questionnaire as soon as you can to Twilight Donkeys.

Discussion

On the plus side, the questionnaire is brief and therefore quick to complete. However, it does make some very important mistakes. These include:

- Q1 is not a simple black and white issue, but it is presented as though it were. People are unlikely to like or dislike the newsletter. Some will like all of it, others only parts only, some will like none of it. How can you answer with a clear-cut yes or no?
- Q2 asks two questions in one, which is confusing. Scrapping the newsletter altogether is a very different option from reducing it to a quarterly.
- Q2 also raises too many 'ifs'. Some members might be happy for the newsletter to be scrapped if the membership fee were halved, for example.
- Q4 is unclear. Do they mean £5 a year? £5 per donkey? £5 a month?
- Q5 is also unclear. What would the poster be of? Donkeys? Cats? A pop group? Would there be a choice of posters? Would the poster be in colour? What size would it be? People might be influenced if the poster were a full colour A1 size donkey, but not if it were an A4 size black and white picture of Gary Glitter.
- There is no closing date for returns, which means that respondents may delay completing it and then lose it or decide not to bother. Alternatively, questionnaires may be returned in dribs and drabs, with returns coming in well after you have begun to analyse the results.
- The return address is not included. If people have to hunt around for the charity's address, they may not get around to sending it back.

Developing a competitive edge

INTRODUCTION

Few charities have hoards of wealthy donors throwing cash at them. It can be hard to attract customers (or supporters) and the ever-growing competition adds to the challenge. You need to demonstrate that you deserve support more than your competitors. You need to show that you are in some way different from, and better than, the rest. In short, success depends on achieving a competitive edge.

Be different, be better

Competitive edge is all about being better than others. There are exceptionally good (and exceptionally bad) charities and voluntary organisations, but the mass of them fall within the 'average' category. The odds are that your organisation will be in that category. If so, you need to identify or develop something that differentiates you from the others – you need a competitive edge. Your growth, your very survival even, may depend on your ability to stand out from the crowd. To have a competitive edge you must offer something that is recognised by the customer and valued by them. This might include:

Quality of Service

Quality of service is a feature that many companies use to differentiate themselves from their competitors. Harrods, for example, use this as a selling point. It is important to ensure that quality claims are matched by reality: if people's expectations are raised by claims of fantastic quality and then dashed by their experience of your service, in the long run you will lose.

Some charities, particularly the smaller ones, are able to offer a higher quality of service because everyone is much closer to that service. It is likely to be your only service, and therefore more important to you than if it were just one of many. The quality service that you can offer should be used as a selling point to give you a competitive edge over some of the bigger name charities which might otherwise have a head start when it comes to attracting funding.

Flexibility

Small charities are often pitched against the bigger ones when it comes to attracting funding for projects. Without the resources of a big organisation behind you, it can be difficult to promote yourself in a way that will attract the interest and attention of funders. Use your size as a strength, not a weakness. Let it give you the competitive edge. Smaller charities can often be more flexible than larger ones, with less bureaucracy to deal with. They can also be more responsive to changing needs.

Personal Service

Smaller organisations generally offer a more personal service. The director of a small social centre for older people is far more likely to know what is happening there than the director of a major national charity specialising in running centres for older people. Use this to your advantage.

Value for Money

Even though administration is an essential part of the effective functioning of any organisation, many donors hate the idea of their cash being used in this way. They want it to go straight to 'the cause'. Some charities spend very little on administration and can use this as their competitive edge – '98p of every pound goes straight to helping Romanian orphans' might be a line that has appeal for potential donors.

Charity Image

Image is a powerful source of competitive advantage, and the larger charities with professional PR, design and advertising expertise find it easier to establish and maintain a good image and a high profile. But even small charities can work on developing and promoting a good image that will help them stand out

TRUE STORY Getting it Wrong

A famous baked beans company promoted itself as having a family image, which helped its brand develop a competitive edge. However, when parents wrote to the company for information to help their children with school projects, many never received replies. This was uncovered when a major piece of independent research was commissioned to expose the gap between organisations' image and reality: the company received bad press as a result. The family-friendly image that was promoted differed from the reality. Proper marketing involves getting both the image and the reality right.

from the crowd. You can present your image through advertising (for donors, staff, volunteers, etc.), publications (such as leaflets and your annual report) and through using the media to gain editorial coverage (by sending news releases or talking to news and feature editors). Remember that a genuine competitive edge involves not just promoting a positive image, but ensuring that your services and products live up to that image.

Finding your competitive edge

Assuming that your competition comprises charities offering the same or a similar service to your own, you need to be better, and to demonstrate that you are better, than your rivals. Perhaps you already have a competitive edge but have so far failed to recognise it. Start by asking:

- Is there anything that we do that is different to/better than our competitors? (For example, perhaps you train all your staff in customer care or disability awareness).
- What's in it for the customer who buys our products/services? (Do they get a friendlier welcome, a lower price, a better deal?)
- What's the gain for them?
- Are we less bureaucratic?
- Are we more organised?
- Are we more client-centred?
- Is our service better? How?
- Do we represent better value for money? How?
- Are we more accountable? How?

Find and use your USP

Your competitive edge might incorporate a USP, or unique selling point. That's the thing that differentiates you, making your product or service unique. You might run the only home for three-legged dogs in the whole of Britain; or the largest recycling charity in Coventry; or the oldest established children's charity; or Britain's very first cats' home; or the only anorexia organisation to offer counselling to all family members. Companies work hard at developing at least one USP and then heavily promote it or build their brands around it.

Not every charity will have a USP, but if you do, use it to your advantage by making it work for you. To find out if you have a USP, answer the following questions:

- Are you the oldest (locally, nationally, internationally)?
- Are you the newest?
- Are you the largest?
- Are you the most cost-effective?
- Are you the only one providing that service or product?
- Are you the only one providing it locally?
- Are you the only one campaigning on that particular issue?
- Is there something about your approach that is pioneering or unique?
- Were you the first to introduce something that is now commonplace?
- Do members get something from you that they do not get with similar organisations? (for example, a daily electronic briefing delivered by email, a newsletter, monthly updates or a free badge).

Remember that a USP must be meaningful to your customers. You may have several USPs: one that appeals to volunteers, one for corporate donors and one for users. For example:

Customer Group	USP
Volunteers	Enviro-parc is the only environmental charity in Anytown to offer volunteers accredited work experience and full expenses.
Corporate donors	Enviro-parc is the longest established environmental charity in the county; this offers companies a unique opportunity to improve the local environment.
Service-users	Enviro-parc is the largest supplier of environmental cleaning services, with a large team of skilled volunteers available at 24-hours' notice to clean up derelict land, overgrown parks and gardens, littered streets and other environmental eyesores. We are the only organisation working for the public sector, business and the community.

Price as your competitive edge

In retailing, price is often the determinant factor. For shoppers who want bargains, the shop offering the best price may have the competitive edge. Sometimes charities find themselves forced to compete on price when it comes to achieving funding for services. The commercial practice of tendering for services is now widespread in the public sector, and many charities have to bid to provide a service. As with retailers (many of which have gone out of business as a result of price wars) so too with charities, price-cutting can be a dangerous route to take. Often it will cost you the same to run a service as it will cost another charity. Offering to do it for less may mean cutting corners and providing an inferior service, thus disadvantaging your users. Given that you were set up to help them in the first place, such a move could be regarded as counter-productive.

Of course, there may be occasions when you can provide the same service for less, because you operate in a more efficient way. Offering to do it for less is legitimate in such circumstances. You are merely making better use of scarce public money.

While you don't want to offer cut-price, inferior services, be careful not to price things too high. If the sort of the children's crèche you would ideally like to run costs £100 per week per child, but your local authority can only afford to pay £70, you will need to amend or alter your service, in a way that is acceptable to you and to them, if you are to achieve your funding. If you find that amending your service (and therefore lowering standards or services) is unacceptable to your organisation, you need either to find a new customer who is willing to pay what you wish to charge, or find a new product that will appeal to your existing customers. Alternatively, you will need to come up with some other way around the problem, such as grant aid subsidy to make up for the shortfall between what the council can afford and what the service costs. Marketing decisions often involve a trade-off between minimising costs and maximising service and customer satisfaction.

Promote benefits, not features

Success depends on being better than your competitors (having a competitive edge) *and* on knowing how to promote this. One major mistake that companies make when it comes to promoting their competitive edge is to focus on the features that differentiate their product rather than on the benefits for the customer of the features. For example, a toaster manufacturer might write in its publicity material:

> Buy this toaster. It boasts a host a unique features including thermal regulator and intelligent eject sensor.

That would be promoting features, but customers want to know the benefits. Focusing on benefits, the text would read:

> Burnt toast is now officially history. Our toaster senses when your toast is done to a turn, and pops it out and straight onto your waiting plate. So take the hassle out of making breakfast, and put an end to bread waste.

Customers want to know what the product will do for them, not what its features are. That also goes for your funders. They want to know that your service will help them make the most effective use of their budget, enable them to meet their statutory duties, and help them to fulfil their commitment to implementing their care in the community strategy on time. That's the benefit to them.

Donors also want to know about benefits. 'Your money can save Pramilla's life and other children like her' (benefits) is better than: 'We have a team of fully qualified doctors on the scene in the Third World administering vital vaccinations to children' (features of your service).

Promoting Your Edge

Once you have developed a competitive edge, which may include a USP, you need to ensure that it is actively promoted. Many organisations undertake impressive projects that really set them apart from the rest, yet it never occurs to them to promote their work. There is no room for modesty. If you've done something that makes you stand out, blow your own trumpet, because you can be sure that your competitors will not blow it for you.

You can promote your competitive edge in all sorts of different ways. The chapters on promotion will give you some ideas.

TRUE STORY   Getting it Wrong

I once did some work for a housing organisation that was a true pioneer, having been the first to introduce no fewer than half a dozen new ideas into the world of housing. But it hid its light under a bushel. I discovered these 'firsts' not from the organisation's literature, but from its archives. The charity was not using them to differentiate itself from other housing organisations, or to create a pioneering and innovative image, which would have helped it attract funds. It is not enough to know that you are good at something – shout it so everyone else knows too.

Image, identity and branding

INTRODUCTION

Image is important. A poor image – whether justified or not – results in smaller donations, you probably won't attract the best staff, and your funders might have doubts about your organisation. A good image can provide a powerful competitive advantage.

In the business world many good products fail because they are not packaged or promoted in the right way. Don't let your packaging and promotion let you down. 'Packaging' concerns not just physical packaging (such as the wrapper around a bar of chocolate or the box in which a jigsaw puzzle arrives), but also the way a product or service is presented. This might involve visible aspects such as design and logo, but principally it concerns things like the name of a product or service, the way its benefits are presented, and the words and images used to explain how it works. In short, packaging is about the many elements that go into creating an overall impression that presents the right image or personality.

Many charitable organisations regard the concept of image development as introspective, narcissistic and irrelevant. The cause is a good one, so why worry about such frivolities as image? Well, if you don't care about your image, you might find that people don't care about you. Image matters, and you can ignore yours at your peril.

Let's start by differentiating image from identity. Image is the way you are regarded, while identity is the visual image you shape for yourself.

Multiple images

No organisation has just one image. Different groups of people will view the organisation from their own unique perspective.

Audiences	Their Image of You
Individual donors	They may see your organisation as comprising caring and compassionate Individuals.
Corporate donors	They may regard you as a professional, efficient and business-like charity.
Staff	You might be seen as a good and fair employer.

Brands

Each of your products or services should have an image and an identity. This is where branding comes in. It is the way goods or services from one organisation or company are distinguished from those of another.

A tin of Heinz baked beans looks different from a tin of Tesco own-brand baked beans. The tins are the same size and shape (and arguably the beans taste the same); simply the label design on the tins is different. Many customers are happy to pay extra for Heinz beans because, thanks to the way the product has been packaged, branded and promoted, they feel they are getting something extra in return.

Non-tangible Factors

Branding involves the way a product looks and is presented, as well as non-tangible factors. Take, for example, tennis rackets. Despite being indistinguishable from racket B in looks, performance and durability, racket A might outsell it tenfold as a result of successful branding. It is the same with many other products. A fragrance costing £9.99 might be outsold by a £50 product with a very similar chemical composition. Why are people prepared to pay five times as much for an almost identical product? Because of branding. In the case of perfume, the consumer is buying more than a pleasant smell: they are buying a lifestyle. Women might prefer the opulent bottle and attractive carton of expensive perfume, or like the sexy and sophisticated images used in its advertising and promotion, and want to be associated with them. Wearing expensive fragrance may make them feel good, in a way that a cheaper perfume from a cut-price pharmacy would not. That shows the power of branding.

Branding as Shorthand

Regard branding as a shorthand, with the name of your charity, product or service coming to represent a host of associations for your 'customers'. Spend time and effort building a brand and when people see your products they should feel confident about them. If you have confidence in the Oxfam 'brand', this confidence should extend to their shops, mail order business, campaigning wing and to other parts of the organisation. Oxfam, having established a brand, do not have to start from scratch when launching a new product; the brand is already established and new products benefit from their relationship and association with the charity. If a new charity called Oxfamine suddenly appeared on the scene, people would regard it with suspicion. It would need to establish its credentials over a period of time before being accepted.

Creating a Brand

What goes into creating a brand? Ingredients include: the product (or service); its packaging; name; promotional activity; and overall presentation. A brand encompasses: physical attributes (such as, with perfume, its smell); aesthetic (the design of a perfume bottle); rational elements (value for money, usefulness); and emotional elements (in the case of an expensive perfume, it makes the wearer feel attractive or glamorous). It is this last point, the emotional one, that is very relevant for many charities. Individuals may buy your product for emotional reasons, and while other factors – such as the value of your work or the probity of your organisation – are important, they may not outweigh the emotional feelings. Put together all of these aspects and you have a brand – but only if your product, and its packaging and promotion, is strongly differentiated from competitors.

Even products that are intrinsically non-brandable, such as bananas, can be branded. Labels are stuck on fruit and vegetables in supermarkets and greengrocers, and point-of-sale material (such as banana mobiles or posters depicting the fruit) are displayed nearby to help develop a sense of brand. People may opt for Fyffes bananas because they have confidence in that brand, even though non-branded bananas alongside taste the same and cost less. People feel they are getting more for their money.

Strong or successful new brands attract 'me toos', imitators who hope to capitalise from copying you. If you devise a fantastic fundraising event, it could easily be copied by other organisations, who may do a better job of exploiting its opportunities than you did. Be aware that good ideas may be copied. Make it difficult for others to steal them by promoting your ideas in a way that closely associates them with your organisation.

A strong brand cannot guarantee success, but it will tip the balance in your favour. Washing machine A might be the stronger brand, but if you have to wait six weeks for delivery, you might plump for brand B thanks to its promise of next day delivery. And so with charities. Your organisation might be the stronger brand in the world of conservation charities, and all things being equal you would probably attract all the potential members, but if a lesser competitor offers a free newsletter, badge and poster to all new members, this might put you at a disadvantage. On the other hand, your USP could be that you never use gimmicks to attract or maintain membership. You could argue that every penny raised goes direct to the cause, with nothing wasted on car stickers, posters and the like. Such an image would be an integral part of your branding and promotion.

Maintaining Brand Values

Brands survive only if they are kept alive by your efforts. You cannot establish a brand and then plod merrily on without any further effort. If you have established your service as innovative and pioneering, you must keep it that way. Otherwise competitors will overtake you and your image will be worthless. If Henry Ford had stopped product development after the invention of the Model T, we would need to look not on our roads, but in the history books, to find out what business Ford was in. Make sure you maintain your position as the biggest, the best, the smallest, the most caring, the most efficient, or whatever it is that you are.

The following companies were brand leaders in 1923: Kodak, Del Monte, Wrigley, Gillette, Coca-Cola and Goodyear. Eight decades on they are still household names, but only because they put time, effort and money into maintaining the brand.

Brand Extensions

When I was a little girl Mars was synonymous with a bar of chocolate that helped you work, rest and play. Now you can buy Mars bar ice creams, mini Mars bite-size snacks, Mars bar Easter eggs and even Mars bar-flavoured milk drinks. This is an example of an established brand extending its product lines into related new products. Because the name and the product are already known, establishing product extensions is not as difficult or expensive as if they were totally new and unfamiliar products. The brand name Mars is used as an endorsement of the quality, origin and value of the new product. The product has credibility merely because of the Mars name and associations.

Charities can do this too. The Vegetarian Society was established many years ago as a charity to support vegetarians and encourage others to give up meat and fish. It now uses the Vegetarian Society name and logo as a brand, and has developed a range of new products and brand extensions which have helped it to raise its profile, campaign on vegetarian issues, raise money and attract new members. It runs vegetarian cookery courses, for example, and sells its logo to companies for use on *bona fide* vegetarian products.

Of course, there can be dangers in brand extension. The value of the brand can be diluted, and there is a risk that if one of your products goes under or attracts negative publicity, the rest of your brands could suffer. If it were discovered that some products carrying the Vegetarian Society logo were not actually vegetarian (because they used animal gelatine, for example) this might damage the Vegetarian Society as a whole, leading to negative media coverage, loss of confidence and a fall-off in membership.

The Charity as the Brand

Some companies have a clear corporate identity, and additionally they have a range of products each with their own branding. Others use their corporate brand to sell all manner of other products, which may in themselves all be quite different. For example, the Sainsbury's 'own brand' is used to sell everything from champagne to toilet rolls. The individual products are not given strong branding of their own; they sell by using the Sainsbury's name.

Sometimes a charity finds, like Sainsbury's, that its brand is the organisation as a whole. The bits that make it up, or the services and products it provides, are not as distinctive as the organisation. For them, their own corporate identity is the brand. The branding and packaging of the whole organisation is what gives definition to the services provided by it. Its unique personality is what differentiates it from the many other charities working in the same field.

There is an Edinburgh housing association called Edinvar – the 'Edin' bit coming from EDINburgh and the 'var' from VARsity. When established in 1972 it housed students from the local university. Since then it has changed dramatically, with thousands of homes, offices in other towns and over 200 staff. It now houses very few students and virtually no one is aware of how it came to be so named. It has worked hard to position itself as a pioneering organisation. That's its brand – Edinvar the Pioneer. It promotes all the 'firsts' it has been responsible for and presses home its pioneering work at every opportunity – whether through newsletters, its annual report, news releases and media interviews, or through job advertising, its business plan and leaflets. So successful has it been that it is now widely regarded in its field as an innovative and forward-thinking organisation. The interest taken in it is far beyond its size, and its reputation has spread to Europe. This has stood it in good stead in attracting funding, doing deals and forging partnerships with the big league, and attracting and keeping the best staff. By ensuring that its innovative work is geared towards providing the best possible service to its users, it protects its brand name. New services launched by Edinvar, such as its community care service, benefit from their association with the Edinvar brand.

Branding Services

Traditionally, branding was associated with products; now the service sector brands services to create a perceived unique and differentiated personality. Personality is promoted via the company's people and the key elements of the provision of its service, such as efficiency, cost-effectiveness, speed and courtesy. For service providers it is important to develop a perception in the marketplace of your individual personality which sets you apart from the competition. Take British Airways (BA), which describes itself as the world's favourite airline. That's quite a claim! How can an airline differentiate itself from the others when the chances are that it flies to the same places as the rest, has the same flight times, the same fares, flies from the same airports using the same planes? BA uses the world's favourite airline slogan to help set it apart. It also does it through its packaging. There is a unity of design from bag tags and tickets through to staff uniforms and the upholstery and colours within the plane. It would be foolish for charities to spend on designer uniforms or expensive interior-designed offices, but there is still a lesson here for the voluntary sector. Visual identity, combined with good quality of service, can be the hallmarks that help you to differentiate what you provide from what is available elsewhere.

Repositioning the Brand

You might find yourself with a brand image that has become out-moded or inappropriate. Many Third World charities used to pro-mote themselves as aid agencies; they raised money for Third World aid and to relieve the symptoms of poverty and disaster. There came a time, however, when this was regarded as paternal-istic, even racist. Progressive Third World charities decided to reposition and reinvent themselves. Instead of using images of emaciated children with begging bowls and swollen bellies, they showed positive imagery. Instead of picturing Third World people as helpless victims they were presented as people who, with assis-tance in the form of money or expertise, could take control of their own destiny. Instead of appealing to people using pity, they appealed using economic and political arguments. Instead of fighting the symptoms they began to address the causes.

Such charities saw their donor profile change. The older, more affluent people to whom their previous approaches had appealed were replaced by younger people with an interest in the political and economic system that maintains underdevelopment and an understanding of the colonial process that caused it. In such cases the charities decided that there was a need to refocus their work; the changed donor profile was a side effect of that, not an aim. Indeed many charities found that their new supporters had less money to give (although many were willing to give up time to campaigning), and that the emotive line they had previously taken had served them well in terms of attracting money.

Companies reposition their brands too, in order to attract new and different customers. Lucozade is the textbook example often cited as the classic repositioning exercise. Developed in the 1920s, Lucozade was a glucose drink for invalids and convalescents, par-ticularly sick children. If you can't remember being unwell and receiving a large bottle wrapped in mustard-coloured cellophane, you must be under the age of 35! In 1983 the drink was dramati-cally repositioned using the British Olympic decathlon gold medallist Daley Thompson. He promoted Lucozade as a dynamic, vital sports drink. Out went big bottles and cellophane; in came cans, one-drink mini bottles, Lucozade glucose tablets and iso-tonic sports Lucozade. Although the composition of the drink is unchanged, thanks to radical repositioning today's youngsters regard it as a healthy sports drink, not something for sick children. So instead of drinking Lucozade on the one or two occasions a year that they are ill, children (and adults) drink it perhaps once or twice a day! Clearly that kind of repositioning has a positive effect on sales of the product.

You too can reposition existing products for a new audience. Consider taking elements of what you offer, but altering them in a minor way so as to appeal to your new audience. Lucozade produced cans in place of large bottles, thus making the drink more practical for sports people. You might find that an alteration to your existing product will make it more attractive or appropriate for your new audience. If you aim to attract students as members, they might find it easier to pay their subscription monthly by direct debit rather than annually via a credit card, for example.

Organisation and product names

Names are a key ingredient of branding. To have a distinct identity, campaigns, appeals and services must be given names. Selecting the right name is vital. People take great care over naming children, books, pets, cars, even hurricanes. Spend time choosing an appropriate name for your product or service.

THE GOOD BRAND NAME CHECKLIST

- ☑ Make sure your chosen name is apt.
- ☑ Select a short, concise name if possible.
- ☑ Try to choose something memorable.
- ☑ Check your name is pronounceable, especially if it is an acronym.
- ☑ Opt for a name that conveys the right image of the organisation and is meaningful, evocative or descriptive.

The Origins of a Name

Everyone has heard of Kodak, but what's it got to do with cameras? Nothing. It is a completely made-up name. Some product names originally had meaning, but while the product name is widely known, the origin of the name is not. Nylon got its name from NY for New York and LON from London: in the days before cheap transatlantic travel these cities conjured up images of glamour and sophistication. In a similar vein, a product called Durex was launched in the 1930s. Its name came from DUrability,

REliability and EXcellence. Everyone has heard of Durex and the name is now used as the generic for condoms, but how many people know how it gained its name?

Generic Names

Most of us call all disposable pens Biros, after the man who invented them. We also call all vacuum cleaners Hoovers, regardless of make. Interestingly, Mr Hoover did not invent the vacuum cleaner, he was simply good at promotional activity! Charity shops are often known by the generic term Oxfam shops. You know that your brand name is a success when it becomes a generic.

Acronyms

You've heard of BUPA, Britain's leading independent healthcare company, which, interestingly, is a not-for-profit organisation. Research shows that there is 75 per cent spontaneous awareness among the public for the name. But do you know what the initials BUPA stand for? Very few would know the organisation as the British United Provident Association.

Which is more important? A name that is memorable, short and snappy, even if it has no meaning or the derivation is no longer known, or a descriptive and meaningful one? There is no right answer. It is up to a charity to select a name that is the right one for them, given what they do, who they do it for, how they are funded and how they would like to be regarded. All of these factors must take into account when deciding on names.

The brand name spectrum

Nucleus	Friends of the Earth Greenpeace	Help the Aged Talking Newspaper Association RSPCA
Completely free-standing, arbitrary or coined ▶	Associative or suggestive ▶	Completely descriptive

Arbitrary	Nucleus is a small, local charity providing support services to parents with children who have special needs. While the name does not directly relate to what the charity does, it is short, strong and memorable, and it suggests a small, close-knit and supportive group.
Associative	Friends of the Earth has associations with empathy for the planet, caring, people who are on the planet's side, who will protect it. However, the name suggests rather than describes.
Descriptive	There is no doubt about what the Royal Society for the Prevention of Cruelty to Animals does.

Changing Name

Changing the name of your organisation is a much bigger step than selecting a brand new name for a totally new service. Yet it is a marketing decision that you may need to consider if your name is working against you. The Anytown Charitable Trust for the Care and Support of Indigent Gentlewomen of Limited Means might be descriptive, but it is far from snappy and it sounds like something from the nineteenth century. Many charities have their roots in Victorian times, which is why their names would not look out of place in a Dickens novel. While some feel that a well-known charity should stick with an established name, a number of high-profile organisations have successfully changed their name to keep up with the times and appeal to a new generation of supporters.

Let's take a fictitious example which illustrates the point very well – the Anytown Charitable Trust for the Care and Support of Indigent Gentlewomen of Limited Means. Suppose the charity does some research to establish its donor profile, and discovers that 95 per cent of donors are reasonably wealthy widows in their nineties. The charity hypothesises that its name is the reason for its almost exclusive appeal to this group (although it could be due to other factors such as where and how the charity promotes its work). What is clear is that when these supporters die, which will be sooner rather than later, the charity will expire too. Without a fresh crop of donors, funds will dry up. To establish why the charity attracts largely from this group, it conducts further research. This reveals that its aged donors offer their support out of a sense of gratitude that they are not gentlewomen of limited means.

Research among a younger age group shows that the work of the charity is regarded as essential and worthwhile once explained, but that the charity's image is a problem. Younger donors are put off helping an outfit that sounds so fuddy-duddy and comes across as remote from their own experience. The charity's name is put before the sample, along with other more cuddly names such as Help Gran, Adopt a Granny and Twilight Life, and radical names like Silver Sisters. It is discovered that potential donors are more likely to support a charity with a more upbeat name and image, even if it is doing the same work as the Anytown Charitable Trust for the Care and Support of Indigent Gentlewomen of Limited Means. Calling the charity Adopt a Granny means something to younger people, who can relate the name to their own grandmothers and therefore to their own experience and emotions.

Your name is an important part of your image. Why do you think Norma Jean Baker changed her name to Marilyn Monroe, or Harry Webb became Cliff Richard? Names say something about a person – they can reveal gender, age, social class, ethnicity. Who is more likely to wear dreadlocks, Crispin D'Arcy-Smythe or Leroy Garvey? Who's more likely to be a pensioner, Gladys Violet Smith or Kirsty Smith? Who's working-class, Gary Richards or Quentin Dorward-Richards? You get the picture.

Names can also reflect a charity's background and values. Which is run by a bunch of 'lefties' – Red Action against Poverty and Injustice or The Royal Society for the Development of Assistance for the Poor and Downtrodden? Which is run by disability activists and which by well-meaning middle-class ladies – Wheelchair Rights Now! and The Anytown Society for Handicapped People? Names say a lot and we base our assumptions on them. The reality might be very different, but that's not the point. If potential customers are switched off by the name, and it happens in sufficient numbers, you should be concerned. People might be supporting you in spite of the name, not because of it.

During the 1980s and 1990s many household name charities underwent name changes. The Spastics Society changed to Scope in 1994. When the Spastics Society was founded, the term 'spastic' was applied to cerebral palsy sufferers. Now it has become a term of abuse, so a name change was inevitable. On the first anniversary of the name change, Scope had attracted nearly 40,000 new donors. It was also in talks with 25 potential corporate donors and sponsors, many of whom steered clear of the charity when it was called the Spastics Society.

The Marriage Guidance Council was set up before co-habitation was widespread. By changing its name to Relate it can more easily show that it can help with married, co-habitational and same-sex relationships. The National Council for Civil Liberties is now Liberty, which is much more modern sounding and has more appeal for a younger generation. If they can do it, so can you!

Visual image

Visual image is important and consideration needs to be given to it as part of your marketing activities. People may be judged by how they look; an organisation will be judged on its letterhead, annual report, office and staff. The way things look counts. The most obvious aspect of your visual identity will be your logo; other elements will stem from this. If you don't have a logo, or you are considering a new one, here's what you need to do:

THE EFFECTIVE LOGO CHECKLIST

☑ Decide what you want your logo to say about you. What sort of image should it portray? Caring? Efficient? Welcoming? Concerned with children? Concerned with trees and the environment?

☑ Write down your ideas for how this could be achieved, or sketch them if you find it easier.

☑ Agree any words or straplines (a brief statement or description of your work) that need to be incorporated into the design.

☑ Decide whether your logo will be a design in its own right, or just a stylised version of your name. Your designer can advise on this.

☑ Decide how many colours your logo will be. The more colours you use, the higher the printing costs for your stationery and other materials. Two-colour logos are quite acceptable.

☑ Brief your chosen designer about your work and your ideas for a logo.

☑ Look over the various options prepared for you by your designer, and if necessary commission further ideas. Make sure you see the logo on letterheads, compliments slips and other materials to get a proper feel for how it will look in use.

☑ Select a design and get the final artwork produced.

---

tip

Ask your designer to design a logo that will also reproduce well in one colour and that will photo-copy and fax clearly.

The colours you select for your logo are known as your 'corporate colours'. You should use them whenever possible to reinforce your visual identity. For example, if your colours are yellow and your staff wear sweatshirts as uniforms, give them yellow sweatshirts. Use pale yellow paper for memos on your notice board, perhaps display yellow flowers in your reception. Gimmicky or monotonous? No. It helps make you more memorable, which is vital to effective marketing.

Promotion: advertising

INTRODUCTION

Although marketing and promotion are often thought of as one and the same, the latter is actually merely an aspect of the former – albeit a very important one. So important, in fact, that six whole chapters of this book have been devoted to its various aspects.

Promotion is one of the four Ps of the 'marketing mix' (the others being product, price and place). Some companies focus their energies and budget on this one P, for obvious reasons. What's the point in having a terrific product, which is in the right place at the right price, if no one knows about it? Promotion is important if you want people to know about your services and products, whether they are users or donors. You need to tell homeless people that you run a free crisis hostel. Otherwise they won't know about it and your beds will remain empty. You must tell donors how well used your hostel is and how there is a pressing need for funding to provide move-on accommodation. Otherwise they won't send in a donation.

This chapter focuses on advertising; the following five chapters cover other aspects of promotional activity. Advertising has a glamorous image and the people who work in it are sometimes regarded with envy. But of course, there's advertising and there's advertising. You don't have to opt for an expensive ad agency in the M&C Saatchi league; a display advert penned in-house for your local paper might suffice – and does for many charities. So whether your budget is big and national press advertising is an option, or whether it is small and you'll be doing everything yourself, there might be space in your promotional strategy for some advertising.

Charity advertising has become both sophisticated and wide-spread. Open up the *Guardian*, *The Times*, a Sunday broadsheet, a tabloid or a trade publication and chances are that you will see charity advertising. Look at a billboard in the street and you may well see something there too. Local and national commercial radio also carries a fair amount of charity advertising. Even TV does some, although cost is the main reason why many charities are kept off our screens – especially during peak viewing.

Use advertising to:

- Publicise an issue, cause or campaign – such as animal cruelty, child abuse or environmental matters.
- Seek money – for an appeal or project.
- Ask for donations of goods – for a project or a raffle.
- Get people to consider leaving you a legacy or other gift.
- Promote your work, publicise your name or remind people that you are still there.
- Attract staff.
- Encourage volunteers.
- Promote membership of your organisation.
- Advertise an event.
- Advertise a service.
- Sell a product.

As this book is a DIY guide, the focus is on press advertising, which you can often do in-house. If you are planning TV or radio advertising, you will probably need to use an advertising agency (you can read how to select an ad agency at the end of this chapter).

Budget is often a primary factor when it comes to selecting an advertising medium. Apart from the obvious considerations such as what you can afford, consider what is appropriate, what will achieve your objectives most cost-effectively and what will reach your target. An advert in *Playboy* might prove effective in terms of attracting donations, but is it appropriate? A TV advert might lead donors to question how you can afford it. A national news-paper advert for a local event would be madness. Targeting is a fundamental advertising issue.

THE EFFECTIVE ADVERTISING CHECKLIST

☑ Establish your objectives – what you want to advertise and what you hope to achieve.

☑ Establish your target audience. Who do you want to reach? (Decision-makers? Wealthy people likely to leave legacies? Animal lovers? People interested in socialist politics? Anyone living in Greater Manchester?)

☑ Establish your key messages. What do you want to say?

☑ Select your advertising medium. What will allow you to promote those messages and reach your target audience?

☑ Establish the frequency required. How often would you need to advertise to get your message across successfully and how big/long would your advert need to be?

☑ Cost out the various options.

☑ Establish a budget.

☑ Work out any hidden costs (placing an advert in the national press involves the cost of buying the space, but you also need to consider the cost of commissioning an ad agency to design the advert, which will include the cost of photography, copywriting, artwork, etc. The same goes for radio adverts. You may need to pay a scriptwriter, commission actors/voice-over artists, and take on singers and/or musicians. That's all on top of the cost of buying the airtime.)

☑ Find out who else advertises there. Is there any clash or conflict? Could you end up in competition with a more 'attractive' or appealing charity?

☑ Anticipate what your supporters may think of your ad campaign. Might they feel that you are wasting their money on advertising when it should go straight to the user?

> **tip**
>
> When examining the cost of advertising, ask whether you could use this money more effectively in a different way. Will a mail shot be cheaper and just as effective?

Advertising channels

When it comes to media advertising, you have various options open to you:

- local and regional paid-for press;
- local freesheets;
- national press;
- trade, consumer and specialist publications;
- local commercial radio;
- national commercial radio;
- commercial TV.

Let's look at each in turn.

Local and Regional Paid-For Press

Pros

- Local and regional newspapers are an excellent way of geographical targeting. Some cover just a town or city, while others – such as the *Yorkshire Post* or *The Scotsman* – cover a whole region or country.

- The newspaper will sometimes help you to design the advert cost-free, although don't expect more than some basic layout of your text and logo.
- A representative from the newspaper will be happy to come and see you to discuss options and ideas.
- As there is no long lead-in time, you can place an advert at very short notice.
- You can use coupon responses – essential if you want people to write in for information or send in a donation.
- If you are using a coupon as part of your advert, it is easy to code it so that you can tell which publication it appeared in, and even on which day. This is invaluable when it comes to discovering which adverts were most effective.
- It can be quite cheap, especially if you are using classified adverts.
- People can re-read your ad as often as they like.

Cons

- Your advert has to compete for attention.
- People buy newspapers primarily for the news, not the adverts. Your ad may just be scanned, or ignored all together.
- Reproduction can be poor, though it is improving all the time.
- Daily and even weekly newspapers have a short shelf-life, which reduces the chances of your ad being seen.
- There is wastage: never assume that because the official readership is 100,000 people, all of them will read your advert. With radio and TV advertising, the ad is played to the viewer or listener. With press advertising the reader must make the effort to read your advert.
- Press adverts are static and two-dimensional.

Local Freesheets

Pros

- They are cheap to advertise in and, because they are free and hand-delivered, they reach most households.
- Many people look forward to their local freebie, enthusiastically reading both news and ads.
- Some free newspapers cover a tiny area, allowing very precise geographical targeting.
- You can use coupon responses.
- It can be very cheap, especially if you are using classified adverts.
- Your advert can be re-read.

Cons

- Their only revenue is advertising, so freesheets carry many more ads than paid-for newspapers. This means that your ad will have to compete harder for attention.
- A significant number of people regard freesheets as rubbish and throw them away unread. When someone has gone to the trouble of buying a paper, they will find the time to read it. They may not place such a high value on something that is delivered free to their door.
- Many freesheets are so localised that they do not reach a good cross-section of the population.
- People do not always regard free papers as 'real' newspapers.
- Not all readers will read your ad.

National Press

Pros

- Decision-makers and professionals read national broadsheet papers, so it is a good way of reaching these audiences.
- Each paper has a very clear readership profile, so targeting is easy.
- There are fewer ads to compete with than in local papers.
- You can place an ad at short notice.
- They are ideal for national organisations to reach a wide audience.
- Coupon responses can be used.
- Although more expensive than local papers, national press advertising can be affordable if you use their classified sections.
- Your advert can be read and re-read.

Cons

- Although some national papers have a geographical bias (more readers in the north of England than in the south, for example), geographical targeting is much poorer than with local papers, so they are generally of less use to local or regional charities. Some papers produce regional issues (such as the *Daily Mail*) or have a Scottish edition, so this does help targeting.
- It is much more expensive than advertising in local papers.
- Reproduction can be poor.
- Daily newspapers have an even shorter shelf-life than weekly freesheets, though the Sunday papers do lie around for longer.
- Unlike a local or free paper, national papers often have a more stylish format and, with the exception of display ads, are more likely to feature professionally designed ads. This

will add to your costs, for you will have to buy in design in addition to paying for the space. Many papers will want 'camera-ready artwork', which you will need a designer to prepare for you.

■ Not all readers will read your ad.

Trade, Consumer and Specialist Publications

Pros

■ Audience targeting is much easier – nurses read *Nursing Standard* and architects read *Architects' Journal*, so you can easily reach a particular profession or interest group.
■ There is generally better reproduction and fewer ads to compete with (except in the trade publications that are given away free).
■ The shelf-life is longer than for newspapers (particularly for monthly and quarterly publications)
■ Most trade publications are passed around the office and therefore read by more than one person.
■ Professional publications may be filed for reference, thus making them even more long-lasting.
■ Coupon responses can be used.

Cons

■ You may have to advertise in a number of journals to reach all of your audiences, whereas a newspaper advert in the right paper would allow you to reach them in one go.
■ The longer lead-in times mean that you have to plan ahead.
■ You may have to provide 'camera-ready artwork', which will involve engaging a graphic designer.

Local Commercial Radio

Pros

■ You can target geographically.
■ It tends not to attract social classes A and B, so if you want to target C1s, Ds and Es, it is ideal.
■ It can work out cheaper than you might imagine, and most stations have a member of staff available to help and advise.
■ Many local stations have a loyal following.
■ Most homes have more than one radio and 95 per cent of all cars have one, so there are many opportunities for people to tune in at home, work and on the move.
■ Unlike press advertising, dimension and life are added to radio adverts with the use of voice, music and sound effects.

Cons

- Local radio is frequently on as background noise, with listeners doing other things while half-listening.
- It is more transient than a newspaper advert, which can sit around for days and weeks, and can be looked at again and again.
- Unlike a coupon response in a newspaper or magazine advert, it is more difficult to respond to radio adverts. Often you need to have a pen and paper handy to take down the details, so it requires more effort from the listener for you to get a response.
- You will need to budget for making the advert, as well as buying the airtime. This will involve a copywriter, a voice-over artist and perhaps costs for music too.
- Unlike both TV and press advertising, radio is not visual. You cannot show your service.

> **tip**
>
> The medium is as important as the message. A brilliant advert placed in the wrong newspaper will be a waste of money. Take the same care when deciding where to advertise as you do when deciding what to advertise.

National Commercial Radio

Pros

- The growth in specialist channels in national commercial radio, such as Classic FM, enables the targeting of certain social groups. In the case of Classic FM, social classes A, B and C1 can easily be reached.
- It offers opportunities to reach a large number of people for a great deal less than TV advertising.

Cons

- Apart from talk radio, such as BBC Radio 4 (which is, in any case, not commercial and therefore does not carry advertising) radio is often not actively listened to.
- All the drawbacks of local radio also apply to national advertising.

Commercial TV

Pros

- Film is a powerful and persuasive medium, and a clever advert can change people's hearts and minds.
- You can reach a wide audience.
- You can target geographically (by advertising on one or more of the local networks) or buy airtime on all of them to ensure national coverage.
- You can decide what time you want your advert to appear and during which programme, so as to reach the right audience.
- You can enter people's homes.

- The viewer need make little effort, as they are presented with your advert.

Cons

- TV is very much at the glamorous end of advertising. It is expensive, both to buy airtime and to make an ad for screening. It is highly unlikely that you could do the job yourself. A few charities do advertise on TV, but for most it is both unaffordable and inappropriate.
- Many people video-record programmes and fast-forward during ads. This is a real concern to the advertising industry.
- Many viewers 'channel hop' using their remote control during commercial breaks.
- It is difficult to get across a complicated message in a few seconds.
- TV advertising is transient; it is over in a flash and cannot be retained in the way that a press ad can.

Setting objectives

Never place an advert just because it seemed like a good idea at the time, or because there was a special offer with reduced rates. Be absolutely clear about your objectives before you advertise. Set objectives that are specific and measurable. It is no good saying 'we want to advertise in order to raise awareness.' That's too general and unfocused. The following objectives are measurable:

We want to advertise in order to:

- Attract 600 new members.
- Attract total donations of £500,000.
- Attract 100 enquiries about our service, leading to 50 people being offered help.
- Generate an increase of 50 per cent in the number of calls received by our helpline.

You also need to incorporate some kind of time-scale:

- We wish to attract 600 new members within one month of our ad first appearing.
- We want to attract donations of £500,000 within six months of our advertising campaign ending, all of them as a direct result of the campaign.

By being clear what you want to achieve from your ad campaign, you can measure whether you have been successful. Objective-setting will also help you to select the right advertising medium to achieve the results you are looking for.

TRUE STORY   Getting it Wrong

A newspaper sent marketing managers some sharp-tipped metal arrows as a gimmick to demonstrate its proficiency at targeting readers. Great idea, but the newspaper landed up in trouble with the Advertising Standards Authority, who said that the mailing of a potentially offensive weapon was not a suitable promotional item.

Ads in isolation

Too many organisations, charitable and commercial, place an advert as a knee-jerk response. They see their membership falling or donations sliding, for example, and regard a hastily placed advert as the solution. If this is your attitude, advertising will fail you. Regard advertising as part of your marketing strategy, and carefully plan it alongside your other marketing activity.

Once you have set a budget and selected your advertising medium, you need to create your ad. Producing effective advertising copy is an art. It has been suggested that we see up to 1,500 sales messages every day – on TV, buses, posters and elsewhere. Of these we remember just seven to ten; the vast majority of advertising just passes us by. Ensure your ads fall into the memorable category.

Before you even put pen to paper, do your homework.

- **Understand your audience** – know whom you are writing for, if you are to stand a chance of communicating effectively with them.
- **Know the competition** – unless you know what they are offering, how can you offer something different or better?
- **Know your UBP** – your Unique Buying Point. This is different from a USP (Unique Selling Point) because it takes as its starting point what is of interest and importance to the buyer. USPs are product-centred. UBPs focus on what counts for the buyer, at whom your advert is aimed.

TRUE STORY   Getting it Right

During the Second World War, Stork margarine was heavily advertised, even though it could not be bought on ration coupons. When the war ended and Stork became available again, the company ran an advert showing a stork in prisoners' uniform being released from prison. Many products were forgotten about during the six-year war, but Stork had no difficulty in making its comeback.

Once you are clear on the above you are ready to start on your advert.

DIY advertising copy

This section explains how to produce copy for the print media. Writing scripts for radio and TV is very specialised and is probably best left to an ad agency.

> **tip**
>
> When you see the artwork for your ad (whether produced in-house or by an agency) ask to see it presented as it will appear. Take a page from the newspaper in which it will be placed, and substitute your own advert for an existing one. An advert on its own has more impact than when seen surrounded by the text of a newspaper.

Obviously, a good professional will produce a better ad than a keen, if talented, amateur. Even so, you can produce effective press advertising in-house – if you can get someone to share a few tricks of the trade. Pick up some useful tips and inside information in this chapter.

Using AIDA

Good advertising should employ the AIDA formula. This stands for attention, interest, desire and action.

- It should attract **Attention** so that people see it and read it. Use strong photographs or other imagery, an arresting headline, bold colours (or striking use of black and white in a colour publication), good design, or a combination of these to achieve something attention-grabbing. Remember that your ad will be competing with many others, so it must stand out and attract attention.
- It must hold the reader's **Interest**.
- It should create **Desire** – to use your service, buy your products, make a donation, take out a membership, to work with you or for you, to campaign for your cause, or support you in some other way. Study commercial ads and see what techniques they employ to stimulate desire.
- It must prompt **Action** – there's no point in producing an ad that is arresting, encourages interest in your service and a desire to use it, if nothing happens thereafter. Make it easy for readers to donate, perhaps with a tear-off slip. Encourage people to ring your free advice line by publicising the number and opening times.

Attracting Attention

Some advertisers attract attention by being deliberately different and unexpected. Take this example. What do you think it is advertising?

> Guinea Bissau is one of the poorest countries in the world and is arguably the most underdeveloped country in Africa. Economic aid was cut in 1989 and the region has been struggling to maintain its infrastructure ever since. The European Development Fund has been helping by introducing a more efficient farming policy, and has created a 50,000 hectare project devoted to maize, cotton and rice ...

The ad continues in this vein for several paragraphs more. Is it an advert for Oxfam? No. Voluntary Service Overseas? No. It is a car ad! I don't normally read car ads but I read this one. Why? Because it was so totally unexpected that I kept reading in order to find out what the economy of Guinea Bissau had to do with the up-market and expensive Land Rover. Six paragraphs later I found out. It is good on hazardous terrains and in monsoons that turn roads to rivers of mud, as happens in Guinea Bissau. I wasn't persuaded to buy a Land Rover, but I did read the sort of advert that I would normally ignore.

Making Action Easy

Your task is to create an ad that makes clear what action is required, and enables respondents to take it with ease. There are various ways you can do this.

1 **Use a coupon response.** This makes it really easy for readers to send in for further information or to mail you a donation. If you are using this device, remember to put your address on the coupon rather than in the body of the advertisement; if a reader mislays the advert having cut off the coupon, they will still know where to send it.
2 **Use a Freepost address** if you can afford to (contact Royal Mail for details).
3 **Use a Freephone number**. Talk to your telecom provider for details.
4 Consider offering a **credit card facility** if appropriate.
5 **Use a return address** that is as short as possible and easy to spell.

After you have written an advert, put it aside for a day or so. Then return to it and ask yourself whether it is clear what the reader has to do. What do you want them to do? Do you want them to:

tip

Caption illustrations: they attract twice the readership of the main text.

tip

If you are using coupons in different publications, code the coupon in the bottom corner so you can tell where it was cut out from. That way you can monitor response to your advert, and assess which publication or which day produced the best response, which is essential if you are planning to advertise again. You can do this for radio adverts too. Ask people to write to Department X for one radio station and Department Y for another.

- Complete a coupon asking for more information.
- Send in a donation.
- Call you for details of a product or service.
- Telephone your counselling helpline.
- Join your organisation.
- Think in a different way about an issue, or change their behaviour (by boycotting certain goods or companies, for example).

Have you made it easy for them to take the necessary action? If not, look at the list above and see if any of them can help you to help your readers.

The eye path

Much research has been carried out to discover how people 'read' an advert. There is a definite route which people's eyes take when they see an ad for the first time.

Picture	Our eye falls here first, so it goes without saying that the picture you choose should be large, dramatic and attention-grabbing.
Headline	Our eye moves here next. Devise a snappy and hard-hitting headline, as only one in five readers make it beyond here.
Bottom right-hand corner	Readers then move to the bottom right-hand corner of the page, which is where most advertisers place their name and logo. The majority of readers will get no further than this.
Captions	The captions on photos and illustrations are read next.
Cross headings	Next, readers scan the cross headings, graphs and other illustrations.
Body text	Last of all, readers focus on the main part of your advert, the body text. By now you have lost most of your audience.

tip

Full colour ads in magazines attract twice the readership of black and white ones, so consider this when making a decision about which to use.

The lesson is simple. Don't rely on your text to get people interested; most won't ever get this far. If your picture and headline are not arresting enough to attract readers into your ad, you are on to a loser.

The picture plus headline formula

Dramatic picture + intriguing (or witty) headline = successful ad.

This tried and tested formula works. An ad for Honda, produced to show how fuel economical the Honda Civic is, showed a car alongside a petrol pump, with the headline: 'Avoid painful fillings'.

Charities use this formula too. Take this advert for the Guide Dogs for the Blind Association. A photo of a man's face with dog's eyes reads: 'No surgeon in the world can help this blind man see. But a dog can.' It works because it tells a story in a picture and a few words, the image is powerful, the headline clever. Here's another clever charity example. The headline reads: 'Like this coat? The last owner was shot in it.' A photograph of a leopard skin coat illustrates the headline.

A picture and headline should work together, with each telling its half of the story. A picture that simply repeats the headline, or vice versa, will not produce the desired effect. Each needs the other to make sense, and together they should produce a strong enough message to stand alone, without any body text. You need body text to give the detail, but aim for something that can work well without it.

Effective Headlines

Your headline is one of the key elements of your advert. Only 20 per cent of readers will read beyond it, so you need to ensure that it does its job well. Neglect your headline and you're wasting 80 per cent of your advertising budget. You can make your headline more effective by:

- Using **why** in the headline – 'Why ten million Britons support charity X' is better than 'Ten million Britons support ...'. The first makes people wonder, the second leaves them thinking 'so what?'

TRUE STORY   Getting it Right

Controversial ads can generate editorial coverage, thus making your advertising budget go further. In 1995 the charity CHILDREN 1ST ran an ad with a photo of a child's frightened face, with the headline: 'If you only give money to animals: she's been treated like one all her life.' As a result of the advert a number of animal charities wrote to newspapers objecting to the implication in the advert, as they saw it, that people who care about animals do not care about children. Other correspondence putting forward different views followed, turning an advertising campaign into something much more high profile that was carried into the letters pages.

- Using **how** – An advert encouraging donors to give by covenant, thus enabling the charity to reclaim the tax, might read 'How to give us 40p in the pound extra – at no cost to you'.
- Using **do** – An effective ACTIONAID advert read: 'Do you really need 50p more than she does?' and was accompanied by an appealing photograph of a child in Southern India.
- Using a **signpost** to alert your intended audience – A fundraising advert for a children's hospice could be headlined: 'PARENTS – How would you feel if your child was dying?' An advert for breast cancer screening might read: 'WOMEN OVER 50 – breast cancer is a real killer in your age group, but free screening ...'.

Some of these headlines could work without an illustration, making them ideal for charities who have a really tight budget and must produce all ads in-house. Sometimes a strong headline and attractive layout may be all that's needed. Another headline that works well without a photo is this one for the Blood Transfusion Service: 'What if they only gave blood to people who were donors?' This is strong enough to stand without any body copy at all, and would make a good advert for the side of a bus, for example, or an effective car sticker.

The body text

Remember that only 20 per cent of those looking at your advert will get this far. However, those who make it are likely to be interested in what you have to say. Your body text needs to explain your headline (and photo, if you used one). It is your chance to give more detail, to offer any facts and information, and generally to draw the reader in. But be careful.

BODY TEXT DO'S AND DON'TS

- ☒ **Don't** waffle.
- ☒ **Don't** say too much; your reader will have trouble taking it all in.
- ☒ **Don't** present too many ideas or propositions; it will confuse.
- ☒ **Don't** use too much unbroken text or small print; it will cause a headache.
- ☑ **Do** use short sentences and short paragraphs.
- ☑ **Do** use questions as subheads, to keep readers' interest. For example: 'Would you like to make the world a better place for your children?'
- ☑ **Do** use the first/second person – lots of 'we', 'you', 'your', etc.

TRUE STORY　Getting it Wrong

One anti-fur campaign produced an ad that met all the criteria for a successful advert. It showed an eye-catching photo of an attractive woman in high heels and a fur coat, headlined: 'It takes 20 dumb animals to make this coat but only one dumb animal to wear it.' The advert was instantly branded sexist and many potential supporters were put off the charity, despite supporting the cause. Be careful not to alienate potential supporters.

Ads for donors

Much charity advertising is aimed at attracting donations. If your attempts at advertising have cost as much as the money you have attracted, you'll know that you are doing something wrong. You may have chosen the wrong publication or the wrong time of year, or perhaps you got the copy wrong. There are various ways of achieving better results from fundraising ads.

Six Ways to Ask for Money

1 Never just ask for cash. Explain how even a small donation can make a difference. For example, instead of simply asking for money to combat blindness in the Third World, why not say: 'Your £5 can make Asuk see his grandson for the first time'. Don't ask for money to help the environment, say: '£10 will plant a tree for future generations'. This way people feel that even though they are giving perhaps just a small amount, it really will help.
2 When asking for money, provide a menu of options. List various items, with a price tag alongside, enabling donors to select an amount: '£1 buys a dozen wild flowers, £10 pays for a tree, £200 enables us to help plant a new forest'.
3 If you are suggesting amounts of money to give, it is best to list the options in ascending order, so that the donor feels more generous the higher up the list they go. Listing in descending order makes donors feel mean if they go too low, and could deter them from giving at all.
4 If you can, try to bring your advert to life by using real people. The example above, 'Your £5 can make Asuk see his grandson for the first time,' is so much more powerful than a headline about the effects of Third World blindness. People can relate to other people, and put themselves in their shoes. It is much harder to be moved by abstract concepts or global problems.
5 Always include an option to give a very small amount of money. To some people £15 is a huge sum, yet many charities

tip

If you plan to run a series of adverts, do not place the first one before starting work on others in the series. You need to have the whole series produced, or at least well advanced, before the first advert is placed.

start their options with this as the minimum. It may encourage some people to give a little more than they otherwise would, but it can also put many off giving anything at all.

6 Keep your copy brief and your request simple. Complex ads fail because many readers do not have the time or energy to tackle an ad with too many messages and too much detail.

Adverts need to be seen to be from the same stable, for they rely on the familiarity factor for recognition. Make it clear that your different adverts are from the same organisation by using a standard layout, the same typefaces in each advert and so on. If each advert looks totally different from the one before it, you have to re-establish yourself with each new one. Your aim is to build on the last one, not start from scratch again.

Advertorials

An advertorial is an ad that tries to look like editorial. The name comes from combining 'advert' and 'editorial' and it is sometimes known as a 'special feature' or a 'promotional article'. Unlike real editorial, it is paid for.

Benefits of Advertorials

- Straight ads should ideally be short and punchy. As an advertorial looks like a feature article, or even a series of articles spanning several pages, it is a good method for getting a serious or more complex message across.
- There is space to go into detail and to illustrate using a range of photos, graphs, case histories and facts and figures.
- Unlike editorial you can, within limits, say what you want to about your organisation, service or campaign.
- Sometimes it can be cheaper to buy half a page of advertorial space than the same amount of display advertising space.

tip

If you decide to place an advert in a trade publication, ask them if you can have some editorial too. Although few publications will admit to their magazine being advertising-led, in practice you can often secure editorial by placing an advert. It is always worth a try.

Advertorials are a good source of revenue for newspapers and magazines and the number of pages devoted to them is on the increase.

Different publications approach advertorials in different ways. Most will get one of their own reporters, or a freelance, to interview you and a feature will then be written about your work or the product/service you wish to promote. Ensure you see this before publication, and amend it if necessary. The publication may also send a photographer to take some shots, or they might ask you to provide quality photographs. Smaller publications sometimes ask you to supply the article. If you are asked to write the copy:

- Find out how many words are required and by when.
- Write in a style that will appeal to the readership (refer to back copies of the publication).
- Ensure that you make the article lively and not too introspective.

The Ethics of Advertorials

Some people regard advertorials as unethical, for in resembling editorial they are attempting to trick the reader. An independent survey, however, has revealed that the majority of readers can distinguish among advertisements, advertorials and editorials. However, the same survey found that 8 per cent of respondents said that the information in advertorials was more convincing than information in editorials! The Periodical Publishers' Association produces guidelines on the labelling of advertorials. The Committee of Advertising Practice advises that advertisement promotions should be designed and presented in such a way that they can be easily distinguished from editorial. Despite this, many advertorials are disguised as ordinary features, even using the same typeface and page layout.

I rarely read advertorials because I know that the chances are that I will not be reading an objective piece. Many journalists share this view and feel that their widespread use erodes a publication's credibility and brings their profession into disrepute. That said, they have their uses, particularly for organisations that would find it otherwise difficult to attract editorial coverage.

Bus advertising

Bus advertising is probably the only form of high-profile advertising that is easily affordable for even quite small charities. You can advertise inside the bus and on the exterior. You can opt for a small panel on the back of the bus, or side panels in a variety of configurations. It works like this:

- Look up 'advertising' in the Yellow Pages and find a company offering bus advertising.
- Arrange for their sales representative to visit you.
- Their rep will explain what bus advertising can do for you and will give you a rate card (this will set out the cost per panel per month for the various types of advertising panel).
- If you want to go ahead, the company will give you advice on your copy, can get artwork produced for you, and will arrange for your adverts to be printed (you can arrange this yourself, but it can be as cheap – and less hassle – to buy a whole package).

> **tip**
>
> You can sometimes get a free ad by using the Listings/ What's On column in your local free newspaper. Most have a column or diary where they publicise community and charity events, and usually there is no charge for this. They often have a help/request column too, which you can use to advertise for volunteers and helpers.

The Benefits of Bus Advertising

- You can specify the type of bus you want your advert on (a double decker, a single decker, etc.).
- You can select which depot(s) you want your bus(es) to run from (but you cannot select particular routes).
- You can specify towns and cities for your campaign.
- You can run a very local campaign (in just one town, or one part of a city) or you can go national (or any combination in between). This makes bus advertising very flexible, and as good for big charities as for smaller community groups.

The Cost

An advert inside a bus can be as little as £10 per month, and it is often possible for a charity to get a discount on published rates. However, you need to add to this the cost of producing artwork (around £50) and the cost of production of your panels. A rear of bus advert (sized 20 × 48 inches) would cost around £65 per panel per month.

Inside or Out?

> **tip**
>
> If you are advertising on a rear panel, your advert will be read by motorists and pedestrians on the move. That's why you must keep it short. If you say who you are, where you are and what you do, that should be sufficient.

Advertising inside a bus is cheaper than placing an ad on the exterior. You need to decide not only what your budget is, but who your target audience is, before you decide which to opt for. Those reading your advert on a bus may be very different to the sort of people who drive along behind buses. But there's another issue. What is your message? External advertising has to be short and sweet, given that you are displaying on a moving vehicle to people who are themselves on the move. Internal advertising, on the other hand, can be more expansive; it will be read by people with time to kill – people sitting on buses.

A charity raising £11 million for a children's hospital known locally as the Sick Kids used bus advertising which centred around headlines alone. One memorable ad read: 'This bus passes by the Sick Kids. Make sure you don't.' It was clever because of the pun and because of the fact that it was displayed on buses passing the hospital, thus serving as a further reminder to passengers.

Bus ticket promotions

Bus ticket advertising is cheaper than many other forms of promotion and is ideal if your target market travels by bus. Tickets must be retained for the duration of a bus journey, so passengers have ample time to look at your ad. Big brand names like Levi jeans use this medium, as well as colleges, small organisations and public sector bodies.

Tickets are produced in full colour for maximum impact. Image Promotions, which specialises in bus ticket advertising (see address section) can help you plan a campaign, whether in just one town or a much wider area. They will make the booking with the bus company, do your artwork, printing, delivery and campaign monitoring. A full campaign starts from £500.

Who Travels by Bus?

Image Promotions, the company responsible for over 95 per cent of all bus ticket promotions in the UK, provides the following figures for what it terms 'typical bus users'.

Socio-economic group		Age group	
A	3 per cent	15–19	9 per cent
B	17 per cent	20–34	22 per cent
C1	26 per cent	35–44	16 per cent
C2	25 per cent	45–54	14 per cent
D	18 per cent	55–64	12 per cent
E	11 per cent	65+	20 per cent

Reasons for bus use			
Shops	56 per cent	Social	12 per cent
Work	18 per cent	School	14 per cent

TRUE STORY

When Save the Children launched its first integrated marketing campaign, Save the Children from Violence, it received support in kind worth £1.3 million. This included help from bus company Stagecoach, who promoted the campaign on bus tickets.

The media plan

If you are placing a one-off advert, perhaps to publicise an event, there is no need to prepare an advertising (sometimes known as media) plan. However, if advertising is a major part of your promotional work, you should produce a programme which states:

- what adverts you will be running;
- when;
- where (in which publications/radio stations);
- at what cost;
- for what effect.

This should be included in your marketing strategy (see Chapter 16).

Legal requirements

All advertising must be legal, decent, honest and truthful. The Advertising Standards Authority (ASA) is the independent body responsible for ensuring that advertising meets the standard and is in the public interest. It has the power to investigate complaints about advertisements and has investigated many about charity advertising. It once criticised many charities for being 'over-zealous' and for 'overstepping the line between presenting a possibly distressing, but accurate, picture of their cause and misinforming people about an issue by exaggerating or stretching the truth'.

If you are a campaigning charity, the chances are that your 'opposition' will want to catch you out as often as possible. They will carefully monitor your advertising for any breaches and will report you with great speed (not just to the ASA, but to the Charity Commission too). Friends of the Earth ran a cinema advert showing a toilet with a mahogany seat overflowing with blood. The voice-over talked about Brazilian Indians who own mahogany trees paying with their lives if they refuse to sell the trees. Complaints were received by the ASA from the Timber Trade Federation and the Brazilian Embassy.

Remember that you can be in breach unintentionally – it is not just unethical businesses trying to mislead the public who have complaints upheld. Many charities have fallen foul of the Codes so make sure that any claims you make in your adverts can be substantiated. The NSPCC ran a Saatchi & Saatchi-designed billboard campaign which read: 'One in every eight people who walk past this poster was abused as a child.' When the inevitable complaints followed, the NSPCC was able to produce independent research to back their claims. However, when they screened a

TRUE STORY   Getting it Wrong

The International Fund for Animal Welfare ran a press ad headed: 'To you, it's a pet. To a Korean, it's a bowl of soup.' It continued: 'Thanks to campaigning from IFAW and its supporters, the South Korean government now has an Animal Protection Act. Regrettably, it's not being enforced. And cats are still being slaughtered at the rate of around 400,000 a year; either butchered, hammered to death, or even boiled to death with herbs to make "medicinal" soup.' The Advertising Standards Authority received a number of complaints that it was offensive to imply that Koreans viewed cats only as an ingredient for soup, and that the 400,000 figure could not be substantiated. The ASA obtained expert advice and concluded that Koreans regarded cats as pets rather than food and that a significant part of the population of South Korea was Buddhist and therefore vegetarian. The complaint was upheld. A potentially powerful advertisement from a charity doing good work had to be withdrawn.

cinema advert showing an unborn baby in the womb reacting to an argument between its parents, the charity could not demonstrate that a foetus can be emotionally disturbed by the hostility around it.

The ASA recognises the problems charities face and has said: 'Limited resources and accountability to supporters means that charities are under particular pressure to produce advertising that makes people sit up and take notice. Those creating such campaigns feel that they weaken their impact if they have to qualify claims or state opinions rather than fact.' The ASA says that often small changes to copy can make the difference between fact and fiction without a charity losing the force of its message.

The Committee of Advertising Practice (CAP) is the self-regulatory body that devises and enforces the British Codes of Advertising

TRUE STORY   Getting it Right

The RSPCA ran four hard-hitting adverts in the national press. They showed how hunting leads to the death of domestic pets as well as wild animals and how the law offers little protection to animals. One, for example, had a headline: 'Wild animals aren't the only victims of hunting' and this was illustrated by a photograph of the stuffed head of a cat mounted on a sporting trophy. It read: 'You won't see this kind of trophy hanging in a country house because it's illegal ... yet every year pets are ripped apart by hunting dogs and garrotted by wire snares ...' Nearly 100 complaints were received from across Britain, presumably orchestrated by the pro-hunting lobby. The RSPCA was able to provide documentary evidence to support each of their claims and so the complaints against them were not upheld.

and Sales Promotion. CAP offers free and confidential pre-publication advice to help organisations ensure that they do not break the Codes. To access it ring 020-7580 4100 and ask for the copy advice team, fax them on 020-7580 4072 or email them at copyadvice@cap.org.uk. CAP also produce a really useful guide to the codes, which is available free of charge (see address section). Ensure that you get hold of one if you are planning any advertising.

The Codes apply to adverts in:

- newspapers;
- magazines;
- catalogues;
- mailings;
- brochures;
- posters;
- Internet advertising (paid-for advertising such as banner ads, commercial emails and online sales promotions on organisations' websites).

They do not apply to:

- broadcast commercials on radio, which are governed by the Radio Authority;
- TV ads, which are policed by the Independent Television Commission.

The main points in the Codes that apply to charities are:

1 All adverts should be legal, decent, honest and truthful.
2 All adverts should be prepared with a sense of responsibility to consumers and society.
3 Advertisers must hold documentary evidence to prove all claims that are capable of objective substantiation.
4 If there is a significant division of informed opinion about any claims made, they should not be portrayed as universally agreed.
5 No advert should cause fear or distress without good reason. Advertisers should not use shocking claims or images merely to attract attention.
6 When it comes to political advertising, the identity and status of such advertisers should be clear. If their address or other contact details are not generally available they should be included in the advert.

'Political' Advertising

The Broadcasting Act 1990 was introduced to deny extremists such as the National Front access to the mass media. Its effect has been to prevent many charities' adverts from being seen and heard. In 1995 Amnesty International was banned from airing a radio advert, which urged listeners to 'break the silence about human rights violations'. This was regarded as a political advert and was banned by the Radio Authority. Amnesty appealed to the High Court, which upheld the ruling. However, a TV advert by Survival International had its ban lifted. Before making an advert for broadcast, ensure it does not fall foul of the Act.

Preparing for responses

When you place an ad, you do so in the hope that people will respond. Be ready for them when they do.

QUICK RESPONSE CHECKLIST

- ☑ Warn your staff, especially your receptionist, that there will be more people than usual calling or writing in.
- ☑ Take on temporary staff if you anticipate the need, or ensure that you are not light-staffed due to holidays.
- ☑ Make sure staff are available so calls can be transferred to them.
- ☑ Ensure that staff know what to say and what details to take down: all calls must be handled professionally.
- ☑ Have information or campaign packs, promotional material, acknowledgement letters and so forth ready to be sent out.
- ☑ Have a distribution/response system in place *before* you place your adverts.

Monitoring and evaluation

When you place an ad, keep a log of enquiries so that you can see where it's best to advertise. This will be invaluable should you decide to re-run a campaign. You will be able to see at a glance whether Publication A or Radio Station B came up with the goods. The sample log on the next page can be adapted to suit your purposes.

Prepare an analysis of your logs. Refer to the sample analysis to see what facts you could draw out.

Once your campaign has ended, sit down with your log and your objectives and take a look at whether or not you have been successful. Another measure of success (in addition to your

Sample advertising response log

Caller's name and address	Advert source	Requested information	Made donation (amount)
Jane Smith 77 Duke Street Anytown	*Anytown Advertiser* (17 July issue)	✗	£10 (credit card)
Seema Desai Flat 3 Meadow Rise Anytown	Bus ticket	✓	No
Paul Wilson The Bungalow 11 Acacia Avenue Anytown	Bus ticket	✓	No. Made no initial donation. Donated £75 after receiving our leaflet

objectives) is to look at income and expenditure. If you have spent a great deal more on your adverts than you have received in donations or subscriptions, perhaps you have failed. On the other hand, if one of your objectives was to build up a database of interested people, and your campaign has achieved this, perhaps you can claim success.

Sample advertising response log analysis

Music Therapy for Blind Children Appeal:
Analysis of Advertising Campaign

The Facts

The main findings of the analysis of the log sheets are:

■ We received 600 donations, 50 per cent from the *Guardian* advert, 14 per cent from Classic FM radio and 36 per cent from *The Times*.
■ In total we received £25,000 in donations.
■ Although *The Times'* readers represented only 36 per cent of enquirers, they gave in total £12,500 (half of all money raised).
■ The average donation was £28.
■ The median donation was £38.
■ As a direct result of the information packs sent out, 107 people so far have taken out Deeds of Covenant. This will represent an income of £10,000 for the charity over three years.
■ *Guardian* readers were more generous when it came to covenants: 75 per cent of all covenants came from them.

The Conclusions

1 Our experiment with radio did not work well, producing relatively few donations and covenants. We failed to cover our

costs and I recommend that we concentrate future efforts on press advertising.

2 While on the face of it *The Times* appears to have produced most money up-front, it produced fewer enquiries and less in covenants. Nevertheless, the amounts given were above average and it could be useful in the future for one-off appeals. It was, however, more expensive to advertise in.

3 The *Guardian* has come up trumps in terms of long-term income from covenants. We have a better chance of developing a relationship with covenanters than we have with one-off donors. Also, the cost of advertising in the *Guardian* was less than *The Times,* so all in all it appears to have been the best option.

The cost of advertising

Various factors affect the price of an ad. For press advertising, they include:

- **Time of year:** there are slack periods when you can get a better deal.
- **Size:** the larger your advert, the costlier it will be.
- **Circulation of publication:** larger circulation generally means a higher price, though it also means that your advert reaches more people.
- **Situation:** a front-page ad is more expensive than one on the back.
- **Colour:** black and white is cheaper than colour, and 'spot colour' (adding, say, a splash of red to your black and white ad) is cheaper than full colour.
- **How you buy space:** whether you go direct or via a media buyer (a specialist who buys media space and can get quite good deals, though generally only for fairly large ad campaigns).

For broadcast adverts, the price depends on:

- which station/network (some are more costly than others, depending on the area they cover, the listening/viewing figures);
- time of day (or night);
- during/after which programme the advert is aired.

Advertising departments produce 'rate cards' which set out the cost of adverts according to size, position and so on. Often rates are negotiable, so always try to get the official rate reduced.

  If you want up-to-date guidelines on current rates, go to your public library and consult British Rate and Data (BRAD), a publication that lists all the UK's advertising media, their rates and their readership.

 tip

If you are planning to place a series of adverts in the same publication, you can generally negotiate a discount.

Don't exploit or patronise

A couple of decades ago most aid charities used images of Third World people that many now regard at best as patronising. Black people stared out from adverts, hungry and poor, waiting for help and assistance from the affluent West. They were portrayed as hapless victims, passive and defenceless. Some people feel that this kind of advertising has created a negative image of the Third World, and that the many positive things happening in underdeveloped countries, and indeed the very reasons for Third World underdevelopment, are underplayed or ignored.

Organisations working for people with physical and mental disabilities have also been on the receiving end of criticism, much of it coming from people with disabilities. The recipients of the charity have in the past (and are still, by some organisations) been portrayed as helpless victims rather than as normal individuals who face particular difficulties because of their disability.

Charities do face a dilemma. Do you exploit imagery on the grounds that the ends justify the means, or do you take the view that advertising should be used to challenge perceptions, not to confirm prejudices and ignorance? A clever ad campaign was run by a cerebral palsy charity. Billboard and newspaper adverts showed a photograph of a mother with her disabled son. The caption said something like: 'My son has a learning age of twelve ... he's only ten.' The advertising was part of a much wider marketing effort to alter and update the image of a charity that previously had a rather old-fashioned image.

Choosing and using an ad agency

If you intend to do a lot of advertising, and you have no in-house expertise, you may need the services of an ad agency. They can:

- Come up with ideas for adverts that will achieve your objectives.
- Advise on where, when and how to advertise.
- Prepare artwork for you.
- Buy advertising space for you.

Approach agencies recommended to you by people or organisations you trust. If you don't know anyone who has used an agency, look at charity advertising in the press and contact the organisations who appear to be doing a good job. Ask them which agency they use. Most agencies specialise in commercial advertising and may know very little about charities, so it is important to try to select an agency that already works, or has done so in the past, for a charity or voluntary organisation. With the growth in the number of quangos, local authorities, NHS trusts and voluntary organisations using advertising, finding an agency with relevant experience is easier than in the past.

Selecting an Agency

1 Contact at least three agencies and tell them what you are looking for.
2 Prepare a written brief. This will give the agencies a clear idea of what you hope to achieve.
3 Ask the agencies to let you know whether or not they are interested in your business. Some may turn you down because your budget is too small, or because of a conflict of interest with another client. If they handle the advertising account for a cigarette manufacturer and you are an anti-smoking charity, you may get turned away – or, of course, you might decide that you can't do business with them anyway in that case.
4 Set a deadline and ask the selected agencies to get back to you by then with ideas on how they would tackle your campaign. Some agencies will ask you for a fee to cover the time and materials involved in preparing ideas for you. Decide whether or not you are willing to see agencies who expect payment at this early stage.
5 Look through the submissions and ask your short-list to do a presentation (or pitch). Ask them to give you a credentials presentation (a talk about themselves and their expertise) and get them to explain how they would approach your assignment and what ideas they have.
6 Ask them to bring to the presentation a document setting out their approach and detailing their costs.
7 Alternatively, go to their premises for the presentation; it is more time-consuming, but you get a better idea of whom you will be doing business with.
8 Select an agency from those you have seen or, if you are still not sure, draw up a new pitch list and start again.

Ask prospective consultants:

■ What experience they have of working for organisations similar to your own. Ask for names of clients and examples of their work. Take up references.
■ What knowledge and understanding they have of your work. If they know little about your field, ask them how they would go about building up their expertise.
■ Who will be working on your account. Ask for their CVs, so you can be sure of their experience. (The people who present to you may not be those who will carry out the work.)
■ How many staff they have.

- How long they have been established.
- What other clients they work for. Ask about actual or potential conflicts of interest.
- How they intend to evaluate the success of the work they carry out for you.
- Whether the agency has won any industry awards.

When assessing the performance of prospective agencies, ask yourself:

- Did they fulfil the requirements of the brief in their tender documents?
- Was their presentation confident?
- Did they have good ideas?
- Did they seem personally committed or sympathetic to our cause?
- Did they seem to understand what we are about?
- Did they handle questions well?
- Do I feel, from what I have seen, that I have confidence in them?

Pick an agency that has relevant experience. If you are doing radio or TV advertising, it is important that your agency has worked in these fields before. Some agencies specialise in press work, and are very good at this, but have limited experience of broadcast advertising

You might find the table below useful for comparing one ad agency with another. Give each agency marks out of ten for each category (replace the given categories with ones that are relevant to your assignment). One is the lowest score and ten the highest. You may decide not to go for the highest overall score, but to opt for an agency that scores well all round. It is up to you.

Sample table for evaluating ad agencies

Criteria	Agency 1	Agency 2	Agency 3
Understanding of our needs			
Experience in this field			
Sympathy to our cause			
Creativity and ideas			
Approach to the ad campaign			
Team involved			
Confidence and competence			
Total cost			
TOTAL SCORE			

Types of Agency

There are three main types of agency:

- creative agencies;
- media independents;
- full service agencies.

Creatives

These are the agencies that deal with the creative side of advertising. They will come up with clever ideas and do all of the artwork for you. They are 'fee-based' – you agree a fee in advance and they will carry out the work on your brief for that agreed fee. They can do more than straight advertising and will take on the design of corporate identities, exhibitions and other publicity material. (Do not confuse them with graphic designers. Graphic designers will do design work for you, but creative advertising agencies have expertise in marketing and advertising that most standard designers do not.)

Media Independents

Media independents specialise in buying space in the media. They do no creative work at all. Because they buy in large volume they can save you money. Media buyers may take as little as 2 or 3 per cent commission for buying space for you, which compares favourably with full service agencies. They will not only buy space for you; they will also help you with media planning.

Full Service Agencies

These agencies combine creative teams with in-house media buyers under the same roof. It generally costs more, but it is less hassle to use a one-stop shop and is perhaps the best starting point if you are new to advertising. Full service agencies get an automatic 10–15 per cent discount from the media when they buy space. Traditionally this money is used to fund the creative work on big advertising campaigns. However, for small campaigns you will probably have to pay a fee for creative work, planning and the management of your account. Generally full service agencies concentrate on 'above the line' advertising (in the media), though they also offer 'below the line' services such as brochures and other promotional material.

Sample advertising brief

The Toy Hospital

Advertising Campaign Brief

About Us

We are a newly registered national charity. We have just registered with the Charity Commission but as yet we have not had a public launch so no one has heard of us; we have no track record and no profile. We want to launch ourselves using a combination of press advertising and editorial obtained via PR (we have already engaged the services of a PR consultant and would expect our advertising and PR people to work closely together to create a complementary publicity campaign).

We aim to get the public to donate old, unwanted and broken toys to us. (A national supermarket chain has agreed to collection points in each of its stores.) We will clean and refurbish the toys and give them free of charge to children whose parents could not otherwise afford them. We need the public to donate both toys and money to refurbish them. We also need volunteers to clean and repair toys and deliver them to needy families. Additionally we must attract finance to cover our running costs and to pay the salaries of our four full-time staff. Thanks to a legacy we have enough to cover our launch costs and to keep the charity going for six months. It is therefore urgent that we orchestrate a high profile launch (launch date is 1 May and Blue Peter have agreed to cover our story on that day) backed up with powerful advertising.

Our Advertising Objectives

1 **To inform the public about our work.** We will commission market research eight weeks after the first adverts appear and we expect name recognition in 65 per cent of our sample and an understanding of our work in 40 per cent of those interviewed.
2 **To get the public to donate toys.** We expect the first toys to be handed into our collection depots on the day the first adverts appear – launch day. By the end of the first month we expect to have collected 50,000 toys.
3 **To attract donations.** As a direct result of the press adverts we expect to get £100,000 in donations by two months after launch date.

Initially we are looking for a set of one-off advertisements to launch the charity and meet the above objectives. Assuming we are successful, we shall be looking to build upon the initial push by developing a rolling advertising programme to maintain awareness and interest.

Our Audience

Our adverts need to be aimed at the widest possible public. American research shows that it is not just children and their parents who give, although they are the main donors, along with schools and Brownies/ Scouts (there is a similar charity operating across the Atlantic). Cash donations come also from childless couples and grandparents, who are the main donors in terms of the amounts they give.

Our Budget

Our advertising budget of £75,000 must cover all media space and all creative work, project management etc. We are aware that this is relatively small, given what we are hoping to achieve, but remember that advertising will be backed up by PR and by displays in supermarkets across Britain.

Have a go yourself

Read through the following advertisement, which has been written for the national press, and itemise what is wrong with it.

Doverstone Donkey Sanctuary

In the 1920s there were no donkey sanctuaries in Britain, but then a donkey-lover by the name of Mr Donald Key founded Britain's very first donkey sanctuary in Bournton. Since that time donkey sanctuaries have sprung up across Britain, run by a range of charities dedicated to the needs of elderly and retired donkeys. The Doverstone Donkey Sanctuary is one such charity, founded in 1991 by Mrs Maria Hee-Haw OBE, who most generously left in her will the handsome sum of £100,000. This has been used to establish the Doverstone Donkey Sanctuary, which has gone from strength to strength and now attracts an income of over £500,000 a year. This month the Sanctuary launches its 'Adopt a Donkey' scheme. It will enable people to adopt a donkey for just £5 a year. Subscribers will receive a photograph of their donkey, a copy of its family tree and history, and a twice-yearly update on how the donkey is faring.

If you would like to adopt a donkey, write to the following address with your details and enclose a cheque for £5:
Mr Steven Reid-Cross CBE, Honorary Secretary, Adopt a Donkey Scheme, The Doverstone Donkey Sanctuary, Donkey House, 27 Green Lane, Doverstone DS12 0BZ.

Discussion

The material contained in the advert is potentially very good, but so many mistakes have been made in the way it is written and presented that it is not likely to be a very effective advert.

- It is a national charity, even though it is based in Doverstone, but because of the way the advert is presented, it comes across as local. By mentioning the network of donkey sanctuaries across Britain, it is almost encouraging readers to support their local one, not this one.

- The advert is not about donkey sanctuaries, though you could be forgiven for thinking so. It is about adopting donkeys. In other words, the advert is selling the organisation, not the brand. It is the equivalent to an advert for Heinz that attempts to sell Heinz rather than baked beans.
- Responding to the offer is made too complicated. First you have to write in; there is no simple coupon. Next you have to fill out a long return address, then you have to contact them to find out to whom the cheque should be made. Could you be bothered?
- Its headline is not designed to attract attention and encourage the reader to read on.
- It contains too much irrelevant background information and facts.
- It fails to exploit the reader's interest in donkeys by throwing in an emotive appeal.
- The copy is dull.
- By writing in the third person the copy is less appealing.
- By mentioning its endowment of £100,000 and its annual income of £500,000 it sounds as if it is doing quite well and does not need the help of the reader. There is no sense in the advert of urgent need, or of how the money will be spent.
- The charity number is missing.

Comparing notes

Adopt A Donkey for the Price of Some Carrots!

Some donkeys have put a lifetime into working to serve humans, but now they find themselves abandoned and alone. You can adopt a donkey for just £5, enabling us to give it a home, shelter, good food, exercise and the company of other retired donkeys.

Helping donkeys in need

As well as the good feeling of knowing that you are helping a donkey in need, your membership of the Doverstone Donkey Sanctuary's Adopt a Donkey scheme buys you a photo of your adopted donkey, its family tree and an account of the life of your very own donkey. You'll even get a progress report twice a year.

Our donkeys urgently need your support, so don't delay. Adopt a donkey today.

www.adopt-a-donkey@doverstone.org.uk

- - - - - - - - - - - - - - - - - - ✂ -

I want to adopt a donkey. Find enclosed my cheque for £5. (If you can afford more than this, your extra donation will help provide new facilities at our new donkey sanctuary.)

Name: ....

Address: ....

Cheques, made payable to Adopt a Donkey, should be sent to:

Doverstone Donkey Sanctuary, PO Box 4, Doverstone DS12 0BZ. IN1

Reg. Charity No. 71261

Discussion

This is much better because:

- The headline attracts attention and is intriguing.
- A subheading is used, which helps encourage the glancer to become a reader.
- It is written in the first person, which gives it more appeal.
- It appeals to the reader direct.
- It quantifies what help costs (a £5 bag of carrots).
- It offers readers the chance to give more if they wish, without making anyone feel mean if they can't.
- It has a coupon response to make replying easier.
- The copy stresses the urgency of the appeal, encouraging people to act.
- It cuts out unnecessary background material and detail.
- It uses emotive words, such as 'abandoned', 'alone' and 'in need', which are designed to appeal to donkey lovers.
- The return address is much shorter, making it easy to reply.
- The inclusion of a web address enables readers to log on and find out more.
- The coupon is coded, so the charity can evaluate its advertising success and work out which newspapers and which days were most effective.

Promotion: media relations

INTRODUCTION

You don't have to pay for advertising to secure first-class media coverage; editorial on radio, television and in the press can be a superb way of
promoting your organisation, a new service, a fundraising appeal or a
campaign. It can raise awareness and your profile, promote your work,
persuade, reach a wide audience, influence, raise funds and attract support. And, best of all, editorial is usually cheaper to obtain than advertising coverage.

Not everyone is clear about the difference between advertising
and editorial. Essentially advertising is paid for, while editorial
coverage is free.

Despite the drawbacks of editorial in terms of control and
guarantees, it does have a powerful edge over advertising in many
respects:

- Editorial coverage carries more weight than advertising
  because it is regarded as more impartial. Statements made via
  editorial are more likely to be believed than statements made
  in adverts, making it a very persuasive tool.
- An article is less likely to be ignored than an advert.
- It puts television within reach of even the smallest organisation.
- It is cheap. Potentially you can secure coverage in lots of publications for little more than the cost of a stamp or an email.

The differences between advertising and editorial

Advertising	Editorial
You have complete control over where and when your advert will appear.	You have no control over when, where or whether it appears.
Coverage is guaranteed.	Coverage is left to chance. If a big news story breaks, your news could be ditched.
You decide the wording.	You have no control over the wording of the story that finally appears; it might take a very different line to the one you had hoped for, perhaps leading to damaging or negative coverage, or a distorted message.
You choose the publication or broadcast outlet.	You choose where to send your story, but there is no guarantee that it will be used.
You select the photographs or illustrations.	You have no say over what, if any, photos or illustrations are used (although you can influence things by submitting suitable material with your news story).
You choose the timing.	You can influence timing according to when you send your release and whether you use an embargo. However, you have no guarantees.
You decide on the position in the publication (for example, front page, top of page 4).	You have no say on where your piece will be placed.
You decide on the size of the coverage (for example, full page, quarter page).	You have no influence on the size of the piece. Sending a long release will not guarantee a long piece of editorial.
You decide whether to go for full colour, spot colour or black and white.	You cannot influence the use of colour.

Attracting editorial coverage

Many people believe that news is found thanks to the efforts of journalists beavering away uncovering stories. In fact, many of the stories you read in newspapers or hear about on the radio or television are placed there by PR consultants acting for central and local government, companies and charities. But how? You can attract media coverage for your services in five main ways:

1 By issuing a 'news release'. This is the principal way of securing media coverage.

tip

You will often hear 'news releases' referred to as 'press releases'. With the huge growth in broadcast media (terrestrial and satellite TV, and radio), press releases have become known as news releases. If you call yours a 'press release', you risk alienating or irritating the broadcasters.

2 By holding a news conference or event.
3 By arranging a feature.
4 By setting up a photocall.
5 By talking to media contacts.

News releases

Newspapers, and radio and TV stations, rely on news releases for a fair amount of their output. Good releases (well written, properly presented, well timed and with a strong story line) will often be used verbatim. Even photographs accompanying releases are sometimes used, though obviously not by radio (no pictures) and television (moving pictures only).

Journalists hate receiving what they dismissively term 'PR puffery' – releases over-selling a product and using exaggerated claims and hyperbole. These releases end up not in the newspaper, but in the wastepaper basket. Aim to write a news release that promotes your service or product and is, at the same time, a 'good read'.

Q: How long, on average, does a news editor spend looking at each news release?
A: 1.5 seconds

Q: What percentage of news releases make it into print?
A: 3 per cent.

So, with only 1.5 seconds to grab a news editor's attention, you have to produce a release that is crisp, targeted, relevant, well written, short and factual. To avoid being among the shocking 97 per cent of news releases that fail to make it into print, you must find something about your product or service that is newsworthy.

Fortunately, you have a head start over commercial companies. Most of the stories they try to 'sell' are too blatantly commercial; the media is not in the game of free advertising. On the other hand, many of the products and services offered by charities and voluntary organisations are of interest to the media. A TV station would be unlikely to run a story on a new commercial business centre, but it would probably broadcast a feature on a not-for-profit business centre set up to help unemployed school-leavers find work or training. Stories with a social edge are generally stronger than stories with a hard commercial one. So while companies might have the advantage of a large PR budget, you have better stories to offer the media.

If you are launching a new product or service, enhancing an existing one or have some other news – and you can produce an interesting release with genuine news value – you have an opportunity of gaining some good coverage in the media.

THE EFFECTIVE NEWS RELEASE CHECKLIST

☑ Capture the news editor's attention in the first paragraph by leading with a newsworthy angle.

☑ Include all the relevant information early on in your release, by covering 'The Five Ws':

What – What is happening? What is being launched? What is the new service?

Who – Who will be doing the launch/opening? What organisation is behind it?

When – When is it happening?

Where – Where will the service/launch be?

Why – Why is the service/product being launched/expanded?

☑ Include a quote in your release from a named person. If the newspaper uses your release, it will appear to readers that they actually interviewed you, when really they just printed your release.

☑ Keep it brief and stick to the point – Ideally one page and preferably no more than two.

☑ Avoid jargon and hyperbole.

☑ Date your release so the news editor knows it is current.

☑ Include two contact names and numbers and ensure that the contacts are available, easy to get hold of and fully briefed. Also include home and mobile numbers so that journalists can make contact outside office hours.

☑ If you need to send background briefing material, put it on a separate sheet (not part of the main release). Also refer journalists to your website for further information.

News Release Layout

The news release overleaf illustrates layout, as well as presenting a strong story-line of the sort that the media would be interested in. There is a convention about how releases should be laid out on the page. To maximise your chances of getting your release used, make sure that your release looks right:

tip

Write your release so that it can be chopped paragraph by paragraph from the bottom up, and still make sense.

■ **Double space** releases – so reporters have space to scribble comments and edit.
■ Use **wide margins** – for the same reasons.
■ Keep them **single-sided** – for ease of reading.

- Make sure your release is **typed**. Hand-written releases are too difficult to read and look unprofessional.
- Use **plain paper** for continuation sheets, but your headed notepaper for the top one (unless you have specially printed news release paper).
- Don't **format** – avoid bold, italics and upper case.
- Don't **split** a sentence from one page to the next. Ideally, don't let a paragraph continue over the page.
- **Staple pages together** – so your top sheet does not lose its companion in a busy newsroom.

Sample news release

Brainwaves

210 Towngate Street, Edinthorpe. Tel. 01884 123456

NEWS RELEASE

For immediate use
Thursday, 11 April 2001

ROCK STAR TONY TINSEL LAUNCHES PIONEERING SCHEME FOR YOUNG PEOPLE WITH BRAIN INJURIES

A pioneering scheme for young people with brain injuries, the first of its kind is Britain, was launched in Edinthorpe today (Thursday) by rock star Tony Tinsel, who has himself suffered from a brain injury. 'BrainBusters', a new rehabilitation programme for young brain-injured people, is run by Brainwaves. It has been devised to meet the particular needs of younger people who have suffered a brain injury as the result of a motorcycle or car crash, sports or play accident. Previously there was no provision anywhere in the country specifically for young people.

Rock idol Tony Tinsel, who last year suffered a brain injury after diving into a swimming pool, launched the new service. He said: 'I know how isolated you can feel when you have suffered a brain injury. Young people often find themselves cut off from their friends, and as a result can miss out on many of the fun things that teenagers do. This scheme will bring together young people and give them a chance not only to socialise, but to learn to cope with their injury and rebuild their lives.'

Brainwaves is a registered charity based in the Towngate area of town. The BrainBusters rehabilitation sessions will be run from the charity's offices, and youngsters between the ages of 14 and 19 will be referred to the service via their GPs.

The £50,000 funding for the service came jointly from Edinthorpe Health Commission and Edinthorpe Council.

ends

Note to Editors:

More detailed information is available on our website at www.brainwaves.org.uk

For further information contact:

Dominic Duckworth,		Andrea Grant,	
Director of Brainwaves		Chair	
Day	01884 12345	Day	01884 99015
Evening	01884 44567	Evening	01884 67656
Mobile	077 177716	Mobile	077 188876

What Will Happen to Your Release?

When a newspaper receives your release, it will do one of the following:

- Use it verbatim or edit it a little.
- Call you for further information, and write an extended article.
- Bin it – perhaps because it is no good, irrelevant for the readership, arrived too late, or because the paper had too much news already.

When a television or radio station gets your release and wishes to cover your story, it may:

- Ask you to the studio for a live or recorded interview.
- Do a recorded or live interview down the telephone (generally radio only).
- Broadcast a news report based on your release, possibly following a brief, informal chat with you on the telephone.
- Send a reporter (and film crew, if it is TV) to you.

Preparing for Distribution

Most of the time you will know where to send your release – the local media, for example, or your own trade publications. There may be times, though, when you need to reach out to other publications or programmes that you are not at all familiar with. There are a various easy-to-use directories which list trade, technical and consumer titles, local papers, TV and radio, national media, European media and business publications. You can find out what publications (or programmes) cover your audience or issue, the names of the editor and any special correspondents; addresses, telephone and fax numbers, and email addresses; circulation details; and frequency of publication. All are available by subscription or as a one-off purchase, although they are expensive. Various titles are available, but the best known are: PR Planner;

PIMS United Kingdom Media Directory; Editors; and Benn's. Most are available on CD-ROM as well as in hard copy.

The needs and interests of your local newspaper will be different from those of a national paper, which will in turn be different from what a radio station might be interested in. Therefore, amend releases slightly according to whom they are being sent. Include local information for a local paper, but omit it in the version for the nationals, for example.

Send releases by post if possible. Faxed releases often go astray. Increasingly, journalists are happy to receive material by email, but always check first. Because of the risk of viruses, you may be asked to include your release in the body of your email rather than as an attachment.

If possible, send your release to a named person – either the correspondent specialising in your field, or the news editor. Where names are not known, and you do not have the time to ring everyone to find out, address your release to a job title, such as the Housing Correspondent, the News Editor, or the Producer of X Programme.

tip

If you are telephoning a newspaper, the best time to call a daily paper is between 10.30 am and 11.30 am; this is the least busy period and reporters will have more time to talk and are therefore more receptive. Try not to call between 4 pm and 7 pm, when journalists are writing and checking their copy – this is when nerves get frayed in the newsroom.

News conferences and media events

Releases are generally the best, easiest and most cost-effective way of using the media to promote a new service or product. However, sometimes it is preferable to talk to the media face-to-face than via a sheet of A4 paper. On such occasions (such as when your story is fairly complex or especially newsworthy), you can either hold a news conference or host a media event.

News conferences (often called 'press conferences') are a lot of hard work to organise, so hold one only if you have good reason. You might, for example, be launching a controversial new service (a free condom scheme for prostitutes, for example) and believe that it is better to face the media than issue a news release that cannot convey the issue in the same way.

tip

The best starting time for a news conference is around 10.30 or 11 am. Make sure that you start and finish on time.

THE EFFECTIVE NEWS CONFERENCE CHECKLIST

☑ Give speakers at the top table name plates which can be seen from a distance.

☑ Issue guests with name badges.

☑ Say what you have to say as succinctly as possible and then throw it open to questions. Don't ramble and bore everyone.

☑ Set aside a quiet side room at your venue for radio and TV interviews.

☑ Be available both before and after the news conference (and possibly even the day before) for radio or TV reporters who cannot attend at the time you have scheduled.

☑ Be as helpful as you can at accommodating the needs of the media if you want to build a good relationship and maximise coverage.

☑ Make parking available if you can, try to find a central venue, and send maps if your venue is off the beaten track.

---

tip

At your news conference give reporters a press pack – an A4 folder containing your news release plus any background briefing material. Also enclose leaflets about your organisation, perhaps your annual report, and relevant captioned photographs and illustrations. If your press pack is a useful one, it will be held on file for future reference.

Whether you are planning a news conference or organising a newsworthy event, you will need to let the media know of your plans in advance so that they can slot it into their schedule. Send them an invitation, ideally about a week before your event/news conference.

Media Invitations

You can see a sample media invitation on the next page. The key points to consider are:

1 Keep it brief.
2 Include a paragraph explaining the purpose of the event/news conference and describing what will happen at it.
3 List all the necessary information – start times, venue, speakers, etc.

Remember that media invitations are designed to attract reporters to your event, not to take the place of a news release. Don't give too much away in your invitation, just enough to get people there.

Sample media invitation

Brainwaves

210 Towngate Street, Edinthorpe. Tel. 01884 123456

FOR OPERATIONAL USE ONLY:
NOT FOR PUBLICATION OR BROADCAST
INVITATION TO NEWS AND PICTURE EDITORS

ROCK STAR TONY TINSEL TO LAUNCH PIONEERING SCHEME FOR YOUNG PEOPLE WITH BRAIN INJURIES

A pioneering £50,000 scheme for young people with brain injuries, the first of its kind in Britain, will be launched in Edinthorpe by rock star Tony Tinsel, who has himself suffered from a brain injury.

Tony Tinsel, Dominic Duckworth (director of Brainwaves, the charity which will run the new scheme), and brain-injured youngsters will be available for interview and photographs.

You are invited to send a representative

Time: 10.30am
Date: Thursday, April 11 2001
Venue: Brainwaves, Towngate House, 210 Towngate Street, Edinthorpe

For further information contact:
Dominic Duckworth, Director of Brainwaves
Day   01884 12345
Evening   01884 44567

Features

Often you can promote your organisation or a new service by arranging for a feature in the press or on TV or radio. The example given above would work well as feature material. A reporter could talk to brain injured people, including the celebrity, about what it is like, how it affects you, and what can be done to help. This could be backed up with facts and figures, information about the new service, quotes from key staff at the charity and so on. If you are launching a service or product that lends itself well to a feature, start by deciding on the best place for it. Radio or TV? The press? Which paper? When? Consider approaching just one publication (or programme) and offer them an exclusive feature which they can run on the day of the launch. Write briefly to the Features Editor in the first instance, outlining your ideas. Follow this up a week later with a call to assess interest. For TV features speak to Forward Planning.

Photocalls

There are three ways of getting photographic coverage for a new service:

1 Arrange a photocall and invite photographers.
2 Ensure that you have a photo-opportunity as part of your press conference or event, and invite photographers to that.
3 Send your own photographs with a news release, but make sure that the quality is really good (by using a freelance press photographer who knows what is expected). Remember that national papers are extremely unlikely to use submitted photographs, though local and trade papers are happy to.

If you have something photogenic on offer, write to picture editors saying when, where and what photographs can be taken. People sitting round tables, 'grip 'n' grins' (people clutching flowers, cheques, certificates, etc. and grinning manically) and other dull ideas will not be considered, so be creative and go for a photo-opportunity with flair. Here are some real life examples that attracted lots of media exposure:

- A pressure group opposed to arms sales to totalitarian regimes hired a tank to make a protest at the AGM of a High Street bank which it claimed helped to finance these deals. Large photos of the stunt appeared in the national press and it was covered by television.
- A Scottish charity was given £50,000 by the Post Office to refurbish a derelict building. It organised a photocall outside the building with a giant replica stamp for the value of £50,000. The stamp displayed an artist's impression of the refurbished building. It got into the press and on to TV.
- A London housing charity wanted to publicise the scandal of the capital's empty properties. It refurbished a room in a derelict house as a 'show house' and invited the cameras (TV and press) to see it.

Using contacts

Build up good relationships with the media. Get to know reporters from your local and professional media. Good contacts can help you secure positive, intelligent coverage. Rather than going through the formality of issuing a news release, you might find it easier and quicker to pick up the phone and chat to a friendly reporter about your new product or service. It takes time to establish trusting and mutually rewarding relationships, but it is worth the effort.

> **tip**
>
> If you can, time your events or releases for a Sunday, as little news happens then. You might have noticed how Monday's papers are often quite thin, and this is why. Newspapers have staff working on Sundays in order to produce Monday's paper, although the day tends to be a fairly quiet one in the newsroom.

Using local radio

tip

Look out for stations that encourage listener response. Phone, fax or email responses to issues raised on their programmes.

There are more than 250 commercial radio stations in the UK, most of them locally-based, plus local BBC stations, providing an excellent opportunity for both big and small organisations to get on the airwaves. You can make news by issuing a news release, or you can suggest subjects or issues to be debated on a phone-in or chat show. By supplying an interviewee, guest speaker or expert, there's a chance to get your point of view across during topical programmes and phone-ins. Some radio stations have What's On slots, offering free publicity for your events. Listen to local stations and make a list of possible openings for your organisation. Make contact with the researcher or producer of each target programme and discuss your ideas. Never rule out national radio if your story is newsworthy enough to merit it (by being of national significance, unusual, quirky or controversial). Many small organisations make national news this way.

THE GETTING ON RADIO CHECKLIST

☑ Do your research by listening to target stations.

☑ Ensure you have a local angle for local stations.

☑ Line up your speakers/experts and ensure they are fully briefed.

Media monitoring

Monitor media coverage. If you attract little media coverage, you can do this yourself. However, if media coverage is one of the main strands of your publicity strategy, you may need to engage a press cuttings bureau and possibly also a broadcast monitoring company. Usually you will pay a retainer plus a cost per cutting, transcript or tape.

Many organisations photocopy press cuttings and circulate them to staff and committee members. You can circulate original press cuttings free of charge, but as soon as you make a photocopy, you are breaching the Copyright Act. The Newspaper Licensing Agency, which is owned by nearly all of the national newspapers, has introduced a fee for organisations photocopying (or even faxing) newspaper articles and cuttings. You must obtain (and pay for) a licence – or risk going to prison for up to two years. For further information and a free explanatory booklet, contact the NLA at 17 Lyons Crescent, Tonbridge, Kent TN9 1EX, or call them on 01732 360555.

Have a go yourself

Read the following made-up news release issued to the local media by a fictitious small community group, the Toddler's Hut, operating from a Manchester neighbourhood. The organisation is not well known, being run by a group of local mothers and providing 20 childcare places on weekday mornings. List what's wrong with the release.

For immediate use
Monday, 2 July 2001

TODDLERS' HUT CAME 6TH
IN VOLUNTARY ORGANISATION AWARDS

The Toddlers' Hut came sixth in the annual Voluntary Organisation awards which were announced last month at Central Hall in London.

Top prize went to the London-based National Community Trust for its pioneering inner city work.

Commenting on their win, Toddler's Hut organiser Vera Lomas said: "Obviously we would have liked to have come first, or even second. However, we're still chuffed to have appeared in the top ten. Naturally we'll be entering again next year, with our sights set on the top slot."

The group's reward for coming sixth is a £3,000 grant.

ends

For further information contact:
Vera Lomas at the Toddlers' Hut on 0161 225 2222.

Discussion
- The group is local and the release has been issued to the local media, but there's no local angle.
- Coming sixth might be good, but it reads more like a failure than a success.
- Stating that the event happened last month is as good as saying 'Throw this release in the bin because it is out of date'.
- Mentioning the winner and their pioneering work helps put the Toddlers' Hut success in the shadows.
- The quote makes the group sound a little disappointed.
- Too many questions remain unanswered, such as: What is the Toddlers' Hut? Who runs it? What are the annual Voluntary Organisation awards? What is their significance and who runs them? How will the grant be spent?
- The only contact number is for the Toddlers' Hut, which is only open weekday mornings.

Comparing notes

Now take a look at this version. What makes it better?

For immediate use
Monday, 2 July 2001

FALLOWFIELD MUMS SCOOP £3000
AWARD FOR LOCAL TODDLERS

A group of community-spirited Manchester mothers has scooped a prestigious award and a £3,000 prize that will be used for the benefit of toddlers in the Fallowfield area of the city.

The mums run the Toddlers' Hut, a free playscheme for local pre-school children. They beat off stiff competition from around 5000 charities and voluntary organisations across the whole of the United Kingdom to be selected as one of the top ten voluntary organisations in the country.

Group organiser Vera Lomas said: "This is the most prestigious award made to voluntary organisations and we have done exceptionally well to have been chosen as a winner. Much bigger and better resourced organisations were up against us, so we are delighted to have shaken off such big name contenders. However, the real joy of being a winner is that we now have £3000 to spend on new toys and equipment for the Hut. This investment will bring real joy to the toddlers who use our playscheme."

ends

Note to Editors:
1 The Toddlers' Hut is run on a voluntary basis by a group of 12 Fallowfield mothers. It is open Monday to Friday from 9.30 am to 12 noon and operates free of charge for users.
2 The Voluntary Organisation awards is an annual event run by the National Committee of Voluntary Organisations.
3 This year's awards attracted over 5000 entries.

For further information contact:
Vera Lomas at the Toddlers' Hut on 0161 225 2222 or at home on 0161 225 2345

Jackie Dolan, Playleader, at the Hut or at home on 0161 225 3443

Discussion
- The local angle appears in the headline and first paragraph, to attract the news editor's attention.
- The significance of the win is emphasised (beating off 5000 others from across the UK).

- The quote conveys how pleased the group is to have won.
- The sixth place win is not emphasised, nor is the fact that the award was made last month.
- No important questions are left unanswered.
- The 'Note to Editors' includes some useful background information.
- Two contact names and home telephone numbers make it easier for a journalist to get in touch.

CHAPTER 10

Promotion: direct mail

INTRODUCTION

Direct mail is marketing jargon for advertising by post. It is the third largest advertising medium in Britain and, according to figures, is growing all the time. You need only look at the heap of so-called 'junk mail' landing on your doormat daily to be aware of that! Charities have long used the humble letter as a way of attracting donations, but charity direct mail is now a great deal more sophisticated. Just look at the quality of the material you receive from good causes and compare it with what was sent out a few years ago.

Charities' use of direct mail is growing. Greenpeace alone sends over a million mailshots every year in Britain and describes direct mail as its 'lifeblood'. Without it, Greenpeace would not be able to fundraise effectively and would therefore not function. Over 80 per cent of Greenpeace's UK fundraising expenditure is on direct marketing and more than 90 per cent of their supporters are recruited through it.

You can use direct mail to:

- Sell – charity Christmas cards or fundraising items.
- Inform – to ensure that people know about a particular issue that they might otherwise not be aware of.
- Fundraise – to seek donations.
- Campaign – to encourage like-minded people to support your campaign and take action.
- Recruit – to encourage people to join your organisation.
- Distribute postal questionnaires.

Benefits of using direct mail

- With a good mailing list, direct mail is a great way of targeting those who are potentially interested, and thus cutting down on wasted effort.
- It can be cheaper than other forms of advertising/promotion, such as TV or national newspaper advertising, as it is more targeted.
- It can be used by very small charities, unlike TV and national press advertising.
- It is harder for other charities to monitor your activities when you use direct mail; unlike press advertising, your message is not slapped across the page for all to see.
- Small mailings can be organised at fairly short notice, so it is a good medium to use where urgency is required; for example, when a charity needs to raise funds following a sudden natural disaster.
- It can be used for 'test mailings' – by sending one mailing to half your list and a different one to the other half, you can discover which approach was more effective.
- You can convey a lot more information that in a press advert.
- You can include enclosures.
- It is as good for small, locally based charities as it is for large national ones.
- It is easy to measure response to the mailing.
- Mailings can be personalised to the recipient.
- The message can be timed to arrive on a particular day or time of year, so it is ideal for seasonal fundraising, such as Christmas mailings (when people are feeling more generous).

Drawbacks of direct mail

- It has a poor image.
- The hidden costs can be quite high – in addition to postage, envelopes and the cost of updating or buying a mailing list you need to add production costs of the mailing (such as design and printing).
- Unless your mailing list is up to date, you can waste money mailing to people who have moved away.
- Unless your mailing list is made up of the right profile, your cost per enquiry might be too high to justify.
- It is unsolicited so the recipients might not welcome it. Some people hate 'junk' mail and discard it unopened.

Test mailings

One big advantage of direct mail is that it enables test mailings. You can systematically change various elements of your mailing,

---

TRUE STORY   Getting it Right

When the Association for International
Cancer research was running a campaign
on prostate cancer, it tested four different
direct mail packs. In terms of response the
highest outperformed the lowest by 8:1.
Thanks to this test, the charity was able to
boost significantly the effectiveness of its
mailings.

---

and monitor the response. This approach could, for example,
help you discover what sort of covering letter or enclosure produces the best results. Do you get a better response when you suggest an amount of money for donors to give, or when you leave the
amount open? A test mailing could help you find out. Does an
incentive such as a free badge or bird box make a difference to the
quantity and quality of responses to your membership drive?
Again, use a test mailing to help you discover.

Test Matrices

You can split your mailing to try out different things at the same
time. For example, let's say you wanted to try a new mailing list
(List X) and to test its performance against the mailing list you
usually use (List Y). You also want to see whether offering a free
wildlife wall chart will increase subscriptions to your environmental magazine. And you want to know whether reducing the
cost of subscription is more effective than offering an incentive.
Your test matrix would look like this:

	List Y (usual list)	List X (new list)
Usual pack (control)	A	B
Wall chart incentive	A1	
Lower price subscription	A2	

To find out whether your new list was better than your existing
list, you would need to compare the results of A with B. This is
done using a control, namely, your standard mailing pack.
However, you also want to find out whether other factors affect
response. Comparing the results of A1 and A2 will tell you
whether the wallchart was more of an incentive than the lower
subscription rate.

You can carry on testing until you find the most successful
combination of factors. To know which mailings are more successful, you need to code the response device. You can do this by
writing or printing a code (for example, M1, M2 or M3) on the
coupon or form that the respondent returns to you.

TRUE STORY   Getting it Right

Greenpeace did a split mailing to test what type of message would recruit more supporters. A message about the work of Greenpeace in general outperformed a pack that focused on just one aspect of the organisation's work. In another test a manila envelope was used alongside a white one. The manila outperformed the white by 94 per cent.

Setting objectives

A direct mail campaign should not be undertaken on the spur of the moment. It should be a part of your overall marketing strategy. You need to be sure that it is the right method, you must establish what you hope to get out of it, and you need to evaluate the campaign at the end. Charities have been criticised for their use of direct mail, both by recipients of the mail and by direct mail professionals. In *Cost-effective Direct Marketing*, Christian Brann said: 'There are few areas of direct response promotion which use direct mail as ineffectively as do some charities.' If you want to ensure that you are not one of the charities that he was thinking of, ensure that you ask the following questions before setting off down the direct market road:

1 **What** – What do you hope to achieve from a direct mail campaign? Be as specific as you can. It is not sufficient to say: 'to attract more donations'. You need to quantify: 'to attract 100 new members and £100,000 in donations' or 'to attract 300 enquiries and to turn half of the enquirers into members within six months'.

2 **Who** – Who is your target audience? Whom do you plan to write to? Be specific. It is no good stating: 'people likely to support us'. You need to say: 'people in the south east of England who have previously made a donation to an environmental charity'.

3 **How** – How will your direct mailing fit into your organisation's marketing work? Will it just be a one-off mailing, one of a series, a mailing backed up by other activity such as editorial or press advertising? A mailing to back up other activity? View your mailing in context.

Direct Mail Fact File

- In the year 2000, 75 per cent of consumer direct mail was opened and 53 per cent was read.
- Women are more likely than men to open direct mail.

- In 2000 charity direct mail accounted for 13 per cent of all direct mail received (way above motor, 2 per cent; health and cosmetics, 2 per cent; and retail, 3 per cent).
- 62 per cent of people say that they enjoy reading mailshots.

Mailing lists

There are two factors that make or break a direct mailing campaign: the mailing list and the mailing pack.

The importance of the mailing list cannot be over-emphasised. It is every bit as important – many would argue more important – as the enclosures. What is the point in sending appeals for money to people who hardly have enough to live on themselves? Don't waste money asking people in the south of England to help a hostel in the north of Scotland; it will seem too remote to them and there are plenty of hostels on the doorstep needing help. They might support polar bears at the North Pole, though. The whole point about direct mail is that you can target. You can write to people with a proclivity to give to your cause, thus maximising your return.

How do you get the right mailing list? Essentially you have three choices:

- Rent a ready-made list.
- Have a list assembled for you.
- Compile your own list.

Ready-made Lists

An off-the-peg list is a bit like a ready-to-wear suit; it will cost you less than its tailor-made equivalent, but the fit might not be quite so good. Mailing lists can be hired quite cheaply via list-brokers. A list broker will advise you on the sort of list that is most suitable for your needs, or which selections from within lists. Their advice is normally free – they earn their fee from commissions paid by list owners.

Generally you will hire a list, not buy it. You agree how many times you will use the list, and the hire charge is set according to this. People on your list are known as 'cold prospects'. Once they respond to your mailing, they become 'warm prospects' and you can add them to your own list.

When you hire a mailing list, it will be 'classified'. The list owner will compile it so that everyone on the list shares certain characteristics. These might be to do with income, lifestyle, attitudes and beliefs, where they live – or a combination of these factors. For example:

- People who live in a certain geographical area, say Birmingham or the West Midlands.
- People who live in a certain type of area, such as a high status retirement area with many single people.
- People who live in a certain housing type, such as new council estates in inner cities.

It is possible to be precise about the type of person you wish to mail to, although inevitably there will be some wastage in even the best mailing lists. There are a number of systems for classifying mailing lists; the two main ones are ACORN and MOSAIC (see Appendix A).

When hiring a mailing list, ask the following questions:

- How was the list compiled? Where did the names come from?
- How has the list performed? What have response rates been for other users of this list?
- How up-to-date is the list? How often is it updated and when was the last update?
- What will the list cost? How often can you use the list and over what period? Are there any additional costs?
- Is the list registered under the Data Protection Act?
- Has the list been cleaned against the Mailing Preference Service's list? (see below).
- Is the list available in a form that suits you best, such as sticky labels or CD-ROM?
- Is the list post-coded, so you can sort it and qualify for Mailsort postage discounts? (see below).

Tailor-made Lists

A tailor-made list will not be made from scratch: it will use parts of one list merged with others, giving you the sort of coverage you require. This is available from a list broker (see above).

Own Lists

Many organisations believe that a home-made list is cheaper than an off-the-peg one, because you have not had to pay for it. But when you take staff costs into account, your own list could be expensive if you are constructing it from scratch. However, research has shown that the names and addresses of your existing 'customers' are, on average, three times as likely to respond to your mailings as 'cold prospects'.

The best home-made lists are those you already have, and if you are at all organised, you should have a database in any case. With personal computers now universal, there are few excuses for not compiling lists as part of your everyday work. (You can buy

software to help you construct mailing lists and databases on
your computer.) You might need to refine a list and you must
spend time keeping lists up to date, but you will already have the
makings of a list. This might be made up of:

- People who have bought from you/donated to you in the past.
- People who currently give to you.
- People who have telephoned or written in for further informa-
  tion, both recently and in the past.
- People who are current members or subscribers.
- People who have entered any competitions you have run (this
  can be a good way of building up a list in-house).

You can also build lists using the local telephone directory, Yellow
Pages and Thomson Directories (for business addresses) and the
electoral register (from October 2001, people will be able to opt
out of having their electoral details used for marketing purposes).

You may find that you need a number of different lists.
Greenpeace group their members into several lists, so they know
which members are interested in supporting campaigns, which
are willing to join local groups, and which are likely to buy from
their mail order catalogue. How do they know all this? They ask. A
welcome pack for new supporters asks them to tell Greenpeace
what interests them. Greenpeace can then target mailings more
accurately and avoid waste and unnecessary expense.

Databases: glorified mailing lists?

A mailing list is simply a list of names and addresses. A database
includes other details too, such as whether people have donated
to you, when, how much, in what form and so on. It might have
someone's sex, age, the number of times they have given and over

TRUE STORY Getting it Right

A small charity launched a 'wills'
campaign, in conjunction with a firm of
solicitors. For a £25 donation to the
charity, the law firm would draw up a will
free of charge. With wills normally costing
from £80 to £100, this was a good deal.
To minimise wastage and maximise
return, the charity asked the firm to
extract from its database those clients
without a will. The charity then wrote to

them, via the solicitors (to protect
confidentiality), pointing out that they had
no will, summarising the benefits of
having a will (and the potential problems
of not having one) and drawing their
attention to the special offer. Take-up was
very high thanks to effective targeting.
There was no wastage and the tailored
approach paid dividends.

what period. A database gives you a more detailed picture, and enables you easily to extract particular groups. A good database would enable you to pull out all female donors over 60 who have donated £10 or more in the last six months, for example. There are various software packages to help you establish databases and many computers now come with the software ready installed.

> **tip**
>
> Don't put every scrap of information you have on your database. This will slow your computer and make information retrieval tedious and frustrating. Record only the information that will be of use to you and keep it all up-to-date.

Staying within the law

Direct Mail already has a poor reputation is some quarters. Don't add to it by misusing what can be an excellent promotional, campaigning and fundraising vehicle. Stay within the law and within the spirit of the law.

Mailing Preference Service

Members of the public can register their details with the Mailing Preference Service (MPS) to help cut down on the amount of 'junk mail' they receive. The MPS produces a list of everyone who has contacted them to say that they do not want to receive unsolicited mail, and this list is available to list owners, who must remove these people from their lists. This makes everyone happy: consumers do not get unwanted mail and organisations do not waste money writing to people who have no interest.

Fax Preference Service

Companies wishing not to receive so-called junk faxes can register their number. It is against the law to fax marketing material to an individual, sole trader or partnership without their prior permission. Call the FPS on 0845–070 0702 for further information.

Email Preference Service

Email mailshots (known as 'spam' by surfers) are governed by a voluntary code. People not wishing to receive spam can opt out by registering their details with the Direct Marketing Association's Email Preference Service. Organisations are advised to check names against the central register before undertaking an email shot, although unlike the telephone and fax preference services, this check is a voluntary one without the backing of law.

British Codes of Advertising and Sales Promotion

Get hold of a copy of the British Codes of Advertising and Sales Promotion (this can be downloaded from the Advertising Standards

Authority's website). If you are unsure whether the wording on your envelope or mailshot enclosures falls within the Codes, free and confidential advice is available from the Committee of Advertising Practice on 020–7580 4100. The golden rule is to ensure that any claims are legal, decent, honest and truthful. You must hold documentary evidence to prove all claims that are capable of objective substantiation. Shocking claims or images must not be used merely to attract attention.

The Data Protection Act

If you keep a database, you are required by law to register as a data user with the Data Protection Register. This is not complicated and a quick call to the DPR on 01625 545740 will provide you with all the information you need. To keep someone's data you must have their specific and informed consent. Individuals may give written notice that you must cease processing personal data relating to them for marketing purposes.

The anatomy of a mailshot

With a good list your mailing will reach people who are likely to regard your charity favourably. But that's only half the battle. The contents of your mailing need to persuade them to help, to join, to buy or to give. Successfully targeted mailings can be let down by a poorly produced package.

A mailshot usually comprises:

- the envelope you send the mailing in;
- the covering letter;
- any other enclosures.

Increasingly, postcards are being used for mailings, doing away with the need for envelopes, letters and other enclosures.

TRUE STORY   Getting it Wrong

I have found my way onto two different mailing lists, in one case as Ms A and in the second case as Mr Moy. Any mail arriving for me so addressed goes unopened into the bin. It is really important to get people's names right when you write to them. If you are hiring a mailing list, find out from the list broker or owner what steps they take to check their lists for accuracy. Addresses can become garbled too. In the same post I have received mail for me addressed to Meadowhead House (my correct house name) and to Meadowhead Farm, Meadowhead Hotel, Meadowhead Villa and Meadowhead Bungalow!

A charity carried out a 'split test' mailing to assess whether the appearance of direct mail has any effect on the response rates. Five types of envelopes were sent out. The one that looked most like a proper letter, with typed address and postage stamp, was found to be twice as effective as the one that looked most like 'junk' mail, even though the enclosures were identical.

The Envelope

Let's start on the outside, with the envelope. You have two options when it comes to envelopes:

- You can use readily available stationers' envelopes, off-the-shelf, as it were.
- You can have envelopes specially printed for you, with a design or message on the outside.

Many charities have envelopes printed specially for them, with messages urging the recipient to open the mailing. In 1995, when the Samaritans launched its 'One Number' campaign to publicise that it now has one local number giving callers access to a network of over 200 branches, it used direct mail to help raise funds to support the new service. The envelopes were printed with the message: 'Please open immediately – time sensitive material' and they brought in £58,000 in donations in just ten days.

Some organisations use photographs to support the message, such as forlorn looking animals, deprived children or other images designed to elicit pity or sympathy. Although this approach can work, many charities are wary of using exploitative or emotive imagery. Charities choosing to produce their own printed envelopes presumably do so because they believe that the cost of design and print are more than recouped by this approach. However, as the true story above shows, at least one charity has

With specially printed envelopes you can get a message across even if the envelope is never opened. I received a mailing from Oxfam, and printed on the envelope were the words: 'Over 90p in every £1 goes to fund our vital work on behalf of the poorest people of the world'. This important message could influence the recipient at some later date, even if they fail to respond to this particular mailing. However, it could be argued that a plain envelope has to be opened, if only to check what's inside. It is easier to throw away mail if you know at a glance that it is unsolicited.

found that mailings that look like 'normal' letters elicit the best response for them. Decide what's best for you. Carefully weigh up the costs and benefits before making your decision, and ideally do a split test mailing to be sure you take the right decision.

Size Matters

Whether you choose ready made or specially printed envelopes, you need to decide on the size (which, of course, will be dependent on the size of the enclosures).

With automated sorting, Royal Mail find it easier to process some envelopes than others. They recommend that envelopes are:

- Between 140 mm and 240 mm (6 and 10 inches) long.
- Between 90 mm and 165 mm ($3^1/_2$ and $6^1/_2$ inches) wide.
- Oblong in shape.
- The longer side is at least 1.4 times the length of the shorter.

The common envelope sizes DL (to take one third A4) and C5 (to take half A4) fall into Royal Mail's preferred range. They cannot handle envelopes smaller than 100 mm × 70 mm ($4 × 2^3/_4$ inches) or larger than 610 mm × 460 mm (24 × 18 inches).

The Enclosures

Most mailings comprise a covering letter and one enclosure. The enclosure may be:

- a mail order catalogue;
- an order form;
- a membership leaflet;
- a questionnaire;
- a promotional or information leaflet;
- a newsletter;
- a pre-paid envelope.

Avoid including too many enclosures: this will burden the recipient and swell your postage bill. Decide on the maximum weight

TRUE STORY Getting it Right

I received a letter in a plain white envelope. Stamped in red ink across the seal were the words 'Opened for inspection'. The envelope had indeed been opened and resealed with adhesive tape. I was furious at this intrusion. On opening the letter myself, I discovered that it was an elaborate gimmick to attract my attention. The enclosure was a mailshot from the *Observer* newspaper. It began: 'Imagine the outrage you'd feel if you discovered your mail had been tampered with.' Promoting a series of articles on censorship, the stunt was highly effective.

TRUE STORY   Getting it Right

The charity CBF World Jewish Relief sent vacuum-sealed sandwiches to over 20,000 Jewish households in the London area. The packaging was printed with: 'This sandwich can feed a family of three for a month.' In place of a filling in the sandwich was a printed appeal setting out the desperate position of people in Belgrade and seeking money to send boxes of food to them. This unusual mailshot was designed to make people take both notice and action.

TRUE STORY   Getting it Wrong

Food was used in a mailshot to promote Scotland. Across Britain freelance travel journalists were sent a small haggis. It certainly attracted attention, but for the wrong reason. The package arrived at the height of summer, when most recipients were away. Heat, humidity and haggis do not mix. Decaying haggis behind the front door is no welcome home. Gimmicks are fine, but always consider what can go wrong.

of your mailing before it is produced, and make sure you do not exceed it to the extent that you are pushed into the next mailing band.

The Covering Letter

Take time over the preparation of your covering letter. It is the thread that holds the whole mailing together, so get it right. This is more important still if your letter is the only enclosure. It must capture the recipient's interest very quickly, or it will never be read.

> **tip**
>
> Aim for your covering letter and contents to emerge from the envelope the right way up. The letter and enclosures should be folded in the same direction, to make opening the mailing that bit easier.

THE EFFECTIVE COVERING LETTER CHECKLIST

☑ Keep your covering letter short and to the point, preferably no more than one side.

☑ If you go onto two sides, end page one with a split sentence to encourage the reader to turn the page.

☑ Keep it personal, so the recipient feels that a real, committed person has written it, and that the letter is appealing direct to them.

☑ Use the words 'you' and 'your'.

☑ Make it persuasive. Put forward clear and strong arguments for why their help/action/membership is necessary.

☑ Use appropriate language to set the tone and appeal to the reader.

☑ Urge action by telling the reader what they can do to help and making it easy for recipients to respond/take action.

☑ Use plain English to explain what a difference the reader's help can make.

☑ Avoid exaggerating how much you need or how serious the problem is.

☑ Use case histories if appropriate (make them anonymous if necessary, to ensure confidentiality).

---

tip

Many organisations print a PS (postscript) on the letter in a hand-written style, so that this stands out from the rest of the letter. It often says something like 'Hurry – offer only available until …' or 'Remember that your help can make all the difference to children like …' Even if recipients do not read all the letter, the PS will stand out enough for them at least to read that. It should have a tone of urgency or aim to encourage action.

Other Enclosures

Your covering letter should signpost readers to the enclosure(s). Both the covering letter and other enclosures should be attractively produced, although it would be counterproductive if they appeared too expensive or wasteful.

Keep the number of enclosures to a minimum, and ensure that each one is as short as it can be. All of us suffer from information overload and there are limits to what we can absorb. Added to that, the increasing pressures on our time, combined with the explosion in direct mail, mean that we have more to deal with than we can manage. Don't add to the burden by sending out jumbo-sized mailings.

Remember that your enclosures need not be written material. Companies, and some charities, now mail videos in place of leaflets and brochures. The RSPCA has been using video for a number of years, targeting high-value donors. Its videos explain how the charity's money is being spent, and appeal for donations. The RSPCA says that the response it gets from video is twice as high as for a standard letter mailing. The average donation is also significantly higher. Of course, you need to remember that producing a video is more expensive, and packaging and mailing costs are also greater (although lightweight video cassettes are available). But for some charities, such as the RSPCA, this is a worthwhile investment.

tip

Design your direct mail letter and other enclosures to reinforce your corporate identity. Make good use of your logo and print in your house colours so that recipients can see at a glance who their mailing is from.

Making it easy to respond

Sometimes direct mail is used merely to inform. Generally, however, it is intended to fundraise or to encourage recipients to take action of some sort. It is in your interests to consider how you can make it easy for them to act. Your success depends on the ease with which you enable people to do something.

Use one or more of the options below to ensure that action can be taken with ease.

Response Device

If you want people to order from you, to send a donation or to join your organisation, you must make it really easy. They are less likely to write you a letter than to complete a simple tear-off slip or coupon. Remember this when designing your mailing. Include a membership form, a banker's order form or another device to allow easy response.

Business Reply

Research by the Direct Mail Information Service shows that paying the postage for your customer's reply will increase response. Royal Mail's pre-paid envelopes or cards printed with your address make it really easy for recipients of your mail to respond. If you think this is likely to increase take-up for you, and that the long-term benefits will outweigh the cost involved, why not try it out?

Freepost

Enquirers or donors can write to you post-free, though you will have to pick up the tab. It will cost you the postage charge, plus an annual licence fee, plus a small handling charge per item. For details talk to the local Royal Mail Sales Centre by calling locall 0345 950 950.

TRUE STORY   Getting it Right

Some charities aim for the best of both worlds: they use a Freepost address, but encourage respondents to use a stamp when replying. Oxfam, for example, includes in its direct mail a pre-printed envelope which says: 'No stamp needed, but using one will save Oxfam money.'

Marie Curie Cancer Care carries a slightly longer message expressing the same sentiment: 'No stamp is needed – but if you kindly use a stamp more of your gift will go to caring for people with cancer. Thank you.'

tip

You can encourage response to your mailing by including a 'speed incentive'. For example, your mailing could say 'Reply before 1 July and get a free "Save the Dolphin" lapel badge'.

Freephone

All phone companies offer Freephone numbers, which work in a similar way to Freepost. Call them for details. Remember that to the cost of such services you need to add the cost of staffing telephone lines to handle responses. Research has shown that people generally prefer to respond by post rather than by telephone.

Credit Card Payment

By offering the facility of paying or donating by credit card, you make it even easier for people to respond. A Freephone credit card hotline makes it easier still. Remember that the costs to you will include the 'merchant fee' charged by the credit card company, which will be a percentage of each credit card transaction. Weigh up carefully whether credit cards are right for your organisation, by working out the costs and the benefits.

Website

Put your web address in mailings and enable recipients to respond online if they prefer. Allow them to access further information from your website, to make a donation, or to download fact sheets, petitions or campaign packs.

Coping with the response

You undertake direct mail campaigns with the expectation that they will be successful – you want people to respond, and respond in numbers. But are you geared up to cope with the response? Do you have enough staff available to process donations/activate new memberships/send out information packs?

THE RIGHT RESPONSE CHECKLIST

- ☑ Tell everyone who needs to know and brief staff who answer the phone.
- ☑ Avoid mailings that coincide with a really busy period in your organisation, such as your Christmas newsletter mailing or summer holidays, when you might be short of staff.
- ☑ Have enough people to answer the phone (your mailing may generate extra calls) and to deal with responses that come in by post and email.
- ☑ Plan your response before your mailing takes place; leave it 'til afterwards and you're in trouble.

The hidden time and money costs of direct mail

tip

If using a designer, copywriter or agency to produce your mailing, give them a comprehensive written brief. This will make their job easier and you will get a more suitable and effective end result.

It is easy to think that the only costs involved in direct mail are postage charges. Here are some others you will need to budget for:

- **The mailing list** – hiring one or building your own.
- **Envelopes** – buying them from wholesalers or having your own designed and printed.
- **Design** – the cost of having envelopes, covering letters and enclosures (such as leaflets) designed.
- **Printing** – the cost of having the above items printed, including the cost of reproduction such as scanning.
- **Copywriting** – if you want your enclosures professionally written, you will need to budget for this.
- **Photography** – if you are producing special enclosures, you may need to commission photography.
- **Response device** – if you are planning to use a Freepost address or other response device to encourage recipients to reply, add the cost of this to your overall budget.
- **Stuffing envelopes** – the time involved in stuffing, sealing and sorting envelopes is immense and you will need to budget for this. There are companies who will do it for you – mailing or fulfilment houses – or you can do it in-house, possibly using volunteers. Never underestimate the time and effort (and boredom!) involved.
- **Project management** – whether you coordinate all of the above in-house, or use a specialist direct marketing agency to oversee it for you, it will cost.
- **Follow-up** – processing responses to direct mail takes time and costs money (though it hopefully generates money too!).
- **Evaluation** – you should always spend time afterwards analysing the success of a direct mail campaign.

Evaluation

Evaluation should be an integral part of the process. You need to measure the cost and effectiveness of direct mail campaigns in the same way as you would measure the success of a press advertising campaign.

Two standard measures are used to measure the effectiveness of mailings:

1 **Cost per response**: add together all the costs associated with your direct mail campaign. Now divide by the number of responses received.
2 **Cost per conversion**: divide the cost of the mailing by the number of 'sales' – or donations, memberships, subscriptions.

The cost per response will inevitably be lower than the cost per conversion. Decide in advance how much you can afford to spend on each 'sale'. This will depend on how much a customer is worth. If you have to spend £25 to get one customer, but each customer will donate around £2,000 to you in their lifetime, and one in ten customers will also leave you a legacy, £25 is a small price to pay.

Based on your allowable cost per conversion, you need to set targets right at the outset. Review these targets as part of your evaluation. Assuming your allowable cost per conversion is £50 and your mailing list is 1,000 people, you will need to receive 20 sales (assuming each mailing costs £1) for you to cover costs. More than 20 sales and you are beginning to see a return on your direct mail investment.

The Post-Mortem

Part of your evaluation should also include a post-mortem to see what lessons you can learn to help improve future mailings. The sample post-mortem checklist will help you identify some of the factors that you may wish to consider when reviewing the success of a campaign.

> **tip**
>
> Royal Mail produce an excellent Direct Mail Guide, full of tips and advice on direct mail. The guide also includes examples of charity direct mail, including mailings by the Salvation Army and Marie Curie Cancer Care. It is available free from Royal Mail Customer Sales Centres (see address list).

Sample direct mail post-mortem pro-forma

Campaign name: ....

Mailing date: ....

Quantity mailed: ....

Number of 'gone-aways' returned: ....

Number of donations received on first mail-out: ....

Number of enquiries for more information: ....

Number of these which then sent in donation: ....

Total cost of mailings (incl. inserts and staff time): £ ....

Cost of sending out additional information: £ ....

Total donations received: £ ....

Cost of mailing per donation: £ ....

Average donation size: £ ....

Percentage of recipients sending in donation (total) .... per cent

Percentage of recipients sending in donation (after first mailing) .... per cent

Percentage sending in donation (after requesting further information) .... per cent

How could the mailing package be improved?

Letter design – ....

Letter content – ....

Enclosed leaflet design – ....

Leaflet content – ....

Envelope design – ....

Other – ....

How did the various suppliers perform? Any comments?

Designer – ....

Copywriter – ....

Printer – ....

Stationer – ....

List broker – ....

Royal Mail – ....

Others – ....

Where could savings be made? ....

....

....

Were there any additional costs we had not anticipated? ....

....

....

How did we handle responses in-house? Could we have done better? How? ....

....

....

Overall how could the campaign's success be rated? Did it meet its objectives? ....

....

....

What are the recommendations for future mailings? ....

....

....

Direct advertising

Be careful not to confuse direct mail and direct advertising. Direct mail is just that, mail that goes direct to a household. By contrast direct advertising is not mailed, it is dropped through people's letterboxes, often though not necessarily in a free newspaper, and is usually in the form of a leaflet without an envelope.

Direct advertising has many advantages for charities:

- It is cheap (especially if you can find volunteers to do the mail-drop).
- It can be used by very small charities.
- It is especially effective for local groups.
- It can be targeted at particular types of neighbourhood.
- You don't need a list of names and addresses.
- Unlike direct mail, it doesn't matter if the previous occupant has moved away.

Toiletries giant Lever was the first company to use door drops, way back in 1952, when it delivered ten million packs of OMO washing powder to consumers.

Royal Mail offer a door-to-door service which enables you to deliver promotional material nationwide (or just in one or two areas, depending on your needs), reaching recipients at the same time as their regular post. The cost depends on the volume and weight of the items you are sending, but is very reasonable. I received a mailing from Oxfam this way; in place of the postmark was a message saying: 'Delivered by hand to save money'. Specialist companies also provide a door drop service. These specialists usually require less notice than Royal Mail and may be cheaper. However, Royal Mail is generally cheaper where remote areas are concerned and it gains higher efficiency ratings.

Your material can be delivered 'solus' (on its own), which will achieve more impact on the doormat. However, distributing it with material from other organisations and companies will mean sharing costs and therefore reducing the bill for you.

Have a go yourself

The following is a made-up direct mail letter written to someone the charity has not had contact with before. According to the database the recipient is female, middle-aged and has a family.

The Action Trust for the Prevention of Sudden Infant Death Syndrome
City Scope House, 2nd Floor, 22 Buccleuch Street,
Easingswold ES10 42P

Tel. 014452 332267 Fax 014452 332268

Philip Davies OBE, Honourable Secretary

Dear Mrs Smith,

The Action Trust for the Prevention of Sudden Infant Death
Syndrome is a national charity registered with the Charity
Commission. Established since 1987, we have invested heavily in
research using the top experts in this field – consultant paediatricians,
pathologists, leading scientists and others – to help uncover the causes
of sudden infant death syndrome (SIDS). We hope that our extensive
and exhaustive SIDS research programme will be successful in
identifying the causes of sudden infant death syndrome. This will
enable us to draw up an action programme aimed at eradicating SIDS
once and for all.

You can help us by funding our vital research. We need to fund a
research worker, which will cost us £25,000 plus national insurance,
car, expenses and other overheads. All of this will come to £40,000 for
one researcher for one year. Since we need to fund the post for two
years, we need £80,000. Please help us by sending in a donation.
Make your cheque payable to The Action Trust for the Prevention of
Sudden Infant Death Syndrome and send it to Philip Davies OBE,
Honourable Secretary, The Action Trust for the Prevention of Sudden
Infant Death Syndrome, City Scope House, 2nd Floor, 22 Buccleuch
Street, Easingswold ES10 42P.

Thank you for reading this letter. We are sure that you will not let us
down in our vital research and look forward to receiving your cheque.

Yours sincerely

Philip Davies

Philip Davies OBE
Honourable Secretary

Reg. Charity No. 767632

Discussion

If that letter landed on my door mat, along with the rest of my
mail, I'm afraid it would rapidly become a resident of the
wastepaper basket. What was wrong with it?

- SIDS is the correct name, but we all talk about cot death. If
  your charity uses jargon, try to speak to ordinary donors in
  plain English.

- The letter fails to engage the reader right at the outset.
- It reads in an impersonal way.
- There is no emotion, no compassion and no appeal to the heartstrings.
- The charity needs £80,000. It might be legitimate expenditure, but the way it is presented, it doesn't sound like it.
- There is no indication of what size of donation is acceptable – 50p? £10?
- The address is too long and does not need to be repeated in the body copy as it already appears on the letterhead.
- It is a bit presumptive to assume that people *will* give! Don't use sentences like: 'We are sure that you will not let us down in our vital research and look forward to receiving your cheque.'

This version is far better:

The Action Trust for the Prevention of Sudden Infant Death Syndrome
City Scope House, 2nd Floor, 22 Buccleuch Street,
Easingswold ES10 42P

Tel. 014452 332267 Fax 014452 332268

Philip Davies OBE, Honourable Secretary

Dear Mrs Smith,

As a mother you'll understand how we feel. Our son, Jason, was born a beautiful, happy, healthy baby. You can imagine our relief. We were the proud parents of a strong and lively boy. But our joy soon turned to despair when our lovely son died suddenly just a few weeks later. It is hard to believe that the child I carried inside me for nine months is now dead. Jason would have been celebrating his second birthday soon. Instead of having a party for him we will be visiting his grave. The pain will always be with us, and nothing can reduce our loss, but you can help to ensure that your own grandchildren do not face Jason's fate. Support The Action Trust for the Prevention of Sudden Infant Death Syndrome and help make cot death a thing of the past.

Jason died suddenly and no one knows why. We didn't even get a chance to say good-bye or to prepare ourselves for the pain. Thousands of parents across Britain know our heartache because they too have lost their babies in this way. The only good thing to come out of our own loss is the establishment of this charity, which will help ensure that other babies like Jason do not have to die so needlessly.

For just 30p per day you can fund our vital research programme, which aims to uncover the reasons for cot death. Though it is still a mystery to scientists the world over, our own research staff have made several important breakthroughs which have brought us all closer to knowing why babies like Jason die. If you can afford to help us, please send a cheque today (made payable to The Action Trust for the Prevention of Sudden Infant Death Syndrome). Donations large and small are very welcome.

Yours sincerely,

Jenny Estelle

Jenny Estelle – Jason's mum

PS For just 30p a day you can help us to help make cot death a thing of the past.

Reg. Charity No. 767632

Discussion
What makes this second letter so much better?

- It is written by someone who has lost a child through cot death, so it is more heart-felt than a letter from a remote honourable secretary.
- It aims to stir the emotions and prompt action.
- Its use of the experience of a real mother talking about her real baby makes it all the more real. Reading about second-hand experiences is never quite the same.
- It is from one mother to another.
- It engages the reader by asking her to put herself in the writer's shoes.
- It refers to SIDS by its popular name, cot death.
- It quantifies what helping means – just 30p a day.
- It reinforces this message using an attention-grabbing hand-written postscript.
- The 'Dear Mrs Smith' bit appears to be hand-written, making it look more personal.

Promotion: printed publicity materials

INTRODUCTION

Even the smallest charity has a publicity leaflet. Bigger charities have impressive suites of leaflets, professionally produced annual reports, posters, brochures, catalogues and a host of other publicity items. Whether you produce a lot of material or just the occasional leaflet, the key is to do it well. To do it well you will need to:

- Produce good 'copy'.
- Ensure clear and attractive design.
- Where appropriate, include interesting photographs and illustrations.
- Arrange production using a professional printer.

Producing effective copy

Most of us have to write as part of our daily lives – shopping lists, a note to the milkman, business reports, emails and other work correspondence typically appear among our regular writing tasks. Copywriting is different – different from both casual daily writing and business writing. For publicity material to do its job, it must be written in 'copy'. Copy differs from business English in a number of ways. If you are used to writing reports and formal documents, you may need to coax yourself out of this business style and into the more relaxed copy style of writing when it comes to penning publicity.

THE GOOD COPY CHECKLIST

☑ Keep it natural and informal in style.

☑ Use contractions – I'd, we'll, you're, etc.

☑ Use plain English – short and familiar words and short sentences.

☑ Have a mental picture of your reader and try to write for a real person.

☑ Use plenty of face-to-face words, more like spoken than written English.

☑ Use the 'first person' and 'second person' – 'I' and 'you' rather than 'the organisation' and 'the service-user'.

☑ Create readable chunks using bullet points, subheadings and pull quotes.

☑ Avoid dense screeds of text.

Although we all learned to write at school, writing is not easy. Many people feel inadequate because they are unable to get it right first time. They are worrying needlessly. Even professional writers (myself included!) struggle at times to get the right words in the right order. The important thing is being able to get there in the end. Never expect to achieve this in just one or two drafts; redrafting is a vital part of effective copywriting.

Establishing the Facts

Before you begin writing, spend a while thinking it through. In particular:

1 Establish your purpose – ask yourself why you are producing publicity material. Do you hope to inform, educate, influence, win support, sell? There can be any number of reasons for producing material. Establish yours at the outset.

2 Establish the size and format – what format will the publicity material take? An A5 twelve-page booklet? An A4 two-fold leaflet? An A2 poster?

3 Establish the outcome – what do you want readers to do? Make a donation? Order a pack of Christmas cards? Join? Specify what action you want readers to take.

4 Establish the tone – all writing has a tone of voice. You might wish to sound friendly and chatty, or serious and authoritative. Be clear how you want to come across to readers so that you can select an appropriate style and vocabulary.

5 Establish the message – be clear what you want to say. What points do you want to make? What are the key messages that must be conveyed?

tip

The first few words are the hardest. Write something, anything, just to get started. You can always go back and polish it later.

Six Steps to Really Readable Writing

1 Collect – Begin by jotting down ideas for content.
2 Group – Organise your ideas into clear themes.
3 Order – Place your themes in a logical order.
4 Place – Try to visualise the finished product and work out what will go where.
5 Write – Put pen to paper or mouse to mat and prepare a first draft.
6 Revise – Redraft until you are happy with the end result.

Preparing a Draft

The biggest challenge you will face is producing the first draft. Good planning can ease this task. After you have produced a draft, put it away for a few days. Return to it when you feel suitably refreshed. You will then be able to read your copy with a more objective, discerning eye. Your mistakes will leap out, enabling you to correct them and to produce an even better version. When rereading your work, look out for the following:

- Repetition – identify any overuse of the same words and phrases. A thesaurus will help you find suitable alternatives. Also seek out repetition of information and edit as necessary.
- Ambiguity – double meanings cloud communication. Check that everything is clear and easy to understand.
- Jargon – check that your chosen words will be understood by the target audience.
- Irrelevancies – delete information that adds nothing to your purpose and intended outcome.
- Omissions – check that you have included all the vital information.
- Consistency – if you spell it 'website' on page 1, don't spell it 'web site' on page 12.

Take it for a Test Drive

Test your text on a few people from your target readership. What do they think about the tone and content? Can they understand it? Is it patronising? Listen to their comments and feedback, and redraft as necessary.

tip

Read your work aloud. Where text sounds stilted and unnatural, rewrite it to improve the flow.

House style guidelines

Newspapers produce 'house style guidelines' to ensure consistency. These guidelines explain points of style, for example:

- How certain words should be spelt – for example, should British 'ise' or American 'ize' word endings be used.
- Whether certain words should be hyphenated – 'co-operate', for example.
- Where and where not to use initial capitals – in words like 'Internet', for example.
- Whether a word is one word or two – 'website' for example.

Many charities have style guidelines for the same reason. They wish to ensure that all of their publications maintain consistency. The Woodland Trust have produced style guidelines which are available to all staff via their computer network. Staff may search an electronic database to check on particular words or points of style. An extract from their guidelines can be found below.

Woodland Trust style guidelines

Inclusiveness – gender, ethnicity and disability

Consider carefully the language you use to ensure that it is inclusive. Always check with your source to make sure that the terminology is correct and will not cause offence.

When referring to either or both sexes, but not specifically to the male sex, try to avoid the words 'man' or 'men'. There are plenty of alternatives such as 'person', 'people', 'human beings', 'men and women'. Avoid 'he', 'his' and 'him'. Use 'he or she', 'his or hers', 'him or her'. 'They', 'their', 'them' and 's/he' can often be used instead. Other words of masculine gender can often be avoided where they do not apply specifically to men. Use 'ordinary people/an average person' for 'the man in the street'; 'chairwoman/chair/who chairs' for 'chairman'; 'people/humanity/humans' for 'mankind'; 'synthetic/artificial/ manufactured' for 'manmade', etc.

Only mention someone's race if it is strictly relevant to the piece, and be alert to nuance. Words that were once in common usage are now considered offensive: for example, 'half-caste' and 'coloured'. Use 'mixed race', 'black' and 'minority ethnic' instead. At a local level, it is best to approach community groups to ask how they wish to be described. The most acceptable overall terms for people living in the UK, but who stem from other countries of origin, are 'ethnic communities' and 'black and minority ethnic groups'.

Never refer to disabled people as 'handicapped', and especially not as 'the handicapped', 'the blind', etc. Remember that they are people first and foremost. Ask groups and Individuals how they like to be described. The RNIB refers to 'blind and partially sighted people', for example, which it says covers the whole spectrum of visual impairment; while some people who use wheelchairs like to be described as 'wheelchair users' rather than 'people in wheelchairs'

(they do not regard themselves as wheelchair-bound). Check, check and check again to avoid causing offence or promoting negative images.

Ensuring attractive design

Some people prefer to commission design first, thereafter writing the text to fit. Others, myself included, prefer to write the copy before commissioning the design. There is no right way; it all depends on what works best for you. The only rule is that whichever you do first, both copy and design must work well together, each enhancing the other.

There are three options when it comes to design:

1 You can do it yourself in-house using desktop publishing (DTP).
2 You can use so-called 'overprint' or 'empty belly' material.
3 You can commission a professional designer.

Desktop Publishing

Most computers come with easy-to-use desktop publishing software. This puts design within your reach, even when there is no budget to pay for a professional designer. It is possible to use this software to produce stunning, professional-looking design. Equally, the same software in the wrong hands can result in publicity material that will do a serious disservice to your organisation. If using DTP, stick to the following rules.

THE GOOD DTP CHECKLIST

☑ Get DTP training before you are let loose with the software!

☑ Stick to just one or two 'fonts' or typefaces.

☑ Limit yourself to one or two 'point sizes' or type sizes.

☑ Avoid small point sizes – at least 10 points, or a minimum of 14 for people with a visual impairment.

☑ Don't go overboard with clipart, which can look amateurish.

☑ Make good use of 'white space', the part of the page without text and illustrations.

☑ Avoid overcrowding a page. Keep it clean, crisp and uncluttered.

☑ Follow a logical layout. Be sure the reader can see at a glance which bits should be read in which order.

☑ Check that your corporate identity is reflected in choice of colours, typeface and by using your logo.

Overprint Stationery

Overprint or 'empty belly' material is a kind of halfway house between producing material in-house and using a professional designer. You can buy overprint stationery from specialist paper suppliers. Leaflets, posters, certificates, stationery and a wide range of other items are available. Each item features a professionally designed and printed element – a border or some other design. You simply overprint this with text using your office printer or photocopier. The benefit is that you can obtain a professional-looking, multi-colour leaflet, for example, for less than the cost of commissioning design and print yourself. For small print-runs this can be a good option. The drawback is that you are buying an off-the-shelf design, something that is not unique to your organisation.

An alternative is to commission a designer to produce empty belly material incorporating your corporate identity. For a one-off design and print investment, you can produce supplies of leaflets or posters by simple in-house overprinting in black.

Commissioning a Designer

Shop around to find a designer you like and can afford. If possible go by recommendation. Alternatively, gather samples from local organisations of publicity material you like. Look on the back to see if you can see the name of the designer who produced it. Ask a few designers to show you their portfolios and discuss costs with them. Try to find someone who is able to show creativity on a small budget. Freelance designers working from home frequently offer design every bit as good as a design consultancy at a fraction of the cost.

Briefing a Designer

Get the best from your designer either by providing them with a written design brief or by sitting down with them to discuss the assignment. Explain in detail what you are looking for and how you will use the finished item. Who is it aimed at? What style do you want? If possible, show your designer samples of designs you like and designs you hate. Should certain colours be avoided because of cultural or political connotations? Give your designer as much information as possible, along with copies of recent material you have produced.

Design Guidelines

Many organisations produce design guidelines to help ensure that all of their published material maintains a unity of design.

> **tip**
>
> Local colleges might be able to put you in touch with freelances who have recently graduated with a qualification in graphic design.

Commonly design guidelines specify such things as which fonts may be used, or where the logo should be placed. They provide a useful reference for both staff and outside design consultants.

Commissioning photography and illustration

Graphic designers lay out text and use typography to create attractive designs. Sometimes you will want to supplement this with photographs and illustrations.

Using an Illustrator

Graphic design uses computer-based layouts. Graphic designers have a good eye for design, but not all designers can draw. That is the role of the illustrator. If you find a designer able both to do layouts and draw, value that person for being rare and doubly talented. An illustrator can provide illustrations using their chosen media. Some specialise in pastels, others in oils, pen and ink, watercolour, charcoal, collage or mixed media. Look at an illustrator's portfolio to see which media they excel in and what their style is. An illustrator who is able to produce attractive work using a range of media and to create many different styles is a sign of particular talent. If you are using a designer, ask if they can recommend an illustrator.

Using a Photographer

Everyone owns a camera, but that doesn't make us all photographers. There is a world of difference between a holiday snap and a professionally photographed image in terms of composition and reproduction quality. If you can afford to, use pictures taken by a professional. As an alternative, use a photo library. You can choose from thousands of images and pay only for what is used. You may want to buy a CD-ROM containing copyright-free photos, although you can sometimes struggle to find an image that is just what you are looking for. Or you can take pictures yourself – if you must!

THE GOOD PHOTOGRAPHY CHECKLIST

- ☑ Look out for extraneous matter, clutter and mess in the background.
- ☑ Remember that close-ups usually work better than wide shots.
- ☑ Shoot from an interesting angle.
- ☑ Avoid shots of people sitting around a table.

☑ Avoid 'grip 'n' grins' – people hand-shaking, holding giant cheques or receiving gifts and awards.

☑ Avoid 'the firing line' – a line up of people, such as your staff or committee.

☑ Avoid group shots, meetings and large gatherings

Arranging production

Once you have written your copy, commissioned photography and had your material designed, it's print time. If you have used a professional designer, they can organise printing, although most will charge a 'mark-up' or handling fee for this service – usually around 10–15 per cent of the final bill. So, it may pay to do your own print-buying.

Give printers as much information as possible so that they can give you a realistic quote. By giving everyone the same information, you can compare quotes and select the best deal. Ensure you tell printers the following:

- The print-run – how many copies you need. It is not economical to get small amounts printed (generally under 400 copies) except by digital printing. Not all printshops will have digital equipment.
- Colours – of ink and paper (ask your printer to show you samples).
- Paper – type (including manufacturer), weight, size and colour.
- Size – give the size of paper (A4, for example) and the length of the document (number of pages – also known as 'extent').
- Special finishes – if you want special effects such as varnishing, embossing or laminating (if you don't know what these are, ask your printer to show examples), say so at this stage.
- Finishing – folding and stitching, for example.
- Extras – including collating, delivery and VAT.

Select your chosen printer, agree a date for the job to start and end, and supply delivery details.

Have a go yourself

The following is a contribution to the National Heart Foundation (a fictitious charity) supporters' newsletter. Imagine your role is to edit the newsletter.

1 Analyse what's wrong with the article.

> **tip**
>
> A run-on (extra copies printed at the same time) is much cheaper than a reprint (extra copies printed at a later date). If you unsure how many copies you require, opt for a few extra: this won't cost much more and it could save you considerable money in the long run.

2 Now edit or rewrite it, including the headline, to make it suitable for the supporters' newsletter. It needs to be relevant, sharp, punchy – and 100 words or fewer.

NURSES HOLD JUMBLE SALE FOR NATIONAL HEART FOUNDATION

A group of twelve staff nurses, who trained and work in Anytown, decided one day last December, during their coffee break at the city's Queen Elizabeth Hospital, that they would raise some money for the National Heart Foundation. They wanted to do their bit to help what they regarded as a very worthwhile cause. After all, being nurses they were only too well aware of the effects of heart disease!

They thought long and hard about what they could do to raise what would amount to a significant sum, but they found it really difficult, impossible even, to come up with anything original. They remembered reading somewhere about a fundraising stunt involving a town declaring independence and issuing mock passports – for a fee, of course. However, they felt that the stunt was too elaborate to work in a large place like Anytown. They considered bungee jumping, parachute jumps and white water rafting – great fun, but a bit too dangerous. Then they decided that perhaps there was no need to be original. After all, why be original when the old tried and tested methods of fundraising – jumble sales, sponsored events, collections and the like – can be just as effective in terms of attracting money. So off they set on their mission to raise some money for the NHF. One of the nurses, Staff Nurse Jackie Nesbitt, suggested that they should take an ordinary fundraising idea – a jumble sale – but give it a novel twist. That's how the team came up with the idea of a red jumble sale.

Uncles, aunts, brothers, sisters, sons, daughters and friends were all roped into the fundraising effort. Their aim was to gather together anything red that could be sold at the jumble sale. To their knowledge there has never before been a red jumble sale in Anytown, or anywhere else for that matter, not even America, where they do the craziest things. The nurses were delighted when, after a busy day running stalls at the jumble sale, they each totted up their takings and added them all together. They had raised an impressive £10,000. What an achievement. Well done.

368 words

Discussion

This article, although not real, is typical of the sort of contribution many newsletter editors receive.

- The headline is boring and descriptive.
- The article rambles like a stream of consciousness.

- It contains too much irrelevant and uninteresting detail and background information.
- The newsworthy aspects, the innovative red jumble sale and the impressive amount raised, are left to the end.
- The style is too loose, waffly and wordy.

Comparing notes

NURSES SEE RED AND RAISE £10,000

It was a red letter day in Anytown recently when the world's first ever 'red' jumble sale netted a staggering £10,000 for the National Heart Foundation. The innovative fundraising stunt, the brainwave of a group of Anytown nurses, involved collecting and selling red-coloured items. Thanks to plenty of local publicity the nurses were soon inundated with all manner of red objects – everything from scarlet lipstick to an imitation ruby necklace! The event was such a success that the nurses plan to hold another one next year on a yellow theme. Watch this space!

100 words

Discussion
This version is so much better.

- The headline is more enticing and humorous.
- The article is more tightly written, more succinct and to the point.
- Boring and irrelevant detail has been omitted.
- It leads with a newsworthy angle.
- The style is more punchy and lively.

Promotion: the Internet

INTRODUCTION

There's a great deal of hype about the Internet and how it will revolutionise our lives. While its impact on day-to-day living may have been overstated, its effect on charity marketing is yet to be seen. What is clear is that the Internet is already changing the way many charities perform a number of key activities, from fundraising to campaigning. Equally clear is the benefit voluntary organisations can derive from a good website.

Use the Internet to:

■ Raise awareness.
■ Publicise your work, issue, service or campaign.
■ Fundraise.
■ Provide information.
■ Educate.
■ Seek feedback.
■ Build support for a campaign.
■ Sell (goods, Christmas cards, etc.).

The pros and cons

The Internet is a great leveller, enabling the smallest voluntary organisations to have the same presence in cyberspace as the biggest multinational company. There are many good reasons why organisations without an Internet site should consider getting one.

The Pros

- Your site can contain lots of information. You are not limited to a certain amount of space, as with a leaflet.
- Visitors to your site can give you instant feedback thanks to the Internet's interactive quality.
- Accurate measurability enables you to gather vital marketing data, such as how many people visited your site, what they looked at and how long they spent there.
- You can use voices, music, sound effects, photos, illustration and moving images.
- The Internet is open 24 hours a day, seven days a week.
- The Internet is a global medium.

While the list of benefits is impressive, do not overlook the drawbacks.

The Cons

- Your key audience may not be online.
- Graphics do not look as good on-screen as in a printed brochure.
- There is a risk of hacking, viruses and fraud.
- For direct selling charities, consumer caution about the safety of Internet buying is an issue.
- Concerns about online credit card fraud may deter people from making donations in cyberspace.
- Unless you have the latest processor, modem and ISDN line (a fast digital phone line), the process can be very slow, especially for sites with complex graphics.

Pulling power

Traditional publicity methods – such as direct mail or press advertising – are pushed at their target audience. With the Internet, consumers pull the information they want. That puts the control in their hands, not in yours.

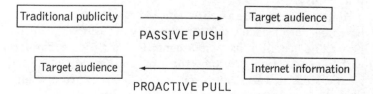

Establishing a website

tip

Contact charities with impressive websites and ask them for their advice. What would they recommend? What works? What should you avoid? Learn from their experience, especially their mistakes.

Spend time working out why you need a website. What will you use it for? What do you hope to achieve? Surf the Net and take a look at other charity websites, both in the UK and in other parts of the English-speaking world. The Americans are ahead of us in cyberspace so you might learn a trick or two from US charities. Look at what other UK charities in your sector are doing with their sites. Also visit commercial sites to see what big companies are doing to promote themselves. Bookmark the sites you like. Make a note of anything you don't like.

Choosing a Web Designer

Based on what you have seen and what you have identified as needing, draw up a brief to give to prospective web designers. Include:

- Some background information on your organisation.
- Details of what you hope to achieve from your site.
- Information on your target audiences.
- Ideas on the content of your site (including graphics).
- An indication of what you will provide and what you want your web designer to provide. For example, will you provide copy? Photos? Other graphics?
- Addresses of websites you like and details of why.
- Addresses of websites you hate and an explanation of why.

Use trusted sources to get the names of three or four specialist web designers. Give them your brief and ask if they would like to pitch to design your site. Ask about their approach to the assignment, their ideas for ensuring that your needs are met, and their costs. Be clear what is included in the quoted fee. For example, ask if the domain name registration fee is included (see below), and whether the fee includes training for staff on managing and maintaining the site. Make your selection and draw up a contract specifying the assignment and stating a completion date. Make sure the contract indicates who is the copyright owner. Work closely with your chosen designer to ensure that your site meets your needs.

tip

Ask your designer to create a site that can be easily updated in-house by one of your staff.

You don't have to use a web designer. Most web space providers have free, downloadable software to help you create your site in-house. The benefit of using a designer is that they are familiar with Internet design, they know the tricks and have a good eye for what is going to work. Unless you are confident and competent, leave the initial construction work to the experts.

Real-life website brief drawn up by charity CHILDREN 1ST

CHILDREN 1ST Website design brief

Aim

- To increase the general profile of CHILDREN 1ST.
- To inform the public and professionals about the services operated by CHILDREN 1ST.
- To raise awareness of fundraising activities in Scotland.
- To reduce the demand for printed leaflets by providing downloadable files.
- To set out the position of CHILDREN 1ST on key issues.

Quotes should include graphic design and structure of the website (see draft site map) in addition to the elements outlined below.

- A system allowing the user to select downloadable files (perhaps Adobe Acrobat) and then print them/save them to disk. Users will have to fill in a brief questionnaire before this can take place.
- A database allowing individuals to sign up as a supporter.
- E-campaigning page allowing for e-petitioning and a description of the issues we are campaigning for – database needed to hold petitioners' names.
- A secure system to allow for credit card donations. This does not have to link into any software at our end, should only generate an email with the details to our fundraising department.
- Map of the regions covered by our fundraising team with a point and click leading to the appropriate email address.
- An easy way of adding in daily press releases with date and publication details.

Content

Think about what you will put on your website. Find out what your target visitors would like to see on your site and then ensure that content is tailored to meet their needs and interests. There's no shortage of things you might want to include. Consider the following as a starting point:

- recent and past news releases;
- fact sheets;
- case studies on how you have made a difference;
- your current newsletter and back issues;
- your annual report;
- an online petition;
- campaigning ideas;
- fundraising ideas;
- information about your organisation;
- contact details for your projects or offices;
- a who's who;

Real life site map for CHILDREN 1ST website

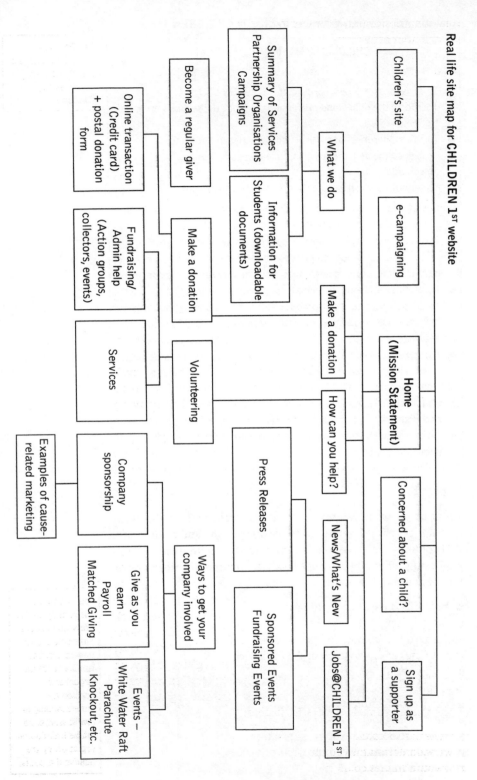

- information about volunteering;
- a calendar of events;
- information on appeals;
- a downloadable screensaver with your branding on it;
- a quiz;
- a questionnaire;
- a letters page;
- job and volunteering vacancies.

Your aim is to attract people to your site, to hold them there and to encourage them back again. The key to achieving this is to provide interesting or useful material that changes or is updated frequently.

Web Writing

Have you noticed how much more slowly you read text on-screen than on paper? We all read around 25 per cent more slowly from a VDU and find that the eye-strain is greater. That's why writing for the Internet is different to writing paper-based material. Sentences must be short and simple. As little as the equivalent of one-third to a half of an A4 page of text can be seen on screen at a time. If a screen looks dense, visitors will be disinclined to scroll down to read the rest. Make your site user-friendly for screen-fatigued surfers by ensuring that visible text is broken up using subheadings, bullet points and bite-size chunks of text. Remember that most people (up to four-fifths, according to research) scan web pages rather than reading every word. Keep text much tighter than in conventional printed publicity and allow readers to get straight to the facts or information they want.

Securing a Domain Name

Every website has a unique address, known as a domain name or URL – for example, www.mediatrust.org. Devise an appropriate domain name (usually your charity or organisation name) followed by .org.uk (for UK not-for-profit organisations) and check that it is available. You can do this by checking with the various registering sites or by asking your web designer or host (see below) to do it for you. If available, you will need to register it in your name (for a fee – around £100) and renew registration annually (for a further fee – around £50 a year). You can register your domain name on various sites, including:

- www.names.co.uk
- www.domainnames.co.uk
- www.netnames.co.uk

THE DOMAIN NAME CHECKLIST

☑ If you operate internationally, register the name for all the countries in which you work.

☑ Choose a name that is intuitive, since many people will guess the name. Someone wanting the Common Purpose website will type in www.commonpurpose.org.uk and they will find what they are looking for.

☑ Try to be unambiguous so that your address can be read out without having to be spelt out.

tip

Many companies and a small number of charities have been targeted with so-called 'suck sites', websites set up by people with a grievance against the organisation. Greenpeace, for example, has been targeted by objectors with a rival website questioning the charity's motives. Web-savvy organisations monitor the Internet to make sure they do not become an unwitting victim.

Finding your Host with the Most

You will need an Internet service provider (or ISP) to host your site. Ask for recommendations, or look in a respected Internet magazine (many publish league tables of good ISPs). Your web designer will be able to make some recommendations. Costs and levels of service vary, so as with any supplier, do shop around. Ask for names of other sites they host and take up references.

tip

Visit competitors' websites and find out what they are up to. Copy and amend good ideas.

tip

Once your site is ready, test it for usability by asking people to navigate their way around it. Ask for feedback. Is it easy to use? Can information be found with ease? Is the content interesting? Revise your site in light of comments before you go live.

THE GOOD WEBSITE CHECKLIST

☑ Easy navigability.

☑ Chunks of text rather than dense text.

☑ Clear, uncluttered home page.

☑ Good use of corporate identity.

☑ Interesting content that is user-driven, not organisation-driven.

☑ Simple yet attractive layouts.

☑ Easy-to-read text.

☑ No complex graphics (which are time-consuming to load).

Creating an interactive site

Good communication is two-way. Communicate with your target audiences through your website and add an easy-to-use interactive element to enable visitors to get in touch with you at the click of a mouse. Make it simple for them to email you with comments on your website, enquiries and requests for information. Preserve your good reputation by ensuring that someone is delegated with the task of replying promptly to emails. Some organisations – including a number of very big companies – are slow to respond to enquiries by email simply because they have no clear system for doing so.

Getting picked up by search engines

People surfing the Net for information rely on search engines to help point them in the right direction. There are a number of well-known search engines, such as Altavista, Yahoo! and Excite. You must register your page titles and page descriptions in order to appear on them. Your designer can help with this by creating 'metatags', hidden lists of key words and descriptions that are monitored by search engines, ensuring that your site pops up on every relevant search. For example, an animal welfare charity might have a long list of key words, including animal, pet, vet, welfare, cat, dog, rabbit, gerbil, and so on. Find no more than ten key words that sum up the content of your website. List them in order of importance.

Another useful trick for leading people to your site is to have links with other related sites. For example, a local children's hospice may ask the Association of Children's Hospices to provide a link to its website. It might also link with specialist websites containing medical information on life-shortening conditions affecting children.

Creating a virtual shop

Many charities have trading arms. The web offers a new vehicle for widening your customer base and securing increased sales. However, before setting up a virtual shop, be sure that you can cope. Can you get the stock and organise delivery within acceptable time scales? An upturn in sales will require you to have sufficient staff to cope with processing orders, invoicing and dispatching. Have you budgeted for this? The global nature of the Internet means that orders may come in from anywhere in the world. Can you organise international deliveries? Think through the implications very carefully before starting to trade online.

Increasingly people are making purchases online, although there is still concern about the security of transactions made on the Internet. If you have a virtual shop, reassure your customers by:

tip
Produce a list of organisations that might be willing to provide links to your site, then ask them if they will. Where appropriate, offer to reciprocate with a link from your site to theirs.

tip

Many charities produce a catalogue, particularly in the lead-up to Christmas, to sell small gifts, cards and wrapping. Consider putting your catalogue online too.

- Providing a link with the real world – promote confidence by supplying details of a named contact person within your organisation, an address and phone number.
- Providing alternative ordering methods – allow people to order by post, fax, phone or through one of your charity shops if they prefer. Publish an order form which they can print out and post or fax.
- Explaining encryption – reassure customers paying for goods over the Internet that credit card information is encrypted as it travels over the Net.
- Publishing a customer care charter – give customers faith in your products by offering exchanges and refunds.

Promoting your site

Tell everyone about your new website:

- Issue a news release.
- Carry an article in your newsletter.
- Put a message on fax header sheets alerting people to your site.
- Remember to put your web address on all of your stationery, including business cards.
- Ensure your www address is on publicity material, adverts, and so on.

Promotion: an A–Z of other ideas

INTRODUCTION

When it comes to promoting your organisation and services, there are only two limiting factors – your budget and your imagination. You can be forgiven for having a small budget, but there's no excuse for lack of imagination and creativity. Good ideas can help a small budget to go a long way. There are hundreds of different ways of promoting your products, services and events and many can be achieved in-house at little or no cost. Admittedly some promotional opportunities require significant expenditure. Select from the ideas featured this chapter according to your budget and add to them with a bit of creative thinking of your own.

A is for...

Answering machines – Use your office answer machine message as a promotional opportunity by recording details of how people can help the cause or make a donation.

Audio cassettes – Many people drive to work and 90 per cent of motorists have cassette players in their car. Audio tapes can be a good way of reaching people with your promotional message.

TRUE STORY Getting it Right

When the Royal British Legion launched its 1999 Poppy Appeal, the charity promoted the event by projecting a poppy onto the Millennium Dome, having a poppy painted on a British Airways tail fin, and having a National Express coach painted with poppies. Think creatively about how you can promote your message.

Tapes can be cost-effective, and they can even be produced in-house. Because they have a higher perceived value than a newsletter or leaflet, as well as novelty value, they are perhaps less likely to be thrown away unlistened to.

Annual Reports

Try not to think of the annual report as a yearly chore; regard it as a first-rate opportunity to promote your organisation and its good work. A series of boring statements written by the Chair, Chief Executive, Director of Finance, and so on will fail to make a promotional impact and may damage the otherwise good promotional work you have achieved.

Use your annual report to promote the organisation as a whole, to explain your approach and philosophy, to present your aims and objectives – and, of course, to review the year. Discuss important issues that relate to your work, look to the future, and flag up important events or new services planned for the coming years.

THE BETTER ANNUAL REPORT CHECKLIST

- ☑ Look at other charities' reports and copy their ideas, suitably adapted.
- ☑ Be imaginative, perhaps writing your report around a theme or issue.
- ☑ Avoid boring lists if you can: they are a waste of valuable space. If including lists, be sure that they are necessary.
- ☑ Use the back page.
- ☑ Present financial information in a lively, interesting, relevant and easy-to-understand way. You do not have to reproduce your full accounts in your annual report; a summary is quite adequate. You must make full audited accounts available to anyone requesting them, but this need not be through your report.

---

tip

Include an appeal for donations or volunteers, either as a part of the annual report itself, or as an insert.

B is for ...

Bins – Some companies sponsor litter bins in town centres and there could be scope for certain charities doing this as an appropriate way of promoting their message.

Bags – Plastic carrier bags with your logo and message printed on them can make useful give-aways.

C is for ...

CD-ROM business cards – The size of a conventional business card, a CD-ROM business card can hold detailed promotional information about your organisation.

Cinema – Cinema advertising is cheaper than TV advertising, it targets a captive audience, and the screen size offers maximum impact for your commercial. On the downside it is expensive to make the commercials, there is the added expense of having to pay for the 'airtime', and you would need to buy-in external help.

Collection sacks – If you drop collection sacks through doors to collect unwanted goods for resale in charity shops or at jumble sales, use the sack to promote your message. Shelter print the following message on their bags: 'Shelter gives advice and hope to the homeless. Why not volunteer in one of our shops and help us raise funds. Your nearest Shelter shop is ...'.

Clocks – Some organisations send clocks bearing their logo and message to key customers. The average person checks the time twice every waking hour – that's 11,680 a year!

D is for ...

Directories – Carefully placed adverts in relevant directories and handbooks can be effective where the readers form part of your target audience. Some charities advertise in legal handbooks to ensure that their charity is known to lawyers, who may be asked by clients for advice on which charities to leave a legacy to.

E is for ...

Eggs – Messages can be blown with high-pressure jets onto the outside of fresh eggs. They offer scope for original and creative advertising.

Exhibitions

Exhibitions allow charities to promote the organisation or a particular issue or campaign. Staffed exhibition stands offer you a face-to-face opportunity to convert interested people, to get them to become members or to make a donation. You can make new contacts which can be followed up later. Exhibiting is a good opportunity for two-way communication. You can tell the people about your charity, as well as picking up views, opinions and feedback from them. Use an exhibition to raise your profile and get your message across. You can exhibit:

- at other organisations' premises;
- at your own premises;
- at conferences, meetings and talks;
- outdoors – for example, in the High Street during a flag day, or at a sports event.

Mobile Exhibitions

A mobile exhibition is one that you take out on the road, perhaps incorporated into a special caravan or vehicle. The National Blood Transfusion Service's blood donor van is an example that you may be familiar with. It visits workplaces and shopping centres to promote blood donating, and it can even take people's blood there and then. Such exhibitions are not cheap, but increasingly charities and public sector organisations are using mobile exhibitions to take their message to people, rather than waiting for people to come to them. My local NHS Trust uses a converted caravan to tour schools and nurseries delivering its oral hygiene message to children. The caravan is called the Dental Dream Machine, it is decorated with bright colours and cartoon characters, and aims to take the fear out of a trip to the dentist. Children go inside the caravan, view the equipment, ask the dentist questions, meet 'Denny the Dentosaurus' and pick up information leaflets.

Portable Exhibitions

These comprise lightweight portable display boards, plus specially produced display material for attaching to them. Display systems cost anything from hundreds to thousands of pounds. Remember to add to this is the cost of commissioning material to display on the boards. (It can be done in-house, although often not to the same professional standard.)

The advantage of a portable exhibition is that you can lend it to other organisations and to libraries and community centres.

TRUE STORY   Getting it Right

Back in the 1990s Greenpeace was concerned that half of all damaging fluorocarbons were leaked by supermarket freezers, in spite of alternative 'planet-friendly' freezers being available. All supermarket chains were receptive to Greenpeace's ideas on reducing damaging fluorocarbons, except Tesco. So Greenpeace transformed a 40-foot articulated lorry into a mobile supermarket fitted out with special 'Greenfreeze' freezers and painted to look like a Tesco lorry. 'Fiasco' was painted on the side using Tesco's corporate lettering. Staff at Tesco's headquarters were invited inside and given leaflets. The lorry then toured Tesco stores across the UK. The cost – around £20,000, not counting staff time – was worth it in terms of impact and exposure.

This makes it a very easy way for you to promote your message. You can also easily take a portable exhibition with you when you attend talks and meetings.

Permanent Static Exhibitions

These are, as the name implies, exhibitions that stay put. Often they are too heavy to move and were designed for a particular place anyway. Many charity head offices have permanent exhibitions of their work.

THE SUCCESSFUL EXHIBITIONS CHECKLIST

- ☑ Offer free coffee at your exhibition stand to attract people across.
- ☑ Have pens and paper to take details of people who want further information.
- ☑ Make your exhibition as appealing as possible using flowers, seating and music as appropriate.
- ☑ If your exhibition is staffed, ensure staff don't look as if they will pounce on anyone stopping to take a look – they should appear friendly and welcoming, but not pushy or suffocating.
- ☑ Have a supply of promotional material available for visitors to take away.

F is for ...

Flags – A number of companies specialise in flag-making (see the Yellow Pages for a company near you). They are surprisingly good value for money and offer a novel way of promoting your message.

G is for ...

Give-aways – Cheap give-away promotional items such as balloons, badges and biros are useful for carrying campaign, educational, health promotion and fundraising messages.

H is for ...

Hoardings – Hoardings form part of a type of advertising known as 'outdoor'. They (and other forms of outdoor advertising) are widely used by the larger charities. Research shows that two

> **tip**
>
> Use your fax header sheet as a promotional tool. Think what campaign, service or other message you could promote with a short and simple message added to your fax header sheet. Big impact for no cost.

weeks is the optimum time for a hoarding advert to be displayed; awareness peaks on the tenth day and then declines. Each poster site has an OSCAR (Outdoor Site Classification and Audience Research) which is an individual score based on traffic flow past the site, position of the board and so on. An OSCAR of 89 (about average) means that the poster is passed by around 89,000 people each week. Motorists seeing your poster have around seven seconds to take it in, so it must be big, bold and very simple.

I is for ...

Inserts – Inserted leaflets in magazines and journals are a cheaper method of distribution than direct mail.

J is for ...

Junk mail – This is the derogatory term for direct mail. You can read more about using direct mail to good effect in Chapter 10.

K is for ...

Key rings – Many charities produce key rings featuring their logo or promotional message. They are useful, cheap to produce, can be sold to recoup the cost, and have a long shelf-life.

L is for ...

LED displays – Some public places such as swimming pools and sports centres offer an advertising service via large LED displays, which flash your message on-screen. It is a cheap and easy way to advertise.

Leaflets

Few organisations are without a promotional leaflet of some sort. For such an important publicity item, the leaflet is frequently given inadequate attention during its preparation. Remember that your leaflets are all-important; they may be the only contact people will have with your charity, so they must be professional and appealing. That's not to say that they ought to be glossy, simply that they should be well written, carefully thought through, and presented in a way that makes them easy to read and attractive to look at. Producing such a leaflet requires investment of time and money. But as with all good investments, there is a pay-off in the end. By spending on an effective leaflet, you hope to improve your chances of donors giving, of individuals using your service, or of people joining your campaign.

THE BETTER LEAFLET CHECKLIST

- ☑ Plan the leaflet before you write it.
- ☑ Establish the aim – is it to persuade, to educate, or to inform?
- ☑ Use clear, plain language.
- ☑ Make it eye-catching.
- ☑ Make it simple – two or three clear messages rather than lots of complex ideas.
- ☑ Break up the text and use illustrations where appropriate.

M is for ...

Meeting rooms – Your meeting rooms should display your promotional material so that visitors can see it and be influenced by it. So should your reception.

N is for ...

Notice boards – Every organisation has one, people do look at them, so get your promotional message up there on notice boards – your own and other organisations'.

Newsletters and Magazines

Regard your newsletter as more than just an information vehicle. It's also an excellent marketing tool. Use it to inform, but also to 'sell' a particular message, to ask for help or donations, to reach out to a particular group with a plea, and to present your image. A campaigning charity might wish to use its newsletter to encourage supporters to keep up their support and perhaps even extend it, to encourage new members to get involved, to educate so that supporters are knowledgeable about the issue, and perhaps even to ask for campaign funds. Naturally there would also be news in the form of campaign progress, updates and achievements.

A fundraising charity might use its newsletter to showcase innovative fundraising initiatives, to suggest ideas for raising money, to thank those who have given, to show how the money has been spent, and to outline the continuing need for more money.

So remember, use your newsletters to promote your new products and services, to raise funds and awareness, and to attract, build and maintain support.

THE BETTER NEWSLETTER CHECKLIST

- ☑ Make your cover page really attractive, to encourage readers to pick up the newsletter and delve inside.

- ☑ Include a list of contents on the front page, again to entice readers inside.

- ☑ Have regular features, such as 'focus on fundraising', 'campaign update' and 'members' news'. This will give your newsletter a familiar feel, which busy readers will appreciate.

- ☑ Edit contributions; most will benefit from it.

- ☑ Use articles of different lengths and remember to include lots of snippets.

O is for ...

Outlets – Use other organisations' outlets (shops, offices, drop-in centres, etc.) as opportunities to promote yourself. Stage exhibitions or displays, or simply leave posters and leaflets.

Open Days

Although open days can provide an effective way of promoting your organisation or its services, many end up a flop, with staff outnumbering visitors and little or nothing to see or do. At such

TRUE STORY   Getting it Right

The National Asthma Campaign won an Institute of Public Relations' award for its membership magazine. The charity uses its magazine in a clever, strategic way. It is used as a mailing system for fundraising activities, a source of advertising revenue, and an opportunity to survey reader attitudes in order to inform the campaigning arm of the charity. Readers receive an annual questionnaire and their comments help shape the content and format of the magazine. By taking readers' views into account, a readership survey showed that 80 per cent of respondents read the magazine in its entirety. Can you match that?

occasions, visitors shuffle about nervously, politely excuse themselves, and rush away vowing never to return. If that's what happens at your open days, you are defeating the object and
damaging your reputation.

THE SUCCESSFUL OPEN DAY CHECKLIST

- ☑ Be clear on why you are having an open day and what you want to achieve.
- ☑ Identify who you want to attend and invite only the right target audience.
- ☑ Offer something to visitors to make their attendance worthwhile.
- ☑ Work out what you want them to go away with (information, for example, or a better understanding of your work).
- ☑ Ensure an appropriate staff/visitor ratio.
- ☑ Follow-up new contacts after the event.

P is for ...

Pay and display car parking tickets – In many towns and cities
you can advertise on the back of these.

Posters – Whether you get them properly printed or make your
own, you can reach a lot of people for very little money with a
poster.

Post Office franks – If you don't have your own franking
machine, you can still get your message across by getting the Post
Office to frank other people's letters with your logo.

Programmes – When exhibiting at a conference you can often
place an advert in the conference programme. Other types of programme may also be available for charity advertising, such as the-
atre programmes. They can be effective in reaching decision-
makers and wealthy donors.

Postcards

Most trendy cafés and restaurants in major UK cities have postcard dispensers. Customers can pick up attractive and free postcards, while organisations and companies can benefit from an
affordable promotional option. The leading name in postcard
promotions is London Cardguide, who invented the idea.

Many charities use postcards to promote awareness events,
such as World AIDS Day, local and national campaigns, and

Friends of the Earth produced a postcard that read on the front: 'You take my breath away. Any chance of getting it back?' On the reverse was the message: 'Air pollution kills up to 24,000 people every year. If you care about me and my family, please do more to reduce traffic and cut air pollution. Then we can all breathe a little easier.' The card was addressed to the prime minister, Tony Blair. This was a clever way of getting an important message across to the British public and providing them with an easy way to take action and register their displeasure, while simultaneously showing the government the strength of feeling about air pollution.

health promotion messages. Household names, such as Oxfam and Action Aid, and less well-known charities like Azafady – Working for Madagascar, have made clever use of this method.

Postcards are a good way of reaching ABC1 consumers aged 20–45 years. Cards are restocked at least three times a week for a month. At the end of this period you receive a report indicating how well your card has performed.

Q is for ...

Questionnaires – Do not conduct a questionnaire survey merely as a way of promoting your organisation, but remember that questionnaires can serve the dual purpose of collecting useful information while at the same time helping you promote your name and your aims.

R is for ...

Railways – Many different advertising opportunities are offered at railways and on Railtrack land. Collectively this form of advertising is known as 'transport advertising' (see below).

Reports

When charities publish reports, they are usually on serious subjects. That does not mean that they must be presented in a dull way or written in impenetrable language. Make reports readable and use them to market your organisation and its beliefs. A report is a 'selling' document; it should sell its findings in order to promote a cause, attract funding, generate interest or make news.

Roadshows

Many charities hit the road with their promotional message. It is not a cheap or easy way to promote your message, but it can be effective, provided you cost the whole exercise very carefully to ensure that the benefits outweigh the costs, and you set clear objectives and design your roadshows around meeting these. Depending on your roadshow – who it is aimed at, where it will go, how long it will last and what materials you already have – you may need to produce promotional literature and exhibition boards, as well are hiring a caravan.

S is for ...

Sandwich boards – These have novelty value and are a cheap way of promoting an event – providing you can find enough amenable volunteers to pound the pavements!

Stickers – Once stuck, stickers have great staying power so your message remains on view for a long time, thus increasing the number of opportunities for it to be seen and read. Don't be anti-social about where you stick them.

Stationery – Your organisation's letterhead, compliments slips and other stationery offer a good opportunity to promote an important message. If your organisation does not have a strapline (a short, clever and descriptive statement of purpose – the World Cancer Research Fund's is 'Stopping cancer before it starts') why not devise one and use it on your stationery to explain your work or promote a cause.

T is for ...

Taxis – Taxi cabs can display adverts, both inside and outside the cabs. Some are also fitted with leaflet dispensers.

Talks and seminars – How better to promote your work than face-to-face? Talks and seminars let you reach out to an already interested audience. Organisations are often asked to present a talk or workshop, and this provides you with a promotional platform. But don't just be reactive; try to get yourself invited to events to talk, and make this part of your promotional strategy. Also, organise your own events as part of your promotional work.

Transport advertising – This covers everything from adverts inside and outside buses (see separate section below) to posters on the London Underground, in lifts, escalators, and trains. The benefit of this method is that you reach an audience that is bored, often stationary, and in need of an interesting diversion, making transport advertising potentially very effective.

U is for ...

Umbrellas – Golfing umbrellas were once synonymous with corporate entertainment, but many charities have since started to produce promotional items of this sort. Unlike those produced by companies, charity umbrellas are usually produced for sale, not as give-aways.

V is for ...

Vehicles – Use your organisation's cars and minibuses as mobile adverts. Also produce car stickers so others can display your message when on the move.

Video – Although expensive, video can be a powerful way of getting your message across in a highly visual and digestible way.

Visors – Visors, baseball caps and other promotional clothing items are available from many different companies at quite reasonable prices. They can be personalised with your logo and message.

W is for ...

Windows – Many charities work from shop front premises; learn a trick from the big department stores and arrange attractive promotional displays aimed at stopping passers-by in their tracks and getting them to peek in. You will need more than a collection of yellowed press cuttings, dog-eared publications and decomposing bluebottles to achieve this!

X is for ...

Xtra curricula work – Your own staff can be living, breathing advertisements for your organisation. What they say about your charity 'after hours' will have a significant bearing on your reputation.

Y is for ...

Yellow Pages – Most charities have an entry in Yellow Pages. If you plan to have more then just a lineage ad, think carefully about its design and content. When going to the expense of paying for a display advert, take care to maximise your return. Look under 'Charities' in the Yellow Pages for examples of what other charities do.

tip

Never overlook the obvious when it comes to promotion. A sign outside your office is a cheap and effective way of promoting yourself, particularly if you are on a busy street. Remember to check about planning permission.

TRUE STORY   Getting it Right

The small charity The Action Group has an excellent Yellow Pages ad. In an attractively laid out ad measuring just 6 × 6 cm it manages to include its contact details; explain what it does (helping children and adults with learning disabilities and their carers); welcome donations; ask for bric-a-brac and quality furniture; and offer a free house-clearance service.

Year Planners – A number of voluntary organisations produce year planners. They remain in use and on display for a whole year, giving them an excellent shelf-life. However, they will only be put on display if they are attractively produced.

Z is for ...

Zany gimmicks – Use your imagination to devise unusual gimmicks that help you promote an important message. When British Telecom cut the price of calls to America, it needed to publicise this to its target audience. As New York is known as the Big Apple, apples were used as the promotional vehicle. The price cut message was printed on small fruit labels, which were then stuck to apples. The apples were handed out to transatlantic travellers arriving at Heathrow. Baskets of apples were also delivered to leading US companies with offices in London. A photocall was staged to secure media coverage too. It was a very cost-effective and imaginative way of promoting a message.

Selecting the right tool

These chapters on promotional activity have presented a wide range of promotional opportunities. Which should you choose? There is no simple answer. It all depends on:

- What you hope to achieve.
- Your budget.

TRUE STORY   Getting it Right

When the charity CHILDREN 1ST launched ParentLine Scotland, a free and confidential helpline on parenting issues, the Scottish Co-op offered help in kind to promote the service. They publicised the helpline telephone number and opening hours on 1,000,000 milk cartons. A photocall featuring a giant milk carton further served to promote this important service.

- Who you are trying to reach (your target audience).
- Over what period of time you need to run a promotion.

You are unlikely to rely on just one method; usually a mix will be called for. Let's say you are opening a hostel for homeless people. To promote it you might choose to:

- Have an opening event and invite professionals likely to make referrals.
- Issue a news release and seek editorial and broadcast coverage locally and in relevant trade and professional publications.
- Send a news release to the publications likely to be read by homeless people, such as the *Big Issue*, and/or advertise there.
- Produce a leaflet on the service and leave copies at soup kitchens, in local authority housing departments and at housing association receptions, at Citizens' Advice Bureaux and other advice centres.
- Write to professionals who work with homeless people, informing them of the service.
- Get yourself listed on relevant databases and in relevant directories.
- Produce a poster advertising the service and display it in places homeless people visit, such as DSS offices, housing association offices, etc.

Select methods that are cost-effective and that will reach the target audience (in some cases, via an intermediary such as a homeless persons worker or a magazine advert).

TRUE STORY   Getting it Right

Some years ago the Health Education Authority needed an innovative way of publicising World AIDS Day to one of its key target groups – young gay and heterosexual men. This group is a light user of the news media, so another way had to be found to reach it with the health promotion message. Given that two-thirds of the millions of people with access to the Internet are male, and two-thirds are under the age of 34, this seemed the ideal vehicle. An attractive website was established (containing AIDS and HIV information), and a Red Ribbon screen saver was produced for downloading onto users' PCs – enabling the World AIDS Day logo to have a presence on people's desks well after the event. Thanks to careful targeting and the right choice of promotional vehicle, the event was a great success for the HEA, with 200,000 people visiting the site.

Sponsorship and cause-related marketing

INTRODUCTION

Not so long ago most large companies had a pot of money for doling out to good causes. The organisations that tended to benefit were the charities with which the chairman's or managing director's wife had a connection. Then, as now, men ran most companies, but some things have changed. In particular, the way that money is allocated to good causes has radically altered over the last few years. Straightforward, no-strings-attached donations have been replaced with a more rigorous and measured American import: 'cause-related marketing' (CRM).

Defining CRM

Basically, CRM involves a company forming a relationship with a good cause for mutual benefit. Although similar in many ways to old-style sponsorship, CRM is a bit more calculated. Few large companies now hand out money simply because a charity undertakes worthwhile work; they expect something back in return. Usually they seek a common link between themselves and the charity, one they can exploit and use to enhance their image or brand.

The organisation Business in the Community (BITC), which promotes CRM, defines it as 'a commercial activity by which businesses and charities or causes form a partnership with each other to market an image, product or service for mutual benefit'.

Here are some examples of CRM:

- Center Parcs, the climate-controlled holiday village, launched a 'flower power' programme in conjunction with a wild plant conservation charity. This involved opening three wild flower reserves for local endangered plants.

■ Andrex toilet tissue use a puppy as their mascot. To celebrate their 25th anniversary they issued a limited edition toy puppy, available through an on-pack promotion, and gave Guide Dogs for the Blind Association money for each toy bought. This raised over £263,000 for the charity.

■ STA Travel, the youth and student travel specialists, teamed up with the Terrance Higgins Trust to promote a safer sex campaign. They asked customers to donate £1 to the charity, in return for a comedy cassette and a booklet on safer sex for travellers.

■ Centrica (British Gas) launched a £5 million programme with Help the Aged to reduce fuel poverty and cut the number of older people dying from the cold. Customer research showed this to be a worthwhile cause for British Gas to support.

According to Business in the Community's CRM guidelines, there are key principles that must underlie any partnership or programme. These are: integrity; transparency; sincerity; mutual respect; partnership; and mutual benefit. BITC stresses the need for a CRM partnership to be approached by both sides (the businesses and the charity) with an open and honest attitude based on a moral and professional code of conduct.

When approaching a company with a sponsorship or CRM proposal, state clearly what the company will get from an association with your organisation. This may include:

■ their logo on your materials;
■ space in your newsletter or magazine for an advert or an article;
■ access to potential new customers;
■ positive media coverage;
■ good internal PR through employee fundraising;
■ the enhancement of their brand values through shared brand values such as, for example, family-friendliness or community empowerment.

While CRM sounds like a good idea, with winners all round, charities must be careful in selecting companies with whom they want an association. Housing and homelessness charity Shelter is highly professional in its approach to CRM. If, for example, discussing CRM initiatives with financial organisations such as banks, Shelter takes time to check that policies around, say, mortgages and repossession, are fair. It would reflect badly on a housing charity if one of its funders was gung-ho about evicting home-owners for small mortgage arrears. Even where charities take the greatest care in their selection of partner, relationships cannot be guaranteed to be problem-free. Amnesty International

TRUE STORY Getting it Right

When Midland Bank (now HSBC) reviewed its £1 million charitable budget, the Bank realised that it was seeing very little return on its charitable giving. Businesses now expect to see a pay-back on their investment, even on charitable donations. Midland decided to make a bigger impact by supporting a smaller number of charities in key fields. A short-list of charities chosen by Midland was invited to tender. Briefed by the Bank, they had five weeks to come up with ideas for specific projects to meet Midland's requirements before pitching for the business. One of Midland's principal aims was to enhance its reputation as a responsible corporate citizen. After the three-year partnership with the successful charities ended, Midland evaluated performance and concluded that all of its objectives had been achieved and that the charities had benefited.

UK entered into a CRM partnership with insurance giant CGU. When the pressure group discovered that CGU had a small share-holding in an arms manufacturer, constructive dialogue followed. Now Amnesty:

- Conducts ethical screening.
- Asks partners to sign ethical declarations.
- Reviews partners' shareholding portfolios annually.

Consider whether there are any requests or requirements that you should make of your potential CRM partners. Make sure that you have a written agreement specifying any conditions, explaining how the partnership will work, how it will be managed and what measures will be used to evaluate success.

> **tip**
>
> See if a local large company will offer you support in kind by seconding someone from their marketing team to provide free marketing advice.

Sponsorship

Few charities have budgets large enough to do all the promotional work they would like. Often you can attract sponsorship for key pieces of marketing literature, such as fundraising materials, supporters' newsletters or your annual review. Getting such materials sponsored is attractive on two fronts. First, it frees money to spend elsewhere. Second, it can show supporters that you are spending your (or their!) money wisely. Supporters sometimes feel uneasy about charities spending their resources on marketing materials. If such literature is sponsored, supporters know that they cost the charity little or nothing.

> **tip**
>
> Make use of personal contacts within companies when seeking sponsorship. Often it's who you know that really matters.

Seeking Sponsorship

Unless you already have both a high profile and a good reputation, it can be really difficult to find a sponsor for your organisation. It is generally easier to secure project sponsorship – where a one-off campaign, publication or event is sponsored – than to attract sponsorship for your organisation as a whole. Some organisations have become so good at attracting sponsorship that they are in the enviable position of being able to ask companies to submit bids, with the highest bidder getting to associate themselves with the organisation. The public sector body Scottish Enterprise does this for its annual report, and has no difficulty in attracting a list of leading companies eager to pay for the privilege. In return they get a page of the report dedicated to them.

It is extremely unlikely that your charity will be so fortunate. Companies receive letters daily asking for money. Some receive thousands each year, with most only getting a standard 'thanks, but no thanks' reply. To increase your chances of successful sponsorship, take the following steps:

Ten Steps to Successful Sponsorship

1 Do your homework – find out who gives what to whom.
2 Approach only those organisations likely to consider supporting you – those with an established interest in the sort of work you do; those who have sponsored you, or a similar charity, in the past; or those with an obvious link (a car manufacturer and a road safety campaign, or a bra retailer and a breast cancer charity, for example).
3 Phone and get the name of the person to write to – letters to a named individual are more likely to reach the right person and they show that you have taken the care and trouble to find out. Don't send unnamed letters and run the risk of your correspondence getting lost in the bureaucracy of a large organisation.
4 Don't send the same letter to everyone – personalised letters stand a better chance of success.
5 Keep your letter brief and persuasive.
6 Explain what's in it for the company – what they would get out of it and how it would enhance their image and help them meet their business objectives.
7 Include any necessary background material, including your annual report.
8 If possible, time your approach for just before the sponsorship budget is allocated.
9 If you have missed this date, try again in the run-up to the year end, when many companies are distributing left-over money from their sponsorship budget.
10 If you are rejected, there is nothing to lose in politely contacting the company to find out why and to learn any lessons you can that will enable you to do better next time.

tip

The Hollis Sponsorship and Donations Yearbook contains an A–Z of the UK's top sponsoring and donating companies, listing names and addresses of companies, the name and job title of the person to contact, their sponsorship budgets, details of who they sponsor, and information on their donations policy. It is also used by companies looking for a charity to sponsor, so you might want to consider placing an entry (for a fee). Consult Hollis at large reference libraries, or buy a copy (a discounted rate is available for not-for-profits).

Setting up sponsorship deals is hard work and very time-consuming. You will get lots of rejections along the way, but don't lose heart or give up. Most good projects do, in the end, get support, but it does take stamina and a thick skin.

Look for ways to use sponsorship to support your marketing activity. Sponsor and be sponsored.

Sponsoring Others

If your charitable objects allow it, sponsoring another body may provide a way of positioning your charity and promoting your name. You could perhaps sponsor a local school football team in order to build awareness in the community. Many voluntary organisations do this. Or you could consider sponsoring an important conference or research report. By being associated with something significant, high-profile or prestigious, you can enjoy both reflected glory and positive media coverage.

Remember that if you plan to use sponsorship as part of your marketing strategy, you should ensure that your chosen project helps you meet your marketing aims. There's probably no point in sponsoring a children's painting competition at a village school if you are a large, national, London-based charity working with refugees. Why? Because however worthwhile the cause you are sponsoring, there needs to be something in it for you. Be clear from the outset about what you are getting out of it. Are you going to gain by association? Will it help you position your organisation? Find out before you commit yourself.

TRUE STORY   Getting it Right

Sponsors expect something in return for their sponsorship. RSPB has a corporate membership scheme which rewards supporters in various ways, such as by offering discounted advertising space in its Birds magazine. What can you offer that is tangible?

Public relations

INTRODUCTION

There is considerable confusion about the difference between public relations (PR) and marketing. Marketing focuses on the four Ps – products (or services) and their price, place (distribution) and promotion. PR is often regarded as the fifth P of the marketing mix, standing for perception. PR is about relationships and reputation, both of which help shape people's perceptions of an organisation. If donors have a poor perception of a charity, they are unlikely to give to it, regardless of the excellent work the charity may undertake. Without effective PR to build a good reputation, effective marketing cannot take place.

PR is about the management of reputation, yet it has done a poor job of managing its own reputation. As a result, PR is too often regarded as little more than 'spin-doctoring'. PR practitioners are seen as experts in putting a gloss on the unattractive, peddling false claims, hyping achievement, whitewashing or concealing mistakes and shortcomings. For sure, some people behave in this way and claim to be in the business of PR. Their actions have led to many worthwhile PR activities being dismissively branded mere 'PR stunts'. Such people do PR a great disservice.

PR is not simply about building a good image; it is about earning a well-deserved reputation. Imagine a building with a superb neoclassical façade. Now picture yourself walking in through the impressive and imposing doorway to find yourself inside a structure riddled with rot, dripping with damp, cracking, collapsing and decaying. What a shock to discover that the breathtakingly beautiful exterior conceals an interior straight from the set of a Hammer House of Horror movie! 'Image' can be likened to the outside of a building, the part that is on show to the casual observer. Reputation is what goes on inside, the real story. Effective PR can help you to present something that is as good on the inside as it looks from the outside. It can help you build an image with substance.

Defining PR

The Institute of Public Relations is the professional body representing people who work in the industry. It defines PR as: 'the planned and sustained effort to establish and maintain goodwill and mutual understanding between an organisation and its publics.'

Many organisations undertake PR activity as a panic reaction to a crisis – negative media coverage, a service disaster or some other mishap. Yet as the definition states, PR must be a planned and sustained activity, an integral part of how you run your organisation. PR as a one-off activity or as a knee-jerk reaction will fail. Planned and sustained PR will succeed; it may even help minimise the adverse effects of disaster on your image.

PR is fundamentally about understanding your 'publics' or audiences (service-users, donors, staff and others) and ensuring that they understand your organisation. Helping them understand you involves identifying key messages to promote to them. Effective PR is targeted, with different audiences receiving different messages.

Establishing a good reputation

Every organisation wants to be favourably perceived. Good perceptions are won by hard work. To be seen to be excellent, you will truly need to be excellent. The positive identity that you promote, and the image that people perceive, should coincide. Where they do not, you have an image gap. This is where people's experience of your charity falls short of their expectations, leading to disillusionment, disappointment and ill will towards your organisation.

To ensure that you do not disappoint, always aim to exceed expectations. If you say that your service is good, make sure it is excellent. If you promise to dispatch charity Christmas cards in fourteen days, try to dispatch them in just seven.

Organisations are made up of real people. Sadly your staff can sometimes let you down and damage your hard-won reputation. Rude or unhelpful personnel cause huge damage to organisations. Encourage staff to adopt a positive, 'can do' approach to

TRUE STORY   Getting it Wrong

I recall a meal recently where the food was excellent, but the service surly. My abiding memory is not of the good food but of the bad service. Now, rather than returning to the restaurant to sample other equally delightful offerings from the menu, I will avoid it (and tell my friends to do likewise) because I resent such rude behaviour.

their work. Provide customer care training. Set standards for staff to meet, monitor their performance and reward staff who are consistently helpful.

Look at every area of your organisation and assess the impact that it has on your reputation. Out-of-date fact sheets, leaflets littered with typing errors, emails that go unanswered or phone calls that go unreturned – all of these things have a negative effect on your image. People judge organisations by little things like this. They might conclude that if you can't be bothered to check leaflets for typos, perhaps your service is shoddy too.

Tackling Image Shortcomings

Where is your image letting you down? Examine everything and identify any shortcomings. Among other things look at:

- Your premises – reception, meeting rooms, any houses, clinics or centres you run.
- Your publicity, information and fundraising material – leaflets, videos, posters, annual report, exhibition boards, etc. (Look at the wording, photos and other images, design, print or production quality and so on.)
- Your website – content, design and usability.
- Your internal communication – the way you communicate with staff and volunteers, including newsletters, memos and briefings.
- External communication – the way letters are written, the way the phone is answered, etc.
- Your staff – are they friendly, professional, warm and helpful?
- Your answer machine message – is it friendly and informative?
- Signage in your premises – is it helpful, welcoming and friendly?
- Notice boards – are they up-to-date and relevant?

Ask key audiences for their comments too. What do they consider to be your weaknesses? What improvements would they like to see? Now draw up a programme of action to tackle weak areas. Decide what specifically you need to do to make improvements. If the list is very long, you may need to prioritise. Assign each activity to a named person who will ensure that improvements are implemented. Agree both a start and a completion date for each item on your list. Where necessary, set a budget. Check on implementation. Remember to look at the fundamentals, such as the services you run, as well as the more visible things. Before long you will see a big improvement in your organisation.

THE GOOD REPUTATION CHECKLIST

☑ Always exceed expectations.

☑ Go that extra mile to be helpful.

☑ Ensure all staff have a 'can do' attitude.

☑ Act professionally at all times.

☑ Aim for excellence in all that you do.

☑ Never accept second best.

PR planning

All PR activity should be part of a planned programme. Set PR objectives and devise a series of timetabled activities to help you achieve your objectives. For example, one of your objectives might be:

Objective:	To improve awareness of our service among professionals who come into contact with young people
Activity:	■ Produce a leaflet aimed at professionals.
	■ Send a mailing to all secondary school teachers in our catchment area.
	■ Send a mailing to all youth workers covering our catchment area.
	■ Send a mailing to all social workers in our area.
	■ Organise an open day and invite teachers, youth and social workers.
	■ Send a news release to our target professional press publicising our drive to promote the service via teachers, youth and social workers.
	■ Book a stand and have a display at the annual local youth workers' conference.

Organise activities into chronological order, with a lead name alongside each. Remember to review your objectives periodically and to monitor success.

Internal communication

Too often PR is seen as external communication, while communication with staff and volunteers is neglected. For any organisation to operate effectively and efficiently, staff must be knowledgeable and informed. Internal communication has a key role in keeping staff in the know, making them feel motivated and ensuring that they are happy. Good internal communication can help reduce stress, absenteeism and staff turnover. It can improve employee relations and output. Contented staff present a good image externally.

All organisations need to communicate effectively, yet some small organisations wrongly believe that internal communication is only relevant for big charities. Often it is in small organisations that communication is at its worst. No formal structures exist, making the spread of relevant information at best haphazard. In such organisations rumour can be rife. In the absence of real information, it's all staff have to rely on.

Find out what staff think about the effectiveness or otherwise of communication within your organisation. Organise focus groups or send staff a questionnaire seeking feedback. Identify where the blockages are and do something about it. Establish failsafe systems for ensuring that staff are told what they need and want to know. Use newsletters, memos, notice boards, email, staff meetings and other methods to keep everyone in the picture.

Coping in a crisis

Reputations are established over many years, yet they can be lost in a split second. PR has a role in identifying reputation-damaging events before they occur, thus averting crisis. Look at all areas of your organisation and paint a worst-case scenario. What could go wrong? Where are your vulnerabilities? Is there anything your organisation can do to prevent a crisis from occurring, or to minimise the likelihood? What action can you take and should you take?

Disaster can come in many forms. Here are a few examples which have affected charities:

- Fraud and theft – for example, fundraisers pocketing some of the money they have collected.
- Dangerous products – for example, a toy in your charity Christmas catalogue being a choking hazard and needing to be recalled.
- Boycotts – customers threatening to boycott your charity shops because it is discovered that some of your overseas goods are made using child labour.

- Gaffes – such as your chairperson making a rude or insensitive remark which is overhead and reported by a journalist.
- Accidents – such as a tenant with learning disabilities being fatally injured in a preventable accident in your supported accommodation.

Crises don't take time off. They may happen at any time – day or night, at the weekend or even on Christmas Day. Although they often strike without warning, good planning and pre-emptive action can minimise their likelihood. In some of the examples given above, it is easy to see how effective checks, systems, practices and procedures could have helped prevent them from happening in the first place. Yet however good your planning, no organisation can guarantee that a crisis will never occur. Where it does, a swift, effective, positive, open and honest response is vital in limiting damage to reputation. Never be defensive or aggressive.

In the aftermath of a crisis, rebuilding reputation and restoring confidence are paramount. Find out what went wrong, learn from mistakes and take action to ensure it will never happen again. Put things right and tell people what you have done to rectify matters.

Work hard on your organisation's reputation because, if it is lost, you may lose everything else with it.

Developing a
marketing strategy

INTRODUCTION

By now you will be aware that marketing is multifaceted. It is not simply about selling your services. To be effective at marketing you need to take a systematic and sustained approach. The marketing of your own organisation cannot be done in an *ad hoc* or casual way – a bit of marketing here, and a bit there. Marketing is an integrated approach, a way of working, and it must be planned and carried out in an organised way. You must also keep your marketing under review, and evaluate success (and failure) as part of that review. To work in this kind of planned way you need to have a clear strategy – a marketing strategy.

There is no simple way of developing a marketing strategy for your organisation, and there are no simple off-the-shelf answers or short-cuts. Marketing is time-consuming and requires long-term commitment. It is up to you to find an approach to developing a marketing strategy that suits your kind of organisation. You may like to take the approach set out below and to amend it to your own situation.

Establishing a marketing team

The best way of getting started with marketing is to involve others. Pull together a team comprising various 'stakeholders' in your organisation – committee members, staff, volunteers and others. This is your marketing team and they will be responsible for shaping your marketing strategy. The strength of the group is that each member will have a different viewpoint. Its many perspectives will ensure that your ideas are questioned and challenged.

It is important that your team understands its role – and understands exactly what marketing is about. You will probably need to hold an information and discussion seminar to make sure that you are all starting from the same knowledge base, with a clear understanding of marketing and its benefits for your organisation.

Reviewing the current situation

Begin by examining where your charity is just now. Carry out a review of what the current position is. This involves looking critically and objectively at how you operate, why you take the decisions you do, what influences your work. You need to look at your market, your products, your customers and your promotional work. In short you are aiming for an understanding of how you currently work and the factors in your operating environment that affect that work.

Only after you have done all this can you focus on where you want to go and on what sort of an organisation you would like to be in, say, five years' time. This is where your objectives come in. The way you get there is your strategy.

Your market

You operate within a market, and you need to understand that market if you are to be successful in it. In looking at your market you need to consider:

- The external variables over which you have no control (which political party is in power, locally or nationally, for example).
- The internal variables over which you have complete control (the set up/structure of your organisation, for example).

This will enable you to have a clear picture of the factors you can influence, and those which will inevitably limit you.

SWOT analysis

It is useful at this stage to carry out a 'SWOT analysis'. SWOT is an acronym, which stands for:

- **Strengths** – What are you good at as an organisation? What do you do better than others?
- **Weaknesses** – What are you poor at? Where is there room for improvement?
- **Opportunities** – What opportunities are there for you externally, either now or in the future?

■ **Threats** – What threats exist externally, now or in the future? Who are your competitors and what threats do they pose?

As part of your strategy you will need to make assumptions about the future market, including the actions of your competitors. You will need to look at how you can build upon your strengths, strengthen your weak areas, take action to minimise threats and ensure that you grasp opportunities.

Your customers

In considering your customers start by listing who they are. Next examine what they want from you. Finally, take a realistic look at what you can offer. Remember that meeting customer needs may involve changing your organisation so that it is better suited to meeting those needs (in other words, altering internal variables) as well as recognising the constraints imposed by external variables over which you have no control, and working to provide the best that you can given these factors.

Looking in turn at each customer type, what are their three main needs? Here's an example: the main needs of the social work department may be to find an organisation that can provide:

1 A professional and high quality community care service.
2 A service that is cost-effective, but does not compromise on quality.
3 A service that is accountable, open and involves residents and relatives.

Another example – the main needs of shoppers in a charity shop may be:

1 To shop in a bright and cheerful place – they do not want dank and smelly shops they are embarrassed to be seen in.
2 To find a good choice of clean, fashionable clothes for all the family.
3 To be able to afford the prices.

You can only begin to meet needs once you understand what those needs are. You will probably find in going back to basics – looking at what your customers actually need, as opposed to what you give them – that research may be required. You may want to ask your customers what they would like from you, what their needs and priorities are. Chapter 5 will help guide you through the research maze.

You must understand what is really important to your customers when they buy. For example, is there a rule that says that the council will buy care services only from organisations where staff have a social work qualification? If so, there is no point in developing such services unless you can fulfil this need from your main customer. If your customers buy from your mail order catalogue because doing so fulfils an emotional need, you need to recognise this and reflect this need in the copy and design of your future catalogues.

Implementing your objectives

Getting started is always the hardest bit. Once you have reviewed where you are now, and worked out where you would like to be, draw up some short-term (perhaps covering the following twelve months) and some long-term (up to five years ahead) objectives. Your objectives should state very clearly what you hope to achieve.

Having done all this, you are ready to work on your strategy – in other words, on the details of how you will achieve your objectives. Draw on the ideas presented in the previous chapters to help you meet your objectives. Look at your marketing mix. See how much time and effort need to be put into modifying your products. How much money can you afford to promote them? Who are you promoting them to and how? Don't forget 'place' and 'price'. Consider all the elements of marketing and see how each one may have a role in helping you do what you do better.

Evaluation

Evaluation is a crucial area of marketing and your marketing strategy should explain how this will be done. Traditional measures in business/commerce have included measurables such as:

- increased sales;
- growth in profits;

TRUE STORY Getting it Right

All organisations need a clear strategy that is well thought out and thoroughly researched. In the Christmas period before the launch of Great Ormond Street's 'Wishing Well' Appeal, the charity was offered a £1 million fundraising campaign by a major newspaper. Many charities would jump at such an offer, but the Wishing Well Appeal had a clear marketing and fundraising strategy into which the offer simply did not fit. The organisers were concerned that if they accepted, the public would say: 'Oh, we gave to that last year.' Eventually the Appeal raised £54 million – £24 million more than the target.

- reduced costs;
- advertising effectiveness.

Some of these measures are very useful to voluntary organisations, such as advertising effectiveness (it would be wrong of a charity to waste donors' money on ineffective advertising). Some are not. For voluntary organisations there is a whole set of other measures that are often a great deal more important than profit:

- **Social need** – It might be very expensive to run a free condom service for prostitutes, and a commercial organisation interested only in profit would be unable to operate it if their bottom line is the balance sheet. However, the price of not running such a service might prove too costly in social terms, leading to the spread of HIV/AIDS among adults, the birth of HIV+ babies, and the transmission of a variety of sexual diseases.
- **Social benefits** – The operation of a service to rehabilitate joy riders and to encourage them not to re-offend may not be profitable in the conventional financial sense, although the benefit to society has an immense value. Often there is a cost to society of not running a service.

'Selling' marketing to colleagues

Developing a marketing strategy is only half of your task. The other half involves 'selling' the concept of marketing to others within your organisation. If you do not do this, all your hard work on the strategy may be wasted. For marketing to work, you need a marketing organisation, and that involves bringing everyone on board. But how?

Many people are very sceptical when it comes to marketing. There are probably people in your organisation who do not understand properly what it is, and may believe that your charity is wrong to invest in something that may appear an expensive luxury. If you are to be a successful service-led charity, it is important that others in the organisation understand what marketing is and why it is so important to you. They need to take it seriously, contribute to the marketing debate and support marketing initiatives. To bring about an attitude like this in your organisation, you will have to work hard and steadily. You cannot expect others to jump up and down with excitement; you must foster that enthusiasm. In short you must 'sell' the idea of marketing within your charity.

How you set about this will depend on:

- the size of your organisation;
- the age of your organisation;
- the kind of people involved in your organisation;

- the amount of marketing-type activity you have undertaken in the past;
- past marketing successes.

Clearly, it is an easier task 'selling' marketing to a small, young organisation with go-ahead people than to a large, traditional, paternalistic and bureaucratic dinosaur of a charity!

THE SELLING MARKETING TO COLLEAGUES CHECKLIST

☑ Explain to everyone what marketing is and why it is important.

☑ Involve a representative group (of staff, volunteers, committee members, etc.) in developing the marketing strategy.

☑ Ensure that the main points of the strategy are communicated to others within the organisation.

☑ Help everyone to see their role in marketing, regardless of their job.

When it comes to explaining what marketing is, employ the marketing techniques in this book to get the message across. This might include an article in the staff newsletter, a talk at a staff meeting, a roadshow (in larger, multi-locationed organisations) or simply a memo to all staff. The same methods can be used to communicate the final strategy, and you may also wish to produce a short leaflet outlining the key points and indicating what everyone's role is in being a marketing-led organisation.

The key points you need to get across to colleagues will be:

- Marketing is not selling.
- Marketing involves being needs-led, not resource-driven. In other words, a marketing approach is entirely in harmony with what most charities exist for: meeting need.
- Marketing is about listening to users and taking action on their views in order to provide the services that are required.

When put across like this, it will be hard for staff not to see marketing's relevance. You can explain to doubters that marketing is needed because:

- Your service-users are generally not in the privileged position of being able to shop around for the service that suits. It is therefore all the more important that you take the time to find out exactly what your users require. Marketing techniques can help you find out what users want.
- You probably have far more 'customers' than you can cope with. In a situation where demand outstrips supply (for example, for affordable housing, cheap nursery provision, Third

tip

Be careful not to get technical when talking about marketing; it is a sure-fire way of switching colleagues off. If you want to sell the notion of marketing, use plain language and arguments that people can relate to and understand.

World aid, etc.) it is easier for voluntary organisations to deliver a second-rate service. A marketing-led approach will ensure that you avoid this and strive for excellence.

■ Limited resources and tight budgets are common in voluntary organisations, and this can lead to charities developing services and products that meet the budget rather than satisfy the need. Marketing-led organisations do not fall into the trap of being resource-driven (though naturally they have to work within their budgets).

Keep Working at it

Persuading colleagues of the value of marketing is not a one-off activity; you need to keep marketing awareness alive in your organisation. So having initially convinced everyone that marketing is a good and necessary activity, you need to feed their interest. Share marketing successes with staff, get them to contribute ideas and feedback, and encourage people to think marketing at every turn. Do all this and you will have a truly marketing-led organisation that attracts the necessary funding to deliver the quality services that your users need and want. And that is, after all, what you were set up to do!

A plain English guide to marketing jargon

Marketing jargon can be impenetrable to the outsider. The aim of this glossary is to give you a reference point. If you are reading other marketing books (see Appendix B for reading list), you can refer to this user-friendly definition of terms to help you. Many of the terms and concepts outlined below are dealt with in more detail in the relevant chapters of this book.

A

Above the Line

This is an advertising term which refers to paid-for advertising using press, radio, TV, cinema and billboards.

ACORN

This acronym stands for A Classification Of Residential Neighbourhoods. It classifies people and households according the type of neighbourhood they live in. People in a particular neighbourhood will probably share similar lifestyles, social characteristics and behaviour. There are 38 different neighbourhood types and eleven different 'family group classifications'. Using the information it is possible to produce mailing lists that will enable you to target very precisely so that you can reach only 'high-status, non-family' areas, or 'unmodernised terraced houses with old people'. There is a similar system called MOSAIC.

Active Customer/Member/Subscriber

Generally an active customer is one who has purchased from you, joined your organisation or sent for information from you within the last twelve months. Many charities keep lists of active customers so that they can mail them during fundraising appeals.

Advertising Rate Card

Newspaper and magazine advertising departments produce a rate card which sets out what an advertisement costs according to where it is in the publication, its size, whether it is colour or black and white, etc. It also contains production information such as deadlines and the form in which you need to submit your advert.

Advertorial

A paid-for advert that is laid out to look like editorial.

B

Below the Line

This refers to advertising and promotion via media other than 'above the line' media – such as direct mail, exhibitions, promotional brochures and give-aways (such as promotional pens, balloons and key rings).

BRAD (British Rate And Data)

This monthly publication (which can be consulted at large reference libraries) sets out the advertising rates of a wide range of publications, from daily newspapers to women's and special interest magazines. It also contains circulation information (see below).

Branding

This is the way goods or services from one organisation or company are distinguished from those of another.

Broadcast Monitoring Companies

A number of companies specialise in monitoring radio and television output, and can ring you up to alert you that you have had a mention. They can also provide transcripts of programmes and video and audio tapes. They are expensive, but can be useful for the bigger charities.

C

Call-out

A designer's trick, where a short extract from the main text is repeated as a sub-head within the text, in order to draw attention to it.

Cause-related Marketing

A company with an image, product or service to sell, builds a relationship or partnership with a 'cause' or a number of 'causes' for mutual benefit. Cadbury's 'Strollerthon' – an annual, sponsored, mass-participation walk through London – is an example of this. Save the Children benefits from the cash raised from the event, while Cadbury's gets publicity, goodwill, a database of participants and a chance to give out product samples at the event.

Circulation

Circulation figures tell you how many people buy a particular publication. 'Readership' figures tell you how many people read a publication. Usually readership figures are higher than circulation ones; a newspaper or magazine will frequently be read by more than just the person who bought it.

Chief Reporter

As the name suggests, the chief reporter is more senior than other reporters and generally gets the best and most interesting assignments. They are usually more experienced than other reporters on the paper.

Classified Adverts or 'Smalls'

These are small adverts which comprise lines of text. There is no design element. They are usually charged by the line, so advertisers abbreviate their copy to fit as many words in per line.

Cold List

This direct mail term refers to a mailing list comprising people who have no relationship with your organisation. When people on the list respond to your mailing, they become 'warm prospects'.

Co-op Mailings

This is when two or more non-competitive organisations come together and have their information or promotional material inserted into the one mailing. By sharing the costs it is a cost-effective exercise.

Copy

The text in publicity material.

Correspondent

This is a specialist media reporter who is an expert in a particular field, such as health or education.

Cost per Conversion

You add together all the costs of a direct mail campaign and divide by the number of orders received/donations made/subscriptions taken out. This gives you your cost per conversion and it is a good way of working out whether your campaign has been a success in terms of the response it generated.

D

Demographics

This market research term relates to population characteristics such as age, sex and family size.

Display Adverts

These are creative adverts which have been professionally designed.

Diversification

This is a growth strategy which involves complete change. You develop new products and offer them to new markets, a risky strategy for charities and businesses alike.

Donor Profile

A donor profile paints a picture of the sort of person who supports your organisation – for example, middle-aged Christian *Guardian* readers with two incomes, grown-up children, living in the south of England and interested in the arts.

Door Drops

These are unaddressed mail packs or leaflets delivered to households by hand, not in the mail. Strictly speaking this is not direct mail, it is direct advertising.

DTP

This is short for desktop publishing, where artwork is produced on a computer using special software. DTP software is now widely and cheaply available, with many computers supplied with it as standard.

E

Early Bird

This is an incentive to encourage people to respond to your mailings promptly.

Editor

This is the top job on a newspaper. On larger papers it is generally a management job rather than a hands-on writing position, although the editor often writes a leader or comment column. On small papers and free papers, the editor can also be a reporter of sorts. The editor is responsible for the content, tone and style of a newspaper.

F

Facing Matter

This is when your advert is placed alongside editorial, rather than being buried in an advertising section surrounded by other adverts.

Friend of a Friend

This is when an existing supporter/donor/member sends in the name of a friend or relative who may be interested in receiving information from you. This technique is used a lot by commercial organisations, who offer incentives to people to get them to send in details of friends. It can sometimes be an effective way of building up a mailing list of interested people. Often it is known as MGM, or member get member.

Fulfilment

This is where you process an order or a request for information following a mailshot or advertising campaign.

G

Gone-aways

This is a term used to refer to mail returned by the Royal Mail to the sender because the intended recipient has gone away or the address is wrong or non-existent. Such mail is also known as 'returns'. Gone-aways are a waste of money: when you get one you must update/amend your mailing list accordingly.

GSM

Paper is referred to by designers and printers according to its weight. Typical notepaper is around 100 gsm, or grammes per square metre. Magazine covers are much heavier, weighing in at around 220 gsm.

I

Initial Caps

This is where a word is in lower case letters, but the first letter uses a capital, such as England or Denise.

ISP

Internet service provider.

J

Justified Text

Justified text produces lines of text of equal length. Unjustified text has a distinctive ragged or uneven right hand margin.

L

List Cleaning

Mailing lists need to be kept up to date if they are to be of any use. List cleaning involves correcting names and addresses, removing those who have moved away or those who have not responded to your mail within a designated period (for example, after four mailings or within one month).

M

Mailing House

You can arrange to have your direct mail addressed, collated and despatched by a mailing house.

Market Development

This is a growth strategy which involves taking your existing products, but promoting them to new target markets.

Market Penetration

This is a growth strategy where you take your existing products to your existing markets. Your aim is to capture a bigger share of this market, or to reach previously unreached potential customers.

Market Segmentation

To be effective you need to 'know your market'. That makes it sound as if you have just one market, made up of one type of person. It is important to recognise that not all markets are uniform. Most are made up of sub-groups or segments. You need to spot the segments in your market and identify what makes one different and distinct from another, and to tailor your approach for these distinct markets. For example, an examination of your donor base might reveal that it is made up of elderly people who leave legacies to your charity, so the style of copy and design for your legacy pack might be different from that for your payroll giving leaflet, which research tells you is most popular with younger people. Spotting the sub-groups in your market is called market segmentation. Your market might be segmented geographically (if you have clear regional differences, for example); demographically (sex, age, life-cycle or family size); socio-economically (income, occupation, social class, etc.); psychographically (in other words, according to the type of person who gives, their personality or lifestyle, for example); and/or behaviouristically (how often they give/buy from you, what they look for from you, etc.).

Marketing Mix

The term 'marketing mix' refers to the four Ps – product, price, place and promotion – and it is important to know which of the

Ps are the key influencing factors for your market. (See also Place, Price, Product, Promotion and Other Ps.)

Media Invitations

If you want to let the media know about an event, news conference or photocall, issue them with a media invitation setting out briefly what is happening, where, when and why.

Media Statement

If you are asked by the media to comment on something, or to answer questions on a particular issue, you might find that you are unable or unwilling to do an interview. By issuing a statement – a written response – you can avoid an interview while at the same time getting your point across.

Methodology

This is market research jargon for how you intend to get the information you need. For example, you may decide to use a postal questionnaire plus depth interviews with a sample of donors.

MGM

See Friend of a Friend.

MOSAIC

See ACORN.

N

News Conference

A news or press conferences is an event held specially for the media to brief them on an important issue, a new product or service, or something that is generally very newsworthy. If you can achieve the same effect simply by issuing a news release, do not go to the trouble of holding a news conference.

News Editor

The news editor selects the news, decides where in the paper it will appear and assigns reporters to follow up particular stories. News editors also work in radio and television.

News Releases

Sometimes referred to as 'press releases', they are stories written in newspaper style by PR people. Releases are issued by companies and organisations to the media in the hope of securing press or broadcast coverage for a story.

Niche Markets

A niche market is one that is small and specialist, for example skate-boarding computer whizz-kids. In business it can be very profitable to cater for niche markets, as they are generally not targeted by anyone else and therefore are crying out for products or services to meet their needs. Often they are prepared to pay handsomely, and with no competition the way is open for companies to make good profits. Many charities cater for niche markets. A charity providing a specialist service for fathers who have lost a child could be said to be catering for a niche. By dealing with something that does not affect a great many people, and by offering a service where currently there may be a gap, a case could be made to funders that you are meeting a very specialist need. If no one else is doing anything quite like you, you could stand a good chance of getting funds. On the other hand, pioneers often find it difficult to attract funding, and projects for minority groups can find it more difficult than those catering for a mass market. Equally, you are more vulnerable, as are businesses catering for niches. If something happens to your niche, or another player (competitor) appears, you could find that you have no other market to provide services to, or that your skills are so specialised that you cannot diversify.

Niche Products

A niche product is simply a product or service developed to meet the needs of a particular niche market (see above).

O

Other 'Ps'

In 1981 a further three Ps were added to the four Ps of the marketing mix: People (the attitude of staff, behaviour, training, commitment, etc.); Physical Evidence (the surroundings in which a service takes place, its furnishings and decor, noise levels, layout, etc.); and Process (policies, procedures, etc.). In 1994 a further P was suggested by charity marketing expert Ian Bruce: Philosophy. This refers to a charity's way of doing things, its beliefs and guiding principles. Norman Hart, Britain's first professor of PR, suggests that P for 'Perception' should be added to the classic four Ps.

P

Pantone Reference

This international system ensures that colours can be matched to exactly the right shade.

Photocalls

If you are organising an event and are seeking publicity for it, consider whether it has 'photo opportunity' potential. If so, set up a photocall, where you invite newspaper photographers (and possibly television, too) to attend at a certain time to take pictures. Invite them by issuing a media invitation (see Media Invitations) – sometimes also known as a photocall notice.

Picture Library

This is a commercial library containing thousands of photographs which cover every conceivable subject. You can borrow photos and use them, as long as you pay a fee and acknowledge the photographer or picture library in your credits. If you need a special picture, your designer should be able to track it down for you through a library.

Piggy Backs

A piggy back is when you enclose your literature in another organisation's existing mailing, for example by inserting a flier into another charity's newsletter. This is a cheaper way of doing a mailing. Charities can make money this way too, by offering a piggy back service in their own mailings.

Place

Place is the bridge that connects buyers and sellers. It ensures that the product and customer are brought together, thus creating an opportunity for the customer to buy. In conventional marketing 'place' refers to distribution – getting the products to the places where they can be available to consumers. If you make baked beans, you need a distribution system that enables you to get your tins out of the factory and into the shops where they will be sold. Clearly in manufacturing the 'place' P is a really important one; tins of baked beans stacked in a factory are of no use to anyone – they need to be placed where they can be bought. 'Place' when used to describe distribution is of use to some charities, for example those that make a product. But it also has a use, as a concept, to service-providers. Just as those making a product need to know how to get it to the customer, you too need to consider how to get the consumer to your service. Is your drop-in centre on a bus route, for example? For fundraisers, too, place is an issue, for they need to ensure that collecting tins are in the right places and that the distribution system operates to collect them up again. Fundraising envelopes and leaflets need to get through the right doors. So even here, 'place' has its role in the marketing mix.

Point Size

Typefaces are measured in points. Most books, magazines and letters are typed in 10 or 12 points. The larger the number, the larger the type size.

Press Cuttings Bureaux

These companies will send you cuttings on your charity from a massive range of publications. They are expensive, as they charge a reading fee and an amount per cutting, so are suitable only for very large charities doing a lot of media work, or for one-off, high-profile campaigns.

Press Officers

Press officers are in-house specialists who deal with media relations and are a contact point for journalists seeking information. Many charities employ a press officer.

Press Releases

See News Releases.

Press Statement

See Media Statement.

Price

If you are selling products, such as Third World crafts, Nicaraguan coffee or second-hand clothes, your products will have a price tag on them. It is not so straightforward with services. Take a youth café, for example. What's the price of a cup of coffee? Is it the 10p you charge, or the 30p it costs you to make it, when you take into account rent, rates, staff costs, etc.? Is the cost the £40,000 you get each year from the council to run the café, or the 15p you charge for a cheese roll? It is both of these things. Part of your operation is selling food and drinks to young people, and it is important that you get the price right. Another part of your operation is providing a drop-in service to local youth, which is paid for by the council; you need to price this service right, too, otherwise the council may feel that they are not getting good value for money.

Primary Data

Primary data is not ready-made. You have to gather it yourself, or commission someone else to do it for you. It is thus more expensive and potentially much more time-consuming than secondary data (see below).

Product

We tend to think of products as things – such as a tin of baked beans or a packet of washing powder. 'Product' here refers to your product or service. It might be a product proper, such as second hand clothing, if you run a charity shop, or a publication or handbook if you run a support service for voluntary organisations. Selling the product may involve an exchange of money. Or it could be that your 'product' is a free service, such as counselling, a drop-in centre, a welfare rights clinic – or one of a host of other services run by charities and voluntary organisations in Britain.

Product Development

This is a growth strategy where you develop brand new products, but offer them to your existing target markets.

Promotion

This is the aspect of marketing that we most readily associate the word with. Indeed, this is often what we mean when we talk about marketing. Promotion involves promoting your service or product, but the question is, 'Promote it to whom?' Are you promoting it to the people who use it or those who pay for it? Those who use are not always those who pay, even in the commercial sector. Children's pasta products, for example, are paid for by adults, but advertising for Postman Pat spaghetti is not aimed at them; it is targeted at children, as they are the major influencing factor on how and what food is bought in a household. Supermarket chain Asda did some research into consumer buying habits and discovered that children exert a strong influence over what their parents buy in supermarkets, to the tune of almost £2 billion a year. But back to the voluntary sector. Promotion involves promoting to the user of your service – teenagers, for example, in the case of the youth club – as well as funders. The council who pay for the youth club need to be as convinced about its use to the town's youth as young people need to be persuaded that it is a place worth going to. The promotional tools used and the messages promoted will differ, but the need for promotion to both audiences remains. Promotion involves advertising, leaflets, posters and other methods to reach target audiences.

R

Recall Tests

Recall tests are used in advertising research to see how many of a sample of respondents remember having seen an advert.

Reporter

On newspapers and magazines there are specialist reporters, known as correspondents (such as housing, health and local government correspondents), and general reporters who have to write about a very wide range of issues but who may specialise in none.

Reversed Out

This term describes the process by which the image or words themselves are not printed, but the surrounding area is. The text or image thereby appears to take on the colour of the paper.

Run-of-Paper

You do not get to choose where in the publication your advert appears; it is placed at the publisher's discretion.

S

Samples

With the exception of the government's ten-yearly census, no survey can cover the whole of the population. Researchers use instead a 'sample', which is a smaller group that is representative of the 'population' they wish to survey. By surveying a representative sample, rather than the entire relevant population, your survey is made more manageable and affordable.

Secondary Data

Secondary data is material that already exists (as opposed to primary data, which you gather yourself). It includes, for example, government publications and statistics (e.g. the Census of Population, the Family Expenditure Survey, reports from the Registrar General, Monthly Digest of Statistics and Social Trends). Large reference libraries are an obvious starting point when tracking down secondary data.

Single Column Centimetre (scc)

This is the unit of vertical measurement that is used to measure the size of an advert and therefore its cost.

Solus Position

This is an advertising term. If your ad has a solus position, there will be no other advertisements adjacent to your own. This means it will not have to compete for attention with other adverts.

Special Position Adverts

You can specify if you want your advert to appear in a special position, such as the front page or near the leader column. If you are running a charity to build schools in the third world, you may opt for your advert to be placed on the education page. The price of your advert will depend on where in the paper it is placed. There can be a waiting list for the best positions, as these are often booked up in advance.

Sub-Editor

Cutting stories to fit the space and headline writing are two of the main responsibilities of the sub on a newspaper.

Surfer

Someone who uses the Internet, or, to use the jargon, surfs the net.

SWOT Analysis

SWOT is an acronym. It stands for:

Strengths: what you are good at, what you do well, what factors are in your favour.

Weaknesses: what you are poor at, what factors are against you.

Opportunities: what external opportunities there are for you to develop new services or to attract new funding, etc.

Threats: what external threats could affect you – new legislation or competition, or a change in government, for example.

A SWOT analysis is simply an examination of your organisation's strengths and weaknesses, and the opportunities and threats which it faces. Once you have carried out a SWOT analysis, you can start to build on your strengths and, where appropriate, do something to address your weaknesses. Remember that a threat to one organisation can be an opportunity to another. The National Lottery has been seen as a threat to some of the big charities, whose donations have dropped since its launch. Conversely, the Lottery has opened up a new source of funding which many smaller charities are benefiting from.

T

Tints

These are made up of tiny dots, which give the effect of a shade. If you are printing in dark blue, your tints would be in shades of lighter blue. For black ink, tints are grey, for red ink they are pink. Effective use of tints can give the illusion of another colour.

U

Upper Case

This is printers' jargon for capital letters.

USP

This is an acronym for Unique Selling Point (sometimes also called 'unique selling proposition') – it is the thing that differentiates you from all the others. For example, there might be scores of children's charities, but your USP is that you are the only one set up exclusively to care for dying children in Sutcliffeville. No one else is offering that service. It is what makes you stand apart from the rest.

W

Warm Prospects

See Cold List.

APPENDIX B

Directory

Further reading

If your appetite for marketing has been whetted, you may be eager to lay your hands on some further marketing books. There's plenty to choose from: a visit to your nearest reference library or decent academic bookseller will reveal shelves heaving with texts on every aspect of the discipline. There's just one problem. Most marketing books are written for commercial bodies. Thankfully, more books are being published on voluntary sector marketing, although the choice is far from large.

Voluntary Sector Marketing, PR and Communication

Meeting Need – Successful Charity Marketing by Ian Bruce

Ian Bruce is Director General of RNIB and Director of VOLPROF at City University Business School. Drawing on his 25 years' experience in the voluntary sector, Ian Bruce's book covers the marketing of goods, service provision, campaigning, pressure group activity and fundraising.

Second edition published in 1998 by ICSA Publishing/Prentice Hall.

Creative Arts Marketing by Elizabeth Hill, Catherine O'Sullivan and Terry O'Sullivan

This comprehensive book covers all aspects of marketing for arts organisations. It uses case studies from community, visual and amateur arts to show how marketing techniques have helped a diverse range of arts organisations.

Published in 1995 (reprinted 1997, 1998) by Butterworth-Heinemann.

Brand Spirit: How Cause-Related Marketing Builds Brands by Hamish Pringle and Marjorie Thompson

Aimed at both corporates and charities, this book examines how cause-related marketing can work. Case studies shown CRM in action.

Published in 1999 by John Wiley & Sons.

Public and Non-Profit Marketing by Christopher Lovelock and Charles Weinberg

This American book covers statutory and voluntary organisation marketing and includes 20 case studies and readings.

Second edition published in 1989 by the Scientific Press, California

Strategic Marketing for Non-Profit Organisations by Philip Kotler and Alan Andreasen

Kotler, a leading academic in the field of marketing generally, was among the first to see the potential of marketing for the public and voluntary sector, way back in the 1960s.

Fifth edition published in 1996 by Prentice Hall.

The DIY Guide to Public Relations for Charities, Voluntary Organisations and Community Group by Moi Ali

By the same author as *The New DIY Guide to Marketing*, this book is full of advice and practical tips on such issues as using the media, campaigning, making videos, photography and event management.

Second edition published in 1999 by the Directory of Social Change.

Effective Customer Care by Amanda Knight

This practical book outlines the fourteen basic rules of good customer care for voluntary organisations.

Published in 1999 by Directory of Social Change.

General Marketing

Marketing Today by Gordon Oliver

This book is more readable than many general marketing texts, though it is still on the heavy side. Unlike many marketing tomes, this does contain a few – though only a few! – pages on voluntary sector marketing (out of over 500 in total).

Fourth edition published in 1995 by Pearson Education.

This is far from a comprehensive list, though it covers the main companies and organisations you may need to contact, as well as the key marketing magazines and handbooks.

Useful organisations

This alphabetic listing contains the details of useful organisations.

Advertising Agency Register
26 Market Place
London W1
Tel. 020–7437 3357

This independent organisation will give you the names of advertising agencies suitable for your brief.

Advertising Standards Authority
2 Torrington Place
London WC1E 7HW
Tel. 020–7580 5555
www.asa.org.uk

Established in 1962, the ASA provides independent scrutiny of the advertising industry. It investigates complaints and ensures that the system operates in the public interest. Independent both of government and the advertising industry, the ASA publishes a monthly report on its website, which includes an auto-response form so you can opt in to receive an email link when specific adjudications of interest, for example, by county or industry sector are published on the website.

AM&M Direct
Studio 3/3
Chelsea Harbour Yard
London SW10 0XD
Tel. 020–7376 5727

This company specialises in charity direct mail, especially fundraising mailings. AM&M Direct offer a range of services to charities, including their Charity Donor Prospects List, which lists over 300,000 people suitable for charity mailings. They say their list is the best performing list in the country for charity donor acquisition mailings.

BRAD Direct Marketing Lists, Rates and Data
Maclean Hunter House
Chalk Lane
Cockfosters Road
Barnet
Hertfordshire EN4 0BU
Tel. 020–8242 3132

This is a guide to lists and direct mail services. It costs around £200 annually.

British Library Newspaper Library
Colindale Avenue
London NW9 5HE
Tel. 020–7323 7535

English, Scottish, Welsh and Irish newspapers from 1700 are housed here.

British Promotional Merchandise Association
Suite 12
4th Floor
Parkway House
Sheen Lane
London SW14 8LS
Tel. 020–8878 0825

This is a trade organisation. It publishes *Promotions News* six times a year, which contains adverts from companies publicising the promotional items they produce. These range from cheap biros, balloons and carrier bags right through to tasteful branded gifts and fundraising items.

Broadcasting Complaints Commission
35 and 37 Grosvenor Gardens
London SW1W 0BS
Tel. 020–7630 1966

For complaints about malicious, damaging or inaccurate television and radio coverage.

Campaign for Press and Broadcasting Freedom
96 Dalston Lane
London E8 1NG
Tel. 020–7923 3671

This pressure group, which campaigns for a more accountable and accessible media, can offer advice on right to reply.

Chartered Institute of Marketing
Moor Hall
Cookham
Maidenhead
Berks SL6 9QH
Tel. 01628–852183

The CIM was established in 1911 and has over 50,000 members. It is a membership organisation offering a range of services including training, professional qualifications, a library and information service, and consultancy. It produces various publications, including a journal, newsletters and marketing reports. The CIM has regional offices at:

29 St Vincent Place
Glasgow G1 2DT
Tel. 0141–221 7700

Chamber of Commerce House
22 Great Victoria Street
Belfast BT2 7BJ
Tel. 028–9024 4113

Eaton Place Business Centre
114 Washway Road
Sale
Cheshire M33 7RF
Tel. 0161–905 1458

Committee of Advertising Practice
2 Torrington Place
London WC1E 7HW
Tel. 020–7580 5555
www.cap.org.uk

The CAP is a self-regulatory body made up of 22 trade and professional organisations representing advertisers, ad agencies, media
owners and service suppliers. It writes and enforces the British
Codes of Advertising and Sales Promotion. These are reproduced in
a free guide, available from the above address or downloadable
from the Advertising Standards Authority's website (www.asa.
org.uk). CAP also offers free copy advice on your advertising and
promotions, to help you ensure it meets the codes. Ring 020–7580
4100.

Craft Emblems
Aspen House
14 Station Road
Kettering
Northants NN15 7HE
Tel. 01536–513501

Craft Emblems will source a variety of promotional items and
specialise in charity work.

Crossbow Research
Aviary Court
138 Miles Road
Epsom KT19 9AB
Tel. 01372–725400

This company specialises in market research for voluntary organisations and comes highly recommended by a number of charities.

Direct Mail Accreditation and Recognition Centre
4th Floor
248 Tottenham Court Road
London W1P 9AD
Tel. 020–7631 0904

Established in 1995, DMARC is an accreditation scheme to ensure direct mail suppliers adhere to the best practices and self-regulatory guidelines of the industry.

Direct Mail Information Service
5 Carlisle Street
London W1V 5RG
Tel. 020–7494 0483

For industry statistics, research and general information on direct mail, contact the DMIS.

DMA Directory of List Owners, Brokers, Managers and Builders
The Direct Marketing Association
Haymarket House
1 Oxendon Street
London SW1Y 4EE
Tel. 020–7321 2525

This body represents the direct marketing industry. It offers a list brokering advisory service.

Direct Mail Services Standards Board
26 Eccleston Street
London SW1W 9PY
Tel. 020–7824 8651

The DMSSB provides a list of approved suppliers and confers recognised status on suppliers who meet the highest ethical and professional standards.

Direct Marketing Association
Haymarket House
1 Oxendon Street
London SW1Y 4EE
Tel. 020–7321 2525

This body represents the direct marketing industry. It produces a code of practice and a list of accredited list brokers. The DMA also runs the Mailing Preference Scheme, which contains the names of 657,700 consumers who do not wish to receive unsolicited mailshots.

Durrants
Discovery House
28–42 Banner Street
London EC1Y 8QE
Tel. 020–7674 0200
www.durrants.co.uk

This company offers a broadcast monitoring service and a press cut-tings service covering over 4,000 national, regional and trade titles.

Fax Preference Service
Tel. 0845–070 0702

Companies wishing not to receive so-called junk faxes can regis-ter their number. It is against the law to fax marketing material an individual, sole trader or partnership without their prior per-mission.

Image Promotions
Units 2 & 3 Maple Works
Old Shoreham Road
Hove
East Sussex BN3 7ED
Tel. 01273–726325

Image Promotions has organised over 95 per cent of all bus ticket promotions in the UK. It has links with over 100 bus companies in all major towns and cities. The company can help you with plan-ning and advice, bus company bookings and liaison, artwork and design, printing, delivery and campaign monitoring.

Incorporated Society of British Advertisers Limited
44 Hertford Street
London W1Y 8AE
Tel. 020–7499 7502

ISBA represents the interests of the majority of British advertis-ers. It can offer organisations help with selecting advertising, pro-motional and direct marketing agencies, and offers training and a range of useful publications and briefing papers.

Institute of Direct Marketing
1 Park Road
Teddington
Middlesex TW11 0AR
Tel. 020–8943 2535
www.theidm.com

Founded in 1987, the IDM is Europe's leading professional devel-opment body for direct and interactive marketing. The IDM organises educational initiatives, including the Direct Marketing Diploma, to improve the knowledge of direct marketing.

Institute of Public Relations
The Old Trading House
15 Northburgh Street
London EC1V 0PR
Tel. 020–7253 5151
www.ipr.org.uk

This is the professional body which represents over 6,000 PR professionals. Profile, its monthly magazine, contains news and articles on the PR industry. The IPR has several special interest groups, including Fifth Estate representing PR consultants in the voluntary sector, and a Marketing Communication group.

London Cardguide Limited
68 Brewer Street
London W1R 3PJ
Tel. 020–7494 2229

This company pioneered the idea of promotional postcards. They will produce postcards and distribute them to selected cafés and restaurants across Britain, reaching ABC1 consumers aged 20–45.

Mailing Preference Service
5 Reef House
Plantation Wharf
London SW13 3UF
Tel. 020–7738 1625

Members of the public can register their details with the MPS to help cut down on the amount of 'junk mail' they receive. The MPS produces a list of everyone who has contacted them to say that they do not want to receive unsolicited mail, and this list is made available to list owners, who then remove these people from their lists. Hopefully this makes everyone happy: consumers do not get unwanted mail and companies do not waste money writing to people who have no interest. You can buy a copy of this list for £100 plus VAT.

Mainline Promotions
Collins Court
High Street
Cranleigh
Surrey GU6 8AS
Tel. 01483–271171

This company produces promotional textiles, clothing and bags and have worked for a number of charities.

Market Research Society
The Old Trading House
15 Northburgh Street
London EC1V 0AH
Tel. 020–7490 4911

Founded in 1946, the Market Research Society is the professional association for those involved in compiling or using research. It has around 7,500 members and offers them a monthly magazine and quarterly journal. The Society produces an annual training programme, which includes such courses as Questionnaire Design, Marketing Skills, and Training the Interviewer Trainer. Courses are open to non-members, though a higher fee is charged. They also produce a free directory of organisations providing market research services.

MarketScan
8 Duke's Court
Chichester
West Sussex PO19 2FX
Tel. 01243–786711

MarketScan will also assemble and post mailings for you. And they can arrange 'shared' mailings, where you share your mailing with one or more non-competing organisations. This can more than halve your costs.

Media Trust
3–7 Euston Centre
Regent's Place
London NW1 3JG
Tel. 020–7874 7600
www.mediatrust.org

The Media Trust is a registered charity that works in partnership with the media industry to meet the communications needs of the voluntary sector. Its website has useful online media guides. The Trust provides one-to-one support and advice, and it runs a training programme.

Office of the Data Protection Registrar
Wycliffe House
Water Lane
Wilmslow
SK9 5AF
Tel. 01625–545700
www.dataprotection.gov.uk

The Data Protection Commissioner is an independent officer appointed by the Queen, who reports directly to Parliament. The Commissioner has the power to enforce the 1998 Data Protection Act.

Paperclip Partnership
Unit 9
The Ashway Centre
Elm Crescent
Kingston-upon-Thames
Surrey KT2 6HH
Tel. 020–8549 4857
www.paperclip.partnership@btinternet.com

Paperclip offers a press cuttings and press coverage analysis service.

Press Association Library
85 Fleet Street
London EC4P 4BE
Tel. 020–7353 7440

This library holds over 14 million news cuttings on every subject from 1926 onwards.

Press Complaints Commission
1 Salisbury Square
London EC4Y 8AE
Tel. 020–7353 1248

For complaints about intrusive or malicious press coverage.

Public Relations Consultants Association
Willow House
Willow Place
London SW1P 1JH
Tel. 020–7233 6026
www.prca.org.uk

The PRCA can help you find a PR consultancy through their free referral service. They will only recommend their members – over 150 firms – who tend to be the more expensive consultancies.

Raymead
13 College Park
Eastfield Road
Peterborough PE1 4AW
Tel. 01733–61799

Raymead sell software to help you set up databases that will enable you to have a clearer picture of your customers.

Rocket Badge Company
Byron Mews
114 Shirland Road
London W9 2BT
Tel. 020–7289 3262

Producing a wide range of badges, this company works for a number of charities and offers registered charities a discount.

Romeike and Curtice
Hale House
290–296 Green Lanes
London N13 5BR
Tel. 0800 289543
www.romeike.com

This press cuttings bureau employs over 150 specialised readers to scrutinise hundreds of newspapers, consumer magazines and technical publications.

Royal Mail Address Management Centre
4 St George's Business Centre
St George's Square
Portsmouth PO1 3AX
www.royalmail.co.uk
Tel. 023–9283 8515

Royal Mail has an address management database on CD-ROM called PAF, the Postcode Address File. It contains 25 million addresses and allows you to cross-reference with census information, local authority ward codes, etc., or to check addresses are correct before adding them to mailing lists.

Royal Mail Mailsort
Sales Centre
Tel. 0345–950 950

Mailsort is a Royal Mail service which offers discounts (ranging from 13 per cent to 32 per cent) for large mailings sorted by you. If you are sending at least 4,000 letters in one go (or 1,000 packets), and you can sort them geographically, you could get a good discount. Royal Mail offer a range of services to support direct mail campaigns, including Freepost, Business Reply and Door to Door. Ask them for details. They also produce an excellent Direct Mail Guide.

TDI Limited
10 Jamestown Road
London NW1 7BY
Tel. 020–7482 3000 or 0800 226633

This is one of the largest bus advertising companies in the country. It can arrange for you to advertise on buses nationwide, regionally or locally.

Telephone Preference Scheme
Haymarket House
1 Oxenden Street
London SW1Y 7EE
Tel. 0845–070 0707

This free service enables individuals to register their wish not to receive direct marketing calls. It is supported by, among others, the Institute of Charity Fundraising Managers and the Direct Marketing Association. It is a legal requirement that organisations making such calls ensure that they do not call numbers registered with the TPS.

Index